■■■ Not in My Family

Praise for

Not in My Family
AIDS in the African-American Community

"AIDS is a deadly disease that is wreaking havoc on our people, especially the younger members of our community. There are a slew of young people who have no knowledge of HIV and AIDS and they need our assistance and encouragement to become informed about this deadly disease. Our community must understand that we don't have any choice but to talk about HIV and AIDS."
   Bishop Andre Merritt, Detroit Straight Gate Church

"HIV has robbed me of some of my most brilliant, colorful, and talented friends and associates. I will never understand how we as a nation can send vessels into space, fight billion-dollar wars, gouge the American people with high gas prices, and yet not be able to end this man-made disease! It's despicable, and yet another poor commentary on our present governing bodies."
   Isaiah Washington, actor, *Grey's Anatomy*

"AIDS has affected the African-American community more than any other. Please read this book to get informed on how you can protect you and your loved ones. Don't hate! Please educate!!"
   Vivica A. Fox, actor

Not in My Family

AIDS in the African-American Community

GIL L. ROBERTSON IV

CHICAGO

Library of Congress Cataloging-in-Publication Data
      Not in My Family : AIDS in the African-American community / edited by Gil L. Robertson IV.
            p. cm.
      Includes bibliographical references.
      ISBN-13: 978-1-932841-24-4 (pbk.)
      ISBN-10: 1-932841-24-5 (pbk.)
      1. AIDS (Disease)—United States. 2. HIV infections—United States.
3. African Americans—Diseases. I. Robertson, Gil L.

      RA643.83N68 2006
      362.196'979200973--dc22

                                                      2006021176

Agate books are available in bulk at discount prices. Single copies are available prepaid direct from the publisher.

Agatepublishing.com

CONTENTS

ACKNOWLEDGMENTS

This book is the culmination of a long journey that began nearly five years ago. It was at that time that I began to conceptualize a book that would give voice to the multitude of experiences felt by the African-American community living in the age of HIV and AIDS. Having watched countless accounts of the virus's impact within the African American community, I was dismayed by how few African Americans were an active part of this dialogue. Although these discussions were informative and made for lively debate, they were not framed in a way that would resonate with the community being discussed. What the black community needed were messages delivered by its own people—messages shaped in the nuances and character that would trigger a true reaction. That brings us to this book, *Not in My Family: AIDS in the African-American Community.*

Once the proposal for this project was completed it was submitted to various publishers. All ultimately passed on the project until Doug Seibold, president of Agate Publishing, said "yes." My most heartfelt thanks go to Doug and his staff for their courage, support, and commitment to sharing my vision about this project.

I would also like to extend generous thanks to the essay contributors, whose efforts have made this project possible. Reading their powerful words of inspiration, faith, and wisdom has been truly awe-inspiring.

Completing this project would not have been possible without the efforts of my team: Kelley Jackson, Angie Fiedler, N. Ali Early, Rahiem Shabazz, Ronda Penrice, Ellene Miles, Ava DuVernay, Melvina Gueye, Kathy Williamson, Rhonda Smith, Pamela Craig, and Jeff Keller.

I wish to also send much love and appreciation to the staff at the Robertson Treatment!

Thanks to ace literary agent Manie Barron for always keeping it real!

Special thanks go to Idris Shone Clark and Logan H. Westbrooks for sharing their guidance and "juice" to make this project a reality!

Special thanks also go to Lee Bailey, Patrick Bass, James Fugett, and Angela Dobson for believing in this project from the very start.

I send a major shout-out to the staff at DVA PR for their support and assistance.

More shout-outs go to Gilda Squire, Ricardo and Stephanie Lozier, Karin Turner, Mr. & Mrs. Rodney Harris, LaTanya Richardson, Sheryl Lee Ralph, Lisa Sorenson, Dena Gray, Candance Sandy, Evelyn Mims, Evelyn Santana, Sharon Robinson, Rhonda Hall, Tina Spigner, Linda Cohn, Sheri McGee, Alvin & Tammy Williams, Qiana Conley, Elvin Ross, William Yarbro, Ed Strickland, Clarence Haynes, Geoff Klosky, Jasmyne Cannick, Enid Bartley, Kim Anderson, Kim Hutchens, Sheri Stuart, Nekidra Shegod, Janet and Martin Miller, and the women affectionately known as "the Council."

Special thanks also go to music visionaries Vicki and Claude Lataillade, and their staff at Gospocentric Records for partnering with me on this project.

Much love goes to Max Siegel, Monique Headley, and Ayana Rivera.

Thanks to my colleagues in the media for the laughs, love, and support.

Thanks to my family and friends for your love and support.

Finally, much love and thanks go to my truest inspirations for this project: my brother, Jeffrey Robertson; my mom, Delmyra Robertson; and my late father, Gil Robertson.

PART I

Introduction

Black America, we have a problem.

HIV/AIDS are running rampant through our communities: globally, domestically, and in our families. Like the Devil himself, it comes to "steal, kill and destroy." It is destroying nations and generations of our people; it is killing our children, our friends, and our family members; and it is stealing our joy. It leaves in its wake a swath of devastation that, if left unchecked, threatens to undermine not just our public health and welfare, but also our culture, our traditions, and our future as a people.

Throughout the last decade in particular, this scourge has trampled on us like an unabated plague, a plague that takes no prisoners and spares no souls. Many of us are sick and dying and living in fear and shame, and many of us who aren't afflicted are living in denial, detachment, ignorance, and glass houses. Worse yet, too many people in our communities act as if they are immune to the problem altogether.

"Not me."

"Not any of my friends."

"Not in my family!"

And that's the problem.

The truth is, if it happens to one of us, it happens to all of us.

I met the face of HIV/AIDS more than 20 years ago when it made a host out of my brother. His diagnosis left me—and my family—with feelings of shock, fear, and regret that have taken us many years to overcome. Fortunately, my brother is alive today and leads a very active life. The threat to his life gave all our lives new meaning, new purpose, and a new perspective. Living with HIV/AIDS could be considered tantamount to walking under the shadow of death. However, there is no shadow without light; together, my family has stepped out of the shadow and into the light.

Learning to live with the reality that AIDS is in our family has not come without tremendous costs. As we've moved through the various stages of this illness with my brother and ridden the emotional roller coaster that comes along with it, we found comfort, solace, and strength in listening to the shared experiences of others. I also realized that we were not alone. There are countless other families, as well as individuals, bearing the same burden of coping and standing on the front lines of the battlefield of survival. As my family did more than 20 years ago when we found the enemy encamped among us like a thief in the night, these families are discovering that they are ill-prepared, ill-equipped, and ill-informed to stop it from invading their territory.

Not in My Family is the result of a desire to stop the enemy in his tracks. It is a weapon of warfare, a tool of empowerment, and a manual on friendship. It includes lessons before dying, lessons on living, lessons on love, and lessons on letting go. It is a call to action from those who have died of AIDS, those who suffer from HIV/AIDS, and those who don't want to get it. It is a collection of colorful stories, hard truths, and differing opinions from people of various lifestyles, strung together to teach us not only how to survive, but how to thrive in the face of HIV and AIDS.

It is a dose of truth to our community.

And hopefully, the truth will make us free.

When I think of HIV/AIDS today, I think of an affliction that has inequitably permeated African-American communities. Although we know that the statistics on blacks and HIV/AIDS are staggering, the human faces of these numbers have eluded us.

Like so many other critical conditions confronting African Americans, we need to raise the platform on this issue. This book is an attempt to provide one such forum. HIV/AIDS can touch the lives of any one of us in a multitude of ways, and thus, *Not in My Family* is really about all of us.

Storytelling has been an important part of sharing history and lessons in the African and African-American communities, and *Not in My Family* is a reflection of that tool at work as our community deals with HIV/AIDS. It is a gripping and heartfelt patchwork of essays reflecting a wide cross-section of ideas, values, and beliefs. And still, despite this diversity, the stories are woven with a common thread of love and good will for our loved ones.

The contributors to this project tell their stories through original first-person narratives. Their messages come from all walks of life: some authors are famous, while others are ordinary people with extraordinary stories. Their stories will make you laugh, cry, and be encouraged with the vibrancy of hope. They will inspire you to move forward, undaunted. The assembled stories offer hope and will edify, cleanse, and heal you with the truth and knowledge of what they reveal, all culled from experience, pain, and faith. Our contributors peel away the layers of ignorance we all have shared about the disease to reveal the truth. These essays break through barriers based upon sex, sexuality, religion, family, lies, myths, and misconceptions to reveal a state of consciousness that is truly empowering.

Despite my intimate connection to the subject matter, compiling this book was at times a challenge. Convincing some of the contributors to break their silence was at times daunting and frustrating. More than once I felt like Sisyphus rolling a rock up a hill that was destined to come crashing down time and again without any further insights. Thankfully, my pains were worth it, and that rock ultimately became the broad foundation of this book! It has been a blessing to meet and cross paths with all of the people who shared their stories for this project. So often I was humbled by these shared experiences; my hope is that this book will motivate readers with lessons that will open further dialogue and action about HIV/AIDS within the community.

African Americans have triumphed over a long history of obstacles: the Middle Passage, slavery, and Jim Crow. So far there has never been an obstacle that together we have not overcome. However, the enemy now is a disease. HIV/AIDS does not need to be a permanent blight upon this generation and its children. We must put forth the priority and sound the call for dedication and hard work to eradicate this disease. Achieving this end will take a relentless assault that gathers the efforts of culture and science against its proliferation. HIV/AIDS is not going to go away by quieting the call of alarm, nor is it something we can outrun.

It's time for a revolution: a change in our thought processes, our actions, and our relationships. The revolution will not be televised, but it will happen, and it's time for black folks to tune in.

It's time that we include HIV/AIDS in our conversations about social change in our communities. It's time to realize that when a crisis hits one of us, it affects all of us.

After all, we are family.

GIL L. ROBERTSON IV

PART II

The Facts of HIV and AIDS:

Plague in the Black Community

Introduction

Dealing with AIDS (acquired immune deficiency syndrome) in African-American communities, either through a positive HIV (human immunodeficiency virus) test, the experience of a loved one living with the disease, or working to educate, organize, and prevent the spread of HIV and AIDS, means encountering a number of dilemmas. Stigma, fear, rejection, denial, invisibility, classism, sexism, homophobia, misinformation, and drug phobia represent some of the palette of cultural issues. In addition, the media-documented consequences such as available treatment, affordable treatment, the eventual loss of independence, and the potential loss of mental and emotional support represent acute challenges in dealing with this disease in the African-American community.

While many of these issues reflect deeper and more complex problems that need attention, as is often the case within marginal communities, the devastating way in which this disease has attacked the African-American community in particular requires that local leaders acknowledge the severity of the continuing epidemic among African Americans and play a greater role in combating HIV/AIDS in their own communities.

Overview

> "In the period October 1980–May 1981, 5 young men, all active homosexuals, were treated for biopsy-confirmed *Pneumocystis carinii* pneumonia at 3 different hospitals in Los Angeles, California. Two patients died. *Pneumocystis* pneumonia in the United States is almost exclusively limited to severely immunosuppressed patients. The occurrence of *Pneumocystis* in these five previously healthy individuals without a clinically apparent underlying immunodeficiency is unusual. The fact that these patients were homosexuals suggests an association between some aspect of a homosexual lifestyle or disease acquired through sexual contact and *Pneumocystis* pneumonia in this population."
>
> MORBIDITY AND MORTALITY WEEKLY REPORT, JUNE 5, 1981

Acquired immune deficiency syndrome (AIDS) is a bloodborne and sexually transmitted disease that weakens the body's immune system, making it susceptible to infections and diseases that under ordinary circumstances would not be life-threatening. AIDS is caused by the human immunodeficiency virus (HIV) that attacks and destroys certain white blood cells.

Few Americans knew of AIDS prior to 1981, when testing and reporting of the disease became mandatory. Some experts believe that HIV was in the United States as early as 1978. By 1995, a milestone was reached as the number of U.S. cases reported since 1981 reached the half-million mark. In 1995, HIV infection was the leading cause of death among persons between the ages of 25 and 44 in the United States.

After seven consecutive years of declining numbers, new AIDS cases in the United States now appear to be rising. According to preliminary figures released by the Centers for Disease Control and Prevention (CDC), there were 42,008 new cases reported in 2001, an 8 percent increase from the year 2000.

Dramatic jumps occurred in Kentucky (59 percent), Georgia and North Carolina (41 percent each), and New York City (47 percent). A decrease in cases was noted in several states, including Michigan

(28 percent) and Kansas (22 percent). While these statistics, based on health department reports, still need to be confirmed, similar early reports over the past six years have been accurate.

The cumulative number of AIDS cases reported to the CDC through December 2002 is 744,467. The total of reported American deaths from AIDS is 448,060. Worldwide, the virus is estimated to have infected 60 million people, killing 22 million.

While U.S. health officials claimed that the overall decline in AIDS deaths was a result of successful new drugs, the rate of decline in these deaths also slowed. AIDS deaths decreased only 20 percent between 1997 and 1998, compared to a 42 percent decrease between 1996 and 1997. In an Associated Press article dated August 30, 1999, Dr. Helene Gayle, director of HIV prevention for the CDC, speculated that the slowed decline in deaths could be due to several factors: patients may develop resistance to drug treatments if they fail to take them regularly, patients may have a difficult time juggling the variety of pills and medications in the AIDS treatment regimen, and those who may be infected could fail to get tested or treated. Dr. Gayle warned that the overall decrease in AIDS deaths masked these more subtle trends and could lead to a false sense of complacency about the disease.

The Human Immunodeficiency Virus

A virus is a tiny infectious parasitic agent composed of genes surrounded by a protective coating. A virus must invade other cells to reproduce itself and grow. The invaded cells serve as their own death chambers. The virus reproduces so proficiently that healthy cells are destroyed and the host (in the case of HIV, a human) becomes diseased. Common colds, influenza, and some forms of pneumonia are also caused by viruses.

HIV Among African Americans

The impact of HIV/AIDS on the African-American community was devastating in 1997. HIV/AIDS was a leading cause of death of African Americans between the ages of 25 and 44. AIDS-related deaths for African Americans by 1998 were 10 times higher than for Caucasians. African Americans comprise 49 percent of AIDS deaths in the U.S., yet they make up only 13 percent of the U.S. population.

More startling, however, is the fact that through December 2000, the CDC had received reports of 774,467 AIDS cases—of those, 292,522 cases occurred among African Americans. African Americans currently make up almost 38 percent of all reported AIDS cases in this country. Of persons infected with HIV, it is estimated that almost 129,000 African Americans were living with AIDS at the end of 1999.

On an international scale, South Africa has one of the world's highest rates of HIV infection. In 2000, 4.2 million people, or 10 percent of the South African population, were estimated to be HIV positive.

A closer look at this raging epidemic in the U.S., particularly for the African-American community, reveals much more troubling realities. In the year 2000, more African Americans were reported to be infected with AIDS than any other racial/ethnic group. Representing nearly half (47 percent) of the 42,156 AIDS cases reported that year, 19,890 cases were reported among African Americans. Almost two-thirds (63 percent) of all women reported as infected with AIDS were African American. African-American children also represented almost two-thirds (65 percent) of all reported pediatric AIDS cases.

The rate of reported AIDS cases among African Americans in the year 2000 was 58.1 per 100,000 people, more than twice the rate for Hispanics and eight times the rate for Caucasians in the United States.

Data on HIV and AIDS diagnoses in 25 states with integrated reporting systems shows the increased impact of the epidemic on the African-American community in recent years. In these 25 states, during the period from January 1996 through June 1999, African Americans represented a high proportion (50 percent) of all AIDS diagnoses, but an even greater proportion (57 percent) of all HIV diagnoses. And among young people (ages 13 to 24), 65 percent of the HIV diagnoses were among those of African-American descent.

Among African-American men reported with AIDS, men who have sex with other men represent the largest proportion (37 percent) of reported cases since the epidemic began. The second most common exposure category for African-American men is intravenous drug use (34 percent), and heterosexual exposure accounts for 8 percent of cumulative cases.

Among African-American women reported with AIDS, intravenous drug use accounts for the infections of 41 percent of all AIDS case reports since the epidemic began, with 38 percent due to heterosexual contact.

Studies of HIV prevalence among patients in drug treatment centers and STD clinics find the rates of HIV infection among African Americans to be significantly higher than those among Caucasians. Sharing needles and trading sex for drugs are two ways that substance abuse can lead to HIV and other sexually transmitted disease (STD) transmission, putting sex partners and children of drug users at risk as well. In a sample of young men who have sex with other men (ages 15–22) in seven major U.S. urban areas, researchers found that overall, 7 percent were infected with HIV (with a range of 2 percent to 12 percent). A significantly higher percentage of African-American men having sex with other men (14 percent) than Caucasian men having sex with other men (3 percent) were infected.

HIV/AIDS Among Women in the United States

Between 1992 and 1999, the number of persons living with AIDS increased as a result of the 1993 expanded AIDS case definition, and, more recently, survival rates improved among those who have benefited from the new combination drug therapies. During that seven-year period, a growing proportion of persons living with AIDS were women, reflecting the ongoing shift in populations affected by the epidemic. In 1992, women accounted for 14 percent of adults/adolescents living with AIDS. By 1999, the proportion had grown to 20 percent.

Since 1985, the proportion of all AIDS cases reported among adult and adolescent women has more than tripled, from 7 percent in 1985 to 25 percent in 1999. The epidemic has increased most dramatically among women of color. African-American and Hispanic women together represent less than one-fourth of all U.S. women, yet they account for more than three-fourths (78 percent) of AIDS cases reported to date among women in our country. In the year 2000 alone, African-American and Hispanic women represented an even greater proportion (80 percent) of cases reported in women.

While HIV/AIDS-related deaths among women continued to decrease in 1999, largely as a result of recent advances in HIV treatment, HIV/AIDS was the fifth leading cause of death for U.S. women aged 25–44. Among African-American women in this same age group, HIV/AIDS was the third leading cause of death in 1999.

Heterosexual contact is now the greatest risk for women, and sex with drug users plays a large role as well. In the year 2000, 38 percent of women reported with AIDS were infected through heterosexual exposure to HIV; intravenous drug use accounted for 25 percent of cases. In addition to the direct risks associated with drug injection (sharing needles), drug use also is fueling the heterosexual spread of the epidemic. A significant proportion of women infected heterosexually were infected through sex with an intravenous drug user. Reducing the toll of the epidemic among women will require efforts to combat substance abuse, in addition to reducing HIV risk behaviors.

Many HIV/AIDS cases among women in the United States are initially reported without risk information, which suggests that women may be unaware of their partners' risk factors, or that the health care system is not documenting their risks. Historically, more than two-thirds of AIDS cases among women initially reported without identified risk were later reclassified as heterosexual transmission, and just over one-fourth were attributed to intravenous drug use.

Scientists believe that cases of HIV infection reported among

13- to 24-year-olds are indicative of overall trends in HIV incidence (the number of new infections in a given time period, usually a year), because this age group has more recently initiated high-risk behaviors; females made up nearly half (47 percent) of HIV cases in this age group, reported from the 34 areas with confidential HIV reporting for adults and adolescents in the year 2000. Further, for all years combined, young African-American and Hispanic women account for three-fourths of HIV infections reported among females between the ages of 13 and 24 in these areas.

Celebrities with HIV/AIDS

Perhaps one of the most famous HIV-infected persons in the world is Earvin "Magic" Johnson, the internationally known former basketball player for the Los Angeles Lakers. When he announced that he was infected with HIV in September 1991, the world was shocked. He had no idea he was infected until he went for a routine physical examination, a requirement for a life insurance policy. He freely admitted that prior to his marriage he had unprotected sexual contact with numerous women, and had no idea who had transmitted the virus to him.

To many, he became a hero for his courage and his immediate public acknowledgement. He became an AIDS spokesman and began working in prevention programs. He was even named to the President's Commission on AIDS (from which he eventually resigned). Others considered him anything but a hero, believing that his promiscuous lifestyle sent the wrong message to millions of young people who admired him. What he has shown others, as one observer noted, is that AIDS is not something you die with; it is something with which you live.

In 1992, former tennis star Arthur Ashe announced that he had become infected with HIV from contaminated blood in the mid-1980s during a coronary bypass operation. His was not a voluntary announcement, but one made necessary when the news media found out and threatened to announce it before he could. Ashe was reluctant to make his condition public, fearing the effect on his then-five-year-old daughter. He maintained that because he did not have a public responsibility, he should have been allowed to maintain his privacy. He subsequently died in 1994.

Mary Fisher, a heterosexual and non-drug user, stood before her conservative peers at the 1992 Republican Convention and announced that she was infected with HIV. A former television producer and assistant to President Gerald R. Ford, she said she considered her announcement to be part of her contribution to the fight against AIDS. The wealthy Fisher was not the image that usually comes to mind when most people think of AIDS—gay, poor, drug-addicted, and lacking access to support systems or adequate medical care and housing. Another well-known celebrity with AIDS is Olympic gold medalist Greg Louganis, who was diagnosed in 1988.

Prevention

Prevention efforts in the African-American community must focus on high-risk behaviors. Looking at select studies among high-risk populations gives an even clearer picture of why the epidemic continues to spread in communities of color. The data suggests that three interrelated issues play a role: the continued health disparities between economic classes, the challenges related to controlling substance abuse, and the intersection of substance abuse with the epidemic of HIV and other STDs.

Substance abuse is fueling the sexual spread of HIV in the United States, particularly in minority communities with high rates of STDs. Studies of HIV prevalence among patients in drug treatment centers and STD clinics find the rates of HIV infection among African Americans to be significantly higher than those among Caucasians. Sharing needles promotes STD transmission, putting sex partners and children of drug users at risk as well. Comprehensive programs for drug users must provide the information, skills, and support necessary to reduce both injection-related and sexual risks. At the same time, HIV prevention and treatment, substance abuse prevention, and sexually transmitted disease treatment and prevention services must be better integrated to take advantage of the multiple opportunities for intervention.

Prevention efforts must also be improved and sustained for young gay men. Previously implemented programs that have proven effective in changing risky behaviors among men and women and sustaining those changes over time should be maintained with a focus on both the uninfected and infected populations within the African-American community.

Increased emphasis needs to be placed on prevention and treatment services for young women and women of color. Knowledge about preventive behaviors and awareness of the need to practice them is critical for each and every generation of young women. Prevention programs should be comprehensive and should include participation by parents as well as the educational system. Community-based programs *must* reach youths outside the educational system in settings such as youth detention centers and shelters for runaways.

Effective female-controlled prevention methods must be developed and widely disseminated. More options are urgently needed for women who are unwilling or unable to negotiate condom use with a male partner. The CDC is collaborating with scientists around the world to evaluate the prevention effectiveness of the female condom and to research and develop topical microbicides that can kill HIV and the pathogens that cause STDs.

The intersection of drug use and sexual HIV transmission must be addressed. Men and women are at risk of acquiring the HIV virus sexually from a partner who injects drugs and from sharing needles themselves. Additionally, women who use noninjection drugs (e.g., "crack" cocaine, methamphetamines) are at greater risk of acquiring the virus sexually, especially if they trade sex for drugs or money.

Better-integrated prevention and treatment services for men and women are needed across the board, including the prevention and treatment of other STDs and substance abuse and access to antiretroviral therapy.

Conclusion

When trying to explain the slow, possibly even negligent, response to AIDS in African-American communities, authors often retreat to a familiar and substantively important list of barriers thought to prevent a more active response from community leaders and organizations. Regularly topping the list is the claim that African-American communities control fewer resources than most other groups, and thus cannot be expected to respond to AIDS in a manner similar to "privileged" groups, such as Caucasian lesbians and gay men. Although there is truth to the assertion that most African Americans operate with limited access to resources, this explanation is based on a very narrow conception of resources available and a very limited understanding of the history of African-American communities. Most of the cities hardest hit by this disease (New York, San Francisco, Washington, DC, Detroit, Chicago, and Atlanta) have been or are currently under the leadership of African-American mayors. Thus, while African-American individuals suffer from limited resources, African-American elected officials control, or at least have had significant input into, decisions about how resources (unfortunately often dwindling resources) will be allocated in their cities.

Others argue that members of the African-American community suffer from so many more prevalent ailments and structural difficulties, such as sickle-cell anemia, high blood pressure, homelessness, persistent poverty, drugs, crime, and unemployment, that few should expect community leaders to turn their political agendas to the issue of AIDS.

Last, many scholars and activists engaged in the fight against AIDS argue that homophobia in African-American communities is yet another reason for the slow response to this disease by African-American elites and organizations.

The harsh and bitter reality is that AIDS, unlike many other medical and structural ailments of the African-American community, has no rehabilitation option. The number of people dying and becoming infected is growing among the African-American community, which is now 13 percent of the total U.S. population. African Americans are at a critical point in their dependence upon community leaders to aggressively participate in the decisions determining the allocation of resources for combating this disease. Doing so is necessary to ensure that these resources actually reach their intended recipients.

The devastation and loss of life in the African-American community from HIV/AIDS is far from over, and will continue until a significant response to this plague transcends political positioning and those unwilling to claim that this disease is a plague threatening all Americans alike.

WILLIAM YARBRO

PART III

Deep From Within

Knots fill their stomachs as their senses shut down
They can't sleep or eat or see or even speak
at night or in the morning
or even during the day
They are so worried ...
So worried that they may let go
and leave as if they don't believe in He
all because of HIV

Deep from within his soul the answer lies
as his heart and eyes cry
For the longest time, knowing was not beautiful
It was rather the death of him and that was reality
He lived life perfectly not knowing if destiny was this disease
He didn't want his life to be altered although this news
would change his life views

Deep from within his soul he didn't want to know
Deep from within her soul the answer lies
All she did was love her husband
Stand by his side during times of need
Did everything she could to build a family
Raise the kids while he was at work
While he sat home she took the kids to church
Gave all she could give to please
and he brought her home this disease

Deep from within her soul she didn't want to know

Deep from within his soul the answer lies
He was living a secret life
as though he was single
Going from hotel to hotel, sneaking around town
Giving every man his hand
Thinking he was only having fun
Then he got a call that said he needed to be tested
and found out he was infected

Deep from within his soul he didn't want to know

Deep from within her soul the answer lies
She was born with it, now she's stuck with it
because of her mother's drug habit
All the kids would laugh, stare, and stay away
Fearing they would be diagnosed that same way
Not knowing they were killing her inside
Flooding her soul and breaking her heart
But they didn't have it and that was the good part

Deep from within her soul she didn't want to know

Deep from within their souls they don't want to know
because when they find out
they begin to die inside
Killing themselves psychologically
Thinking they have no reason to live
but they do, so they can help me and you
become more aware of what they could and couldn't help

Deep from within their souls they didn't want to know

Deep from within my soul I didn't want to know
because I feared the worst so I stopped eating

and almost stopped breathing, then I realized that it was me
that was killing me, not the presence of HIV
I didn't know for a fact, my friends kept telling me
I needed to find out, so I got tested
The test came back negative, so the enemy was me ...

Deep from within my soul, I'm now happy I know

JANUARY 18, 2006
MICHAEL J. BURT

Michael J. Burt is the author of *Experience Is Impossible Without a Chance: A Collection of Poems*. Visit www.mjburtpoetry.com for more information about this writer.

PART IV

The Essays

Chapter 1

Time to Break the Silence

HIV/AIDS is devastating our community, and unless we stand up and fight for our right to live, we will continue to suffer and die because of this preventable and treatable disease.

- We know that African Americans are disproportionately affected by HIV/AIDS. We know that African-American women are increasingly bearing the brunt of this disease, so much so that AIDS is the leading cause of death for African-American women between the ages of 24 and 34.
- We know the low down about the "down-low" men leading double lives, having sex with other men and passing the virus on to women—and we've gotten over the hype.
- We know that our so-called "criminal system" is breaking apart the black family by sending our men to prison to serve as the entry point for HIV, hepatitis C and other diseases into our communities.
- We also know, and the statistics show, that our kids are the ones at greatest risk of getting infected.

In short, we know what the problem is. Now we have to act. We have to mobilize ourselves, our families, our friends, our church leaders, our communities, and our government to take action.

It is time to break the silence!

We can begin by rejecting the stigma and embracing and showing compassion for those who are already living with HIV/AIDS. As our beloved, late Coretta Scott King said: "To eradicate AIDS, we must first and foremost cure our own hearts of the fear and ig-norance that leads to the ostracism of people with HIV and AIDS. The real shame falls not on the people with AIDS, but on those who would deny their humanity."

Only by de-stigmatizing those with HIV/AIDS can we begin the critical dialogue about this disease, which is the first step to de-veloping community awareness and understanding and making it easier for people to get tested, seek voluntary counseling, and learn how they can protect themselves.

Protecting our community means taking the responsibility to talk openly and honestly about HIV. That means men and women have to talk to each other about HIV and about the need to use protection. It means we've got to encourage open dialogues in churches, so that pastors can have honest discussions with their congregations, and it means that we've got to have open and hon-est discussions about homosexuality within the African-American community.

Our challenge is not just to rally ourselves and our community against this disease, but to elevate our cause in the national con-sciousness. As African Americans, we have a special role to play in making sure our nation understands that we are all in this to-gether, and that this is a global pandemic.

Let's be clear. This virus does not pick and choose who it will infect. On a purely medical level, we can all be infected, regardless of race, gender, sexual orientation, age, or income.

So this discussion has to be more than just about HIV/AIDS. It has to be a comprehensive discussion about poverty, about dis-crimination, and about the willful marginalization of whole seg-ments of our population.

- We need to examine why homophobia, the aura of stigma, and taboos about sex and sexuality are preventing us from having an honest discussion about how we can prevent people from getting infected.
- We need to examine the way that sexism, objectification and commodification create an environment where women and

girls don't feel like they have control over their own bodies or their own relationships. Women must be empowered.

- We need to examine the ways poverty and discrimination contribute to a criminal justice system where poor people and people of color are at greater risk of getting HIV/AIDS because they are more likely to go to jail. We must demand HIV/AIDS awareness education and condom distribution in prisons and jails.
- We need to examine the factors that make the crises in our communities invisible. It is totally unacceptable that when African-American journalist Gwen Ifill asked Vice President Dick Cheney what the administration planned to do about the fact that black women are 13 times more likely to die of AIDS than white women, he didn't know what she was talking about.

Make no mistake.

This is a political struggle that warrants political action on our part.

It involves building grassroots organizations, building coalitions, and electing candidates who support making HIV/AIDS a priority for their public policy agenda. It means holding our elected officials accountable.

To me, working to put an end to the HIV/AIDS pandemic is a personal commitment. When I think about those whose lives have been cut tragically short by this devastating pandemic—our brothers and sisters, husbands and wives, sons and daughters, and all the other faces behind the statistics—I am reaffirmed in my belief that, together, we can eradicate this disease from the face of the earth. We must.

THE HONORABLE BARBARA LEE (D-CA)

Congresswoman Barbara Lee's accomplishments in promoting effective, bipartisan measures to stop the spread of HIV/AIDS and bring treatment to the infected have earned her recognition both at home and abroad as a leader in the fight against HIV/AIDS. In 2005, the House of Representatives unanimously passed her legislation in support of National Black HIV/AIDS Awareness Day. Lee was also a leader in the bipartisan effort to designate $15 billion for the prevention, care, and treatment of HIV/AIDS, TB, and malaria. She authored the bill to establish the framework for the Global Fund to Fight HIV/AIDS, Tuberculosis and Malaria in 2002, as well as other recent legislation designed to address the needs of orphans and vulnerable children, many of whom are victims of the HIV/AIDS pandemic.

Chapter 2

I Know the Face of AIDS

I have touched it, kissed it, comforted it, listened to its voice cry out in anguish, tried to find a hopeful word to soothe its fears, and wiped the tears from its eyes.

I have lived it, buried it, loved it, and lost it, but never will I forget it.

The first face of AIDS I knew was that of my younger brother, who died in 1991 at the age of 28. No, my brother was not gay, to answer the question that so many stupidly ask (as if that factor should somehow justify the person having the disease).

Back then, in some way that train of thought may have led our young people to look at AIDS as strictly a gay disease. They never paid attention because they were led to believe that only the "gay boys" were dying. The only thing you needed a condom for was to protect you from having a baby, and any STD could successfully be treated with a shot or a tube of ointment.

No one told my little brother that he would be fighting for his life, that he would be leaving his parents, his sisters and brothers, his five-year-old son, and his girlfriend because he had AIDS. No one told us that we would be standing around his hospital bed watching him struggle to breathe, touching his handsome face, and wiping the tears from our eyes as we said goodbye. No one told us that in a couple of years, his girlfriend would also be dead.

The next face of AIDS I knew belonged to my dearest friend of twenty-five years, a talented fashion designer. Every Friday after work, we would hit the "happy hour" at our favorite club, sip our drinks, catch up on the latest gossip, and share our dreams and our secrets like only best friends could do. The bar would be packed with the beautiful people, who were drinking, cruising, and dancing the night away.

You could always tell what season it was at the club by the posters on the wall; an invitation for the "Summer Boat Cruise", tickets being sold for the "New Year's Eve Gay-la," and my favorite, the "Sunday Night Talent Shows." But all too soon, it would become the season of AIDS.

As the virus began to take its toll, the atmosphere at the club began to change. The "happy hour" crowd grew smaller, and old familiar faces began to disappear. My best friend quietly slipped away a week before his forty-fourth birthday. The thump-thump-thump of the house music that had once beckoned us to dance the night away reverberated like a heartbeat, and then the music died.

Within the gay community, AIDS could not and would not be ignored. What started as a silent whisper would soon be heard loud and clear, like an air-raid siren warning you that a bomb was about to drop. One by one, the faces of my friends began to change. One by one, when asked, they denied being sick. One by one, the minds and bodies of those beautiful people were ravaged by the sickness. And one by one, those happy vibrant faces stared back at me from the pages of their obituaries. Happy hour was never the same, nor would it ever be again.

Twelve years would pass before I would once again see the face of AIDS, and that face belonged to my sister. My sister, who is a mother and a grandmother, was diagnosed three years ago. She contracted the virus from a former boyfriend; no, he was not a brother on the "down-low," but instead a brother on drugs.

The passing of time has brought about change: new medicines that prolong and sustain the quality of life, community AIDS programs that provide comfort and support, and media campaigns to remind us that AIDS does not discriminate.

On my sister's behalf, I am thankful for the progress that has been made.

On my brother and my best friend's behalf, I am sorry that it took so long.

S.M. YOUNG

A native of Washington, D.C., S.M. Young currently resides in Los Angeles. An African-American baby boomer, Young is a songwriter and freelance writer.

► *Chapter 3*

"Sexy" and "Safe" Aren't Mutually Exclusive

If you don't believe it, just ask Iona Morris, Lola Love and Mariann Aalda (also known as *3 Blacque Chix*), who wrote, produced, and star in the naughty, bawdy play, *Herotique-Aahh* ... The groundbreaking theatrical production, which they call "a sexistential comedy," celebrates the joys of sex for women over 40 and those planning on living to be older than 40, and the men (and sometimes the women) who love them.

"As rampant as AIDS is in the African-American community ... and especially with black *women* in the highest risk group, it would be irresponsible for us to talk about sex and not talk about protection," says Morris, who plays Lady I, Goddess of Love & Sexual Freedom. "Right," insists Love, who plays Lady L, The Dominatrix, "we don't dwell on it, and we don't preach on it ... but we had to bring it up."

"Absolutely!" chimes in Aalda, who plays Lady M, The Ex-Stepford Wife. "If you're gonna *bring it up* ... then you've *got to* bring it up!" Ba-dump-bump. The following excerpt from their show is how they (ahem) *cover* the subject in the spoken word ...

Lady I: Oh, and ...
Lady L: ... don't
Lady M: ... forget
All: ... Your rubbers!!!
Lady I: You've gotta make sure you're both covered ...

Lady L: Put a cap on it, baby. Keep it sexy and tight ...

Lady I: Lots of varieties to satisfy your *voracious* appetite!

Lady M: Ribbed, tipped, neon ... and choc-o-late tasting!

Lady I: And there are so many more of those fun dick casings!

Lady L: Full Body ... SUPERMAN!!! ... and Peter-Meter condoms ...

Lady I: And if he doesn't put it on before the entrance is made ...

Lady L: TAKE CONTROL!!!...so YOU won't later pay!

So, Do They Practice What They Preach?

MARIANN AALDA (Lady M): Well, I'm the only one of the three of us not in a committed relationship right now, so I'll go first.

I was already married when AIDS was first identified some 25 years ago, and I remained married—albeit to two different husbands—for most of my adult life. And I have to tell you, being divorced and in the dating scene right now and trying to have any kind of sex life can be tough to negotiate, especially when you discover that middle-aged men don't like wearing condoms any more than teenage boys do.

And, yes, I have allowed myself to be intimidated into having unprotected sex, but it was an *internalized* threat. I was concerned that the man I was dating would be insulted! Now, how dumb is that? And it wasn't even a man that I had a great love, or even a great passion, for. It's just that it had been a really long time, and I was really horny.

And then, of course, having done it with him *once* without a condom, I figured the cow was already out of the barn, so why go through *the embarrassment* of having "the conversation" with him after that?

I'll tell you why ... because waiting for the results from an AIDS test is *pure hell,* that's why! The relationship ended, but the *fear* lingered interminably. Every time I got a cold ... a sore throat ... a rash ... I would wonder, could it be?

Yeah, I was stupid; but thank God, I was lucky. I also smartened up enough to know that *I didn't want to press my luck*. So, after I got my results, I went right out and bought myself some condoms. Hopefully, I'll get a chance to use them sometime before their expiration date.

▌▌▌

LOLA LOVE (Lady L): When I was younger, my partners made demands about how, why, and when they wanted to have sex. And, being an obedient slave, I acquiesced. Why? The reasons were endless: afraid of being alone, wanting to please, scared of being rejected, 'cause he or she was "soooo fine," marriage, peer pressure, social pressure, religious pressure … blah, blah, blah.

But no more! Now *I'm* in control … as we *all* should be. Each and every one of us must master the role of restraint … and I'm not just talking handcuffs or silk scarves on bedposts. And it doesn't matter if you're mature or young and tender, female or male, black or white, or gay or straight. No one … and I mean NO ONE, should be having unprotected sex—not today, not tomorrow, not ever … NEVER! !

You see, role-playing as a dominatrix is more than just a sexual fantasy to me. In addition to insisting that my partners be sexy and obedient, I *command* them to be securely covered. That's right, baby, they've got to put a cap on it. *I want it sexy and tight!* I demand that. Because when you've been around for a while, like I have, and actively read the multitude of information about HIV/AIDS, and heard and witnessed the testimony from family and friends sharing their personal stories of the devastation, disruption, and destruction this epidemic has caused in our community, you don't want to put a decision that could cost you your life in someone else's hands. You ask questions and you TAKE CONTROL to protect yourself. So, if the man you're with says he doesn't like to wear rubbers … well, let me just say that I know a lot of men who have acquiesced with the promise of *a good spanking!*

Now that I'm a seasoned and empowered woman, I want to

make sure that I'm around to enjoy life's magnificent treasures. I am in a committed relationship ... with life! And as a woman over 50—yes, I said 50! But, just in case you didn't hear me the first time, let me say it again ... I said, I am an intelligent, sensual, black woman over 50! And I love every year that I'm here, and I plan to be around for a lot more, so I *always* play it safe. And I have never, ever found that it interfered with me being *sexy* ... and believe me, I've never, ever had any complaints.

▌▌▌

IONA MORRIS (Lady I): Having sex is one of the greatest pleasures in my life. But I've got to be safe, so I've developed some fun, sexy ways to talk about it, get that condom on, and still have great pleasure with my mate.

First of all, I ALWAYS carry my own rubbers. You can also have some fun. Go to a sex shop and pick out a variety to try. Make a sexy game of it. Or carry several different varieties with you and have fun choosing in the moment.

If this is a casual encounter, I try to keep the conversation about protected sex and AIDS tests in the flirtatious, pre-"doing-it" stage. For example, we're sitting on the couch, the moment is thick with sexual desire, and I whisper, "Baby, I've gotta ask you, have you had a recent AIDS test?" If he balks, I keep it sexy-sweet: "Ah, baby, I'm not trying to break the mood. It's not easy to talk about it, but we really have to." I smile. Your sweetness should relax him. But, if he doesn't talk, send him home and take care of yourself, yourself. After all, an intimate moment alone is the safest sex I know.

However, if he is responsible, you'll have a terrific conversation about being safe. I find that women are the ones who usually take the lead in this regard, but men, too, can use this approach with that special someone, be it a woman or another man. Even in a woman-to-woman relationship the HIV/AIDS virus can be transferred, because it's not transmitted by penetration, but through the exchange of bodily fluids. *THAT* is the culprit.

If I sense that I want to have a deeper relationship with the man,

I suggest that he and I, together, get an AIDS test to make sure that we can be secure in delving into many sexual pleasures without restraint. We'd also have to agree to be exclusive.

My favorite part is putting on the condom. Use this opportunity to do something else sexy with your partner. Sure, those "rubber things" can challenge the fingers, but I have ways that won't break the moment. (Tip: Put the condom within arm's reach, and if it ends up across the room, sashay slowly or sensuously crawl over there to get it.)

You be the judge of when you need to put the condom on. (I make sure it's on before I let that beautiful thing get close to my legs.) So, in a very sexy moment, subtly begin opening the package while sensuously diverting his attention with sexy whisperings or kisses. Then, move the condom down his shaft, massaging him the entire time, continuing with nibblings and sexy talk, or just keep your focus on admiring your man's "appendage." This allows you to get the condom on, hopefully, with as little difficulty as possible and with more excitement for both of you. But, if it all goes to hell in a hand basket, laugh together, keep it fun, and make him hurry up and put that thing on!

Live ... to make love ... another day.

3 BLACQUE CHIX

Lola Blank is president and CEO of LHB Entertainment in Los Angeles, CA, and has over 20 years of experience in the entertainment industry. She heads her own management company, LHB Management, where she specializes in guiding the careers of a very select group of young up-and-coming talent. In addition to entertainment consulting, lecturing, teaching and managing, she is the President of BX Girl Productions, a video and music industry production company.

Iona Morris is an accomplished actress with credits on stage, in TV, and in films. In 1997, Iona won a Hollywood NAACP Theater Award for Best Supporting Actress and the Best Ensemble Cast DramaLogue Award for her work in Kevin Arkadie's play *Up the Mountain.* In the same year, she won a second DramaLogue Award for *Home* and *Piano Lesson,* which were staged at the Denver Center Theatre Company and *Blues for an Alabama Sky* at The Sacramento Theatre Company. Iona is a child of black Hollywood royalty; her father was Greg Morris, who played Barney Collier, the highly intelligent engineer on the hit '70s series *"Mission:Impossible."* She is self-publishing her first book, *Love, Death & Rebirth,* and has a new collection of poetry and short stories due out soon.

Mariann Aalda is a graduate of Southern Illinois University and the Negro Ensemble Company theater-training program. She made her New York stage debut with Ruby Dee and the late Ossie Davis in The New Federal Theatre production of *Take It from the Top.* She is best known for her work in television: a long-running role in the ABC soap opera *Edge of Night* as DiDi Bannister; she costarred in the films *Class Act, Nobody's Perfect,* and *The Wiz* (now cult classics because of endless TV reruns); and she had a regular role on the CBS sitcom *The Royal Family* as the daughter of Redd Foxx and Della Reese. Aalda also writes a humor-infused "ethnic etiquette" advice column with writer-producer Karen Greyson for BlackBerrySpeak.

For more information on these dynamic ladies, visit www.3BlacqueChix. com.

▶ *Chapter 4*

Who Will Step Up?

I was first introduced to the subject of HIV/AIDS back in the days when I was in grad school at Harvard Law School and working on a project that helped people who were getting evicted from their apartments when the landlords found out that they had AIDS.

I learned about the discrimination side of the disease before I actually learned about the disease itself.

Sometime thereafter, I ended up doing a short film about HIV, *One Red Rose,* which I co-wrote with my cousin, Charlie Jordan. Starring Victoria Rowell, the film addressed how quickly HIV was spreading amongst young black women.

I did that film as I was completing grad school, but it was really the film *The Visit* that had me meeting people living with HIV and talking about it with them. While preparing for the role of someone who was HIV positive, I did a great deal of research on the disease.

I met one man that had 80 friends or associates who were in-fected with either HIV or AIDS. He had full blown AIDS, as well. Having conversations with him, and talking about the pain, really made me aware of another side of the problem.

Then Phill Wilson of the Black AIDS Institute asked if I would get involved to help raise awareness in the community. Interacting with that organization increased my awareness of the statistics and what's going on with treatment and outreach.

There still seems to be a stigma and so much homophobia in the African-American community. It was once considered a "gay disease"; therefore, many were fearful of having that label applied to them, and as such avoided being tested. There is still a wide gap between truth and perception.

Now, I think that as more people find out that it's treatable, they will be encouraged to get tested. With increased awareness comes decreased transmission. AIDS no longer has to be a death sentence unless it is kept quiet in our community.

As a single adult male, the key is to practice safe sex no matter who you are with, whether or not it is a long-standing partner. Even with my girlfriend, I practice safe sex.

Condoms aren't free, so it takes a commitment to use them. If people say that condoms take the fun and spontaneity out of it, they are attaching a false and negative message. I remember when it wasn't cool to wear seatbelts. Now, it's not even a thought. People get in the car and buckle up. It not only has to do with laws, but also retraining people's minds. The same thing has to happen with using condoms. It has to become a necessary part of the whole sexual experience.

Leadership in the black community could do more. There are some church and religious leaders who are also guilty of falsely identifying AIDS as the "gay disease."

Rev. Jesse Jackson is widely respected as a leader, but he and other charismatic leaders like him don't get out in front of this issue enough.

Drawing maximum attention to this disease will take the re-direction of organizations that once focused only on apartheid to now look at AIDS in Africa.

It will take the voices of Oprah Winfrey, Bill Cosby, Tavis Smiley, and others like them to reach the general public.

To reach young people, it will take the artists to get behind the message. They will pay attention to someone like Alicia Keys and other performers who are clearly politically active. You've got to get someone like The Game or 50 Cent and get them to do a public-service announcement. I think that it is assumed that these artists won't do them, but a lot of them are receptive. It's about asking people and getting their voice involved.

The good news is that African Americans are survivors, and we are going to make it.

HILL HARPER

Hill Harper is a popular stage, film, and television actor. Currently starring in the television drama *CSI: NY,* Harper is a graduate of Brown University and Harvard Law School. He is the author of the best-selling motivational book *Letters to a Young Brother: MANifest Your Destiny.*

Chapter 5

Ms. Different

Bodies collide as huge drops of hot sweat fall to the floor. Hearts are racing, thoughts are carefree, and the moment has full control. They're ready to get drunk, have fun, and forget it all. She tells herself she's earned it, that she's young and *now* is the time to live spontaneously. He's in his prime—the more he gets, the more he's worth, and let's be honest, she's good enough to sample. So he does.

It only takes a moment, a silent lock of the eyes. The question—the answer—yes. They don't know where they are. A vacant room—a car—a closet. It doesn't matter. All we know is that she wants him and he wants her and in that special moment she will ...

She will ... what do *you* put in the blank? As varied as the answers will be, almost all of them will be wrong. In moments like these, when we feel it is understandable and almost right for us to lose control, we forget about the risks. The last thing we think is "in that special moment she will ... be infected with AIDS."

As an American woman living luxuriously in the suburbs of Los Angeles, I can say that being infected with the AIDS virus was one of the last things that I ever thought about. Even though I was born in 1984, in the height of the first epidemic, my relation to the AIDS virus was very tangential. I recognized the virus for the repulsive horror it was, I empathized with its victims, I watched the movies and campaigns, I knew both people living with and those who had succumbed to the virus, but I never truly considered the fact that it could one day attack me. How is it that when young adults like myself think of the clichés our mothers told us involving unprotected sex ("A moment of passion may lead to a lifetime of pain"—or death, in this case), we are still more petrified of K-I-D-S, the fruitful offspring that will sacrifice our bank accounts and vibrant social lives, instead of being deathly afraid of A-I-D-S, the devastating virus that could sacrifice our lives? How can this still be the case, considering all the campaigns, the plays that come to high schools, Tyrese on BET, and Bono?

Tony Kushner's *Angels in America* and Bono's campaigns in Africa, as progressive as they are, helped me to maintain my distance and ignorance. I could contribute to the funds and watch the play and HBO movie while compartmentalizing these groups away from myself. As a black woman, I can safely say it was the first time I was excited to not be included. I was comforted by the fact that I was not. I am not a homosexual male, I do not share needles, nor do I live in a Third World country, and if I ever visited Africa, we can all be sure I would not have sex, protected or not, with a native. By these standards, I would never be infected with AIDS.

The largest group currently being infected with the AIDS virus in America is black women. That makes me Target #1. How did this happen? How did a virus whose favorite victim was homosexual white men develop a taste for the complete opposite—heterosexual black women?

This virus seems to be extremely successful in attacking marginalized groups. AIDS first attacked homosexual men and drug addicts, arguably two groups that the hegemony of this white, heterosexual, and patriarchal society tells us we can do without. Next, it globally attacked poverty, or shall we say, Third World countries. If that wasn't enough, it attacked Africa, wiping out nearly an entire generation of people. Only a mass genocide could have been as swift. Now, American black women, who are known globally for their music video roles as females who can be objectified and degraded and enjoy it, are also under attack.

I am not trying to ring the bells for some incredible conspiracy theory. I am just trying to point out the fact that it is interesting. When I look at the hot spots in this country for AIDS and I see that most of them have historically-black colleges and universities as epicenters. I can't help but scratch my head. What does this information really mean? Are black college students more promiscuous then their white counterparts, or are they less willing to use protection? I attended a predominantly white university and can say that in my four years, legions of virtuous white women and chaste white men were not to be found. Most importantly, races mixed and slept together. So what is it? What makes the difference between an outbreak at Howard and an outbreak at the University of Pennsylvania? What makes the difference between life for some and certain death for others?

These questions aren't easily answered, and blame can prove to be a vacant game. This virus doesn't care which group you think you're a part of, or which group you choose to blame. Eventually, rich, poor, young, old, white, black, Asian, and other ... our names can all be on the list.

NADIA LATAILLADE

A recent graduate of the University of Southern California, Nadia Lataillade is pursuing a career as a professional writer.

► *Chapter 6*

Reality Check ...

Whether we choose to admit it or not, AIDS has definitely made an impact on how we live our lives. I know it's definitely changed the way that I view having an intimate encounter with someone. I have always been responsible, but the idea of AIDS has certainly taken the spontaneity out of it. You have to consider a person's life before you met them. You have to consider what's come before you. It's very real.

In the last five years, AIDS has become even more real to me. My family and I have lost two close relatives to the disease: my mom's sister and her cousin. My mom's cousin was more like her brother, so we called him Uncle Jimmy. He was gay and was infected ten years ago by his partner. My aunt was infected by her husband, who had had a bout with drugs. She left behind four children and five grandchildren.

Because of her untimely death, my mother, siblings, and I all take turns raising her youngest son, who is now 14. He lives with my mother; my brother had him before that, and I have him on the weekends.

It's affected his life in every way, and he has to deal with it on a daily basis. He's lost his mother. He's lost his father. He's lost his grandmother. He's lost everyone who's loved him. As a result, he gives my mom trouble—he's trying to not get too attached to her. His pain runs very deep, and he's going through therapy.

His mother was already infected when he was born, but he was spared. Dealing with that is so hard; he's wondering, "Why not me?" There's a lot of thoughts like that that go through his mind, and I'm certain it's affected his life in many ways; only he, in his head, deals with it on a daily basis. As a result of these great emotional losses, he lashes out at those who are closest to him—and now, that person is my mom. But it stems from his fear that if he gets too close to her, death may take her away from him as well ... the pain runs very deep.

His sister is 21 and has a five-year-old son. She was a teenage mother, like her mom. She knows that you can get the disease through unsafe sexual encounters, but I don't know how much she understands, because she is so young.

It hasn't always been so easy to talk about it. When I first learned about the disease and realized that I knew someone personally who was infected with it, there was still a lot of misinformation out there. No one really knew how you contracted it; some were afraid to touch an infected person.

My uncle Jimmy would often make an African dish called peanut chicken that was one of my favorite dishes; he would make it for me whenever I asked him to. One Christmas after his diagnosis, I asked him to make it—but I asked him to make it before we'd discovered that he was HIV positive. He made it for me, but I was the only one who ate it; no one else would eat it, which made him feel horrible. The rest of the family loved him, but they didn't know any better.

I accepted my uncle's diagnosis easily because I had already lost two friends to AIDS. However, that didn't mean that things went any smoother between us.

When my friend was sick, he had told me that he longed for touches, hugs, and kisses, because people had stopped touching him. Whenever I would kiss him goodbye, he would thank me.

Once my friend passed, my uncle expected me to do the same things for him. I had spent almost every day at the hospital and later, at the hospice, with my friend. My sister and I were with him for everything—to celebrate when his T-cell count was up, and then to console him when the report was not so good. We were there when he took his last breath, and the experience of watching someone you love unconditionally die—all the while hoping against hope that the illness will reverse and he will beat the odds—was emotionally and physically draining. I went through a long mourning period for my friend and wasn't sure if I could do it again. This made my uncle feel like I wasn't there for him as I had been for my friend. It was unfair, but it was a part of his anger.

Everyone knows someone who has had it, but there's still that attitude of "That's not me," or "I'm far away from that and am not susceptible to it." I don't know where that's coming from. Maybe having HIV and AIDS is still thought of as someone else's disease that can't happen to "regular" people. I don't know what it's going to take. But we've got to stop it. We cannot let those numbers continue to rise. I'm not letting my children grow up in a world where everyone is infected. We've got to stop this thing in its tracks. I remember reading an article in the 1980s that said that in 20 years, everyone would know someone infected with HIV/AIDS or who had died from it. At the time, I thought, "No way," but it's been less than 20 years, and I know more than one person; two of them were members of my family.

Although the task is daunting, there are certain things that I think I can do on an individual level and within the entertainment community to help bring awareness to the problem. I have a responsibility to teach because I have two young children of my own. I have tried to maintain a strong Christian foundation and love for God in my house. I stress more than anything to love yourself and to wait for the right person. I understand curiosity—we've all been there. I tell my children that as much as they think they know, I know more. I stress to them that if the flesh must have its way, explore it safely.

The responsibility to teach doesn't just rest on my shoulders, however. I believe there is much that the entertainment community can do as well. I try my best to live the life I preach to them. For me, it boils down to my relationship with God, and whether I choose to abstain or not. I tell my children that if a potential partner makes an issue about practicing safe sex, then they need to rethink their relationship with that person. We realize that it is clearly an intimate, sensitive, and difficult issue to discuss, but it goes beyond that.

Black Hollywood could definitely be doing more. Writers write, directors direct—they can make characters that aren't too idealistic. TV is a powerful medium. Certain shows have done AIDS arcs; when I was casting *Girlfriends,* there was a two-story arc that dealt with HIV/AIDS. We need more of that on shows that our children watch. We need more of that in the characters that they are watching, listening to, and trying to emulate. Throw a storyline in there to inform them. There are definitely more things we could be doing.

For us as a community, information is power. Even though we know that AIDS kills, there's really not that much information given out or driven home to young people. The enormity and extent of what can happen is not being understood. I don't know what it will take for our people to realize how serious this is; I hope it's not going to take losing a great public figure to AIDS.

We need to view the threat of HIV/AIDS as if it were in our own families. That could mean taking part in the Black AIDS Institute's next big fundraiser, or joining the 100 Stars' Fight Against AIDS, or going to schools and speaking, or just mentoring a child. No action is too great or too small.

ROBI REED

Robi Reed is an Emmy Award–winning casting director who has worked with many of Hollywood's brightest stars, including Vanessa Williams, Eddie Murphy, Stevie Wonder, Janet Jackson, Michael Jackson, Richard Pryor, Danny DeVito, Tupac Shakur, and Denzel Washington.

Chapter 7

The Power of Truth

When I first heard about HIV and AIDS, like most people, I was shocked, and I tried to figure out what it was. In the black community, I think we became particularly cloudy and homophobic. Too many people in the black community foolishly believe that AIDS is a gay thing or an African thing, but not an African-American or a heterosexual problem. Not only is neither true, but these assumptions exacerbate the impact of this disease. The more you ignore a problem and compartmentalize it, the more it can grow. AIDS is not "over there." It's right here. And I'm not even talking about our neighborhoods; it's right in your house.

How does any intelligent, sane person ignore what's right in front of him or her? We started a campaign, The Black Church Forum, because the black church was absent from the forefront of HIV/AIDS education. Denial and homophobia have contributed to AIDS becoming such an epidemic in the African-American community. The denial hurt our people. It hurt our congregants because we act as if we don't engage in any behavior that causes HIV/AIDS, especially gay sexual activity.

We have to start with the truth. First, HIV/AIDS does not just impact homosexuals; it touches people of all backgrounds and sexual persuasions. Second, we've all known about gay life, even if we didn't acknowledge it. The first gay people I knew were in the church. I am alarmed by the hypocrisy of some leaders in the black church who don't want to deal with their own homophobia and denial. People in their congregations are gay. People in their congregations are also being exposed to AIDS. One guy said to me that if we put everybody out of the church that had had a gay experience, we would probably have empty pews. Our gospel music departments and half the pulpit would be gone. So why are we playing with this? We are just coming into an era where people are openly challenging the black church to deal with sexuality and sexually transmitted diseases. It's not yet to the degree that it should be, but it's a beginning. I see signs of progress.

Black political and church leaders should try to solve problems, but not in an accusatory way. We should be publicly testing and publicly dealing with this disease in a way that embraces families and individuals impacted by HIV or AIDS. We must avoid perpetuating feelings of abandonment and isolation by interrogating victims about how they got the disease. "Oh, you must have done this that or the other to contract the disease." That kind of blame game really doesn't matter. If we offered solutions and more comfort we might have avoided the phenomenon of the "down low." Men are on the "down low" because they were pushed down low. They didn't jump up and volunteer for this; they were psychologically pushed down low. If I came into your house, beat you up, brought you to the bedroom, and put you under the bed, I couldn't then ask what you were doing down there. I put you down there. I made you afraid to be branded with another scarlet letter. We have done the same in responding to homosexuals. They live part of their lives in secret and in the process they are affecting innocent, unsuspecting women in a black community already disproportionately affected by AIDS.

The black community's hostile message is not very different for black lesbians. I grew up with a sister who was gay. She had to struggle with bias as a black person, bias as a woman, and bias within the black community as a lesbian. Witnessing the trinity of pain she faced made me more open-minded than most. Many black homosexuals are on the "down low" because of the message they receive from the society at large. Look at how members of the political right dealt with the same-sex marriage phobia of the last election. These political trends make black homosexuals even more fearful of being marginalized and ostracized. This is one of the moral impediments the church must address. Even if the black clergy believes that homosexuality is outside the church's teachings, we have a moral obligation to protect people against bias and discrimination.

Part of the impetus for black homophobia is our desire to imitate and surpass the white homophobia. Blacks always want to be accepted by the white world, and the white world is homophobic. In turn, we believe that we have to be even more homophobic, because we have to be more acceptable to be accepted. However, as white America has dealt with the gay issue, we have slowly followed suit. Given our history, we should be leading white America, not following it. Homosexuals were the scapegoat of 2004. The United States has 50 million people with no access to affordable health care, a war going on with no weapons of mass destruction, a broken public-education system, and all this drives the right wing to attack homosexuals to win major elections. "They are going to destroy marriage!" That's the sort of rallying cry that helped bring Bush back.

I was incredulous when I asked black preachers, "How can you be so stupid?" Being president has nothing to do with gay marriage. Heterosexual adultery breaks up many more marriages than the presence of homosexuals in the community and their desire to have committed relationships with other homosexuals. So why fall into the trap of demonizing the gay community?

Black homophobia is simply a way to try to make ourselves more acceptable to bigoted people—people who will not accept us anyway. We should be paying attention to the reality of our own community and families instead. The lowest scum of our community, those individuals who have done terrible things to other people, can find forgiveness. But a homosexual, even a close family member, has to hide and pretend to be something she or he is not? That's not right. It is completely unthinkable that we put such a burden on people; we are a community that knows more than others about what being rejected and ostracized feels like.

The shame exhibited in the black community regarding AIDS is an illusion. It's manufactured shame, because truthfully, what are we really ashamed of? Something that we always knew was there? AIDS is not something that we created or brought on ourselves. It is a disease that has surfaced like many others, and now we must deal with it. We should be ashamed that, to date, we have not done enough to combat AIDS. Many black people have developed a sense of shame for having this disease, but the shame belongs to all of us for not doing enough about it.

The hope is that we are now investing resources to find a cure and tearing down the societal walls that we have put in place. I spoke at two of the three memorials for Rosa Parks. Sometimes, it takes just one person to be a catalyst for change. It was acceptable to sit in the back of the bus before Mrs. Parks helped change people's minds.

Now that some of us are coming out and challenging AIDS, maybe we can get past this backward mentality. It is not going to happen overnight, but it won't take 50 years either. Mrs. Parks made America come to terms with its beastly attitude towards black people in a dramatic way. When she refused to give up her seat, it led to change in America that was accepted. The Civil Rights Act of 1964, the Voting Rights Act of 1965, and many other accomplishments were all possible because of the movement led by Dr. Martin Luther King that was sparked by Mrs. Parks. Now, there is a national holiday honoring Dr. King. Rosa Parks was honored posthumously by lying in state in the Capitol rotunda. It is an accepted idea that overt racism and indecent behavior towards blacks are deplorable things.

What is still not as accepted, however, is that blacks should have a sense of their own ownership, destiny, and self-definition. This is why someone like John Johnson, the founder of publications including *Ebony* and *Jet* magazines, among others, is not yet an icon like Dr. King or Mrs. Parks. As successful as Mr. Johnson was, America is not ready for black people to define and own ourselves. John Johnson taught the power of black self-definition. Whites in Hollywood, in "TV Land," and in books still don't want us to have that power. Mr. Johnson was like Rosa Parks in that way.

Johnson's message was, "No, I'm not going to let you tell us who we are. We aren't all like Stepin Fetchit." That was a revolutionary act just like the one that occurred on December 1, 1955. America can accept blacks staying at hotels like the Four Seasons, but is reluctant to allow blacks to define themselves. That's what John Johnson represented, and it may take a few more decades for white America to realize that self-definition is just as significant as being able to sit at the front of the bus.

It's going to take the black community a lot of time and a lot of honesty to overcome the psychological damage of our experience in America. Many of us just don't want to deal with it. And many of the most successful among us are the most confused, and the most vulnerable. We won't acknowledge the demons we inherited from our parents and grandparents. If those of us who are most visible continue to run from the invisible demons, it is more likely that these demons will persist into succeeding generations. We have to finish the journey for real justice, because it does not yet exist. We often act as if the Middle Passage didn't happen.

One positive thing that arose from Mrs. Parks' passing is that it forced us to acknowledge that there was a struggle for us to get somewhere. And therefore we are responsible to struggle today. But now some of us say, "The struggle is over. I am successful now. I am in the suburbs now. I have made it. We don't need to struggle anymore. We don't need to struggle against the AIDS and HIV epidemic. We don't need to struggle against the other social ills crippling the black community." We might have better accommodations and accoutrements, but we are still in an uneven situation.

And then there are the conspiracy theories. Some people believe that HIV/AIDS was created in a laboratory and disseminated to destroy us. I'm definitely one to believe some conspiracy theories, but I'm not convinced of the accuracy of this claim. How or why the disease got here does not excuse us from dealing with the fact that it is here and devising ways to defeat it. My problem with some of these conspiracy theorists is that they spend more time on the theory than on creating solutions.

To adequately fight AIDS in the black community, we need both mass education and mass testing. We also need to attack AIDS on the political front. We need to demand more from those people who are competing for our votes, and force them to make AIDS a prominent issue. That means allocating public resources for HIV/AIDS research and expanding access to healthcare. We cannot afford to take AIDS off the table, especially as our community is impacted more than anyone else. When people seek our support as they run for office, we have to demand that as part of their commitment to us, they must put public funds into research and healthcare for HIV and AIDS victims. It impacts us disproportionately, but we don't make it an issue when we have the opportunity.

It is the responsibility of real political leaders (and so-called political leaders) to pressure the government and start corralling the resources within our community, in the church community, in the business community, and in the entertainment world. We should have drives to raise money for HIV/AIDS research the same way we had drives for Hurricane Katrina relief; AIDS is a healthcare Katrina. Researchers who wish to conduct studies on HIV and AIDS in our community cannot get the financial support they need. That should not happen.

We have the economic resources in our community to do a lot, but these potential solutions are not mutually exclusive. We can use our own resources, and make demands of the government. Why do I say that? Politicians often ignore our issues, but at the same time they all come to us for votes. If we speak up, we can force the government to deal with issues that it might otherwise ignore. We've had huge gatherings like the Million Man March and the Millions More Movement. We've had an international audience at our disposal. Why wasn't the AIDS epidemic a prominent issue at these events? We have not yet done enough when we have had the world's attention.

In addition to talking to our elected officials and the rest of the world, black Americans must also talk to each other. Abstinence is one message that we can give our youth to prevent the spread of AIDS, but it should not be the only one. Our AIDS prevention programs for the young should include everything from safe sex to abstinence to testing. But it must start with compassion, research, and understanding.

Caution must be taken with the message of abstinence, as it has the potential to direct arrogance and insensitivity toward those already affected. Abstinence cannot be preached as the only righteous choice. We cannot assume that everyone will subscribe to abstinence. Again, we are forcing people "down low." A lot of people will say, "Yes, it's the right choice," about abstinence, and surreptitiously become sexually active anyway. We have to be real. The parents of my generation preached the message of abstinence to us as children. At the time, we weren't necessarily talking about homosexuality and AIDS, but the singular focus on abstinence didn't lead to less sex; instead, it led to more abortions. Let's not repeat the mistakes of previous generations. There has never before been a generation of young people that has abstained from sex.

But still we can make it. The fact that we survived our journeys through the Middle Passage, slavery, and Jim Crow is evidence that we can make it. The question is not if we can make it, but when are we going to make it? When will we stop telling ourselves what we want to hear and deal with the reality of HIV and AIDS in our community? You can never change reality if you are living under an illusion. We must stop wondering *if* we can win our battle with AIDS and move forward determined that we *are* going to win. We have no choice but to defeat AIDS. Our very lives and the future of our race are at stake.

I have two daughters. As a father, it's frightening to think about them entering into adulthood with something like AIDS around. Of course, it makes you tell them to be careful and to be safe. But the only way you can be completely comfortable is if the disease is eradicated. Each time you admonish your children, you remember the admonitions your parents gave you that were not heeded. And now they only have to make one mistake, and it's all over. So the only real solution is to eliminate AIDS at the same time that you guide your children, because as long as it exists, one slip-up can mean everything.

Black people in America must recognize that no one on the planet went through what we went through as a people and survived. Therefore, there must be something within us that is stronger than anybody else on the planet. We need to harness that strength towards solving existing problems like the AIDS epidemic. But as long as we are ashamed of our struggle rather than proud of it, we will have misplaced self-definition and self-worth. I am proud to be a part of a race that, for all practical purposes, should have been wiped off the face of the earth. We are still here. We are still thriving and setting the tone for culture in the world. That's why I know we can beat AIDS. Look at what we have already overcome. There is no way we should have come from the opposite end of the Atlantic Ocean to where we are now. If we can take that journey, we can certainly turn this corner.

THE REV. AL SHARPTON

The Rev. Al Sharpton is a Pentecostal minister and a political and civil rights activist. In 2004, he sought the Democratic Party nomination for president of the United States.

▶ *Chapter 8*

Standing United Behind a Cause

I don't know anyone in the black community who hasn't been touched in some way, shape, or form by HIV/AIDS. The devastation of losing someone to this disease affected my life early on; a close family friend, Keith Barrow, died in 1983. Back then, it was considered a gay disease, so no one had a full appreciation of the negative impact HIV/AIDS would have on the entire community. Today, we have more and better information, so we must do three things: spread that information faster than the disease, call on all levels of government to contribute appropriate resources, and work with health-care concerns to make sure they do the same.

HIV/AIDS remains a pervasive problem in our community. This is not a gay disease. It is largely spread in our community via heterosexual contact and intravenous drug use. Many people in the African-American community are aware of this significant information about HIV/AIDS, but they are still uncomfortable about sharing it. We shouldn't find comfort in the darkness of ignorance; we should find comfort in the bright light of information.

The statistics should force us out of our silence: HIV/AIDS is the number one cause of death for African-American women 25 to 34 years of age. According to the Centers for Disease Control and Prevention (CDC), 49 percent of all new HIV/AIDS cases are among African Americans, and we are 10 times more likely to contract it than our white counterparts. We need more of our churches and ministers to use their pulpits to share the information. Our mass-media educators must use their outlets to create greater awareness. Our civil rights leaders must use their platforms. Our federal, state, and local elected leaders must use their voices to talk and legislate about HIV/AIDS. Individuals who are at the center of influence in our communities must use their voices to talk about this disease, educate others about how it spreads, and come up with programs that offer solutions to this problem.

But we also need to hear from our everyday heroes. When a person who has been personally and tragically affected by AIDS steps forward and commands the nation's attention, lives can be saved. Celebrities can also make a big difference. When Earvin "Magic" Johnson announced that he was HIV positive, we were forced to think about this disease and its consequences on all of our communities. All the recent attention paid to the "down-low" phenomenon has taken us on another path, but the bottom line is that it has helped spark crucial dialogue about sexuality and its impact on health. The bottom line is that we need all hands on deck for the battle against HIV/AIDS.

While we're doing what's necessary within our community, we must continue asking tough questions of those on the outside. Is the African-American community receiving a fair share of federal money to educate its people about HIV/AIDS? Is that level of funding enough? African-American health advocates should have every weapon at their disposal to fight this disease, as well as the overall general health concerns that make treating African Americans living with HIV/AIDS so challenging. Along with other members of the U.S. House of Representatives, Congresswoman Maxine Waters and I have been working to make sure that whatever funding exists is distributed in ways that are most effective in, and supportive of, the African-American community.

We must also remain vigilant because the government has not been naturally sensitive to the particular needs of African Americans, from individual needs to physical infrastructure. In August 2005, Hurricane Katrina merely pulled a scab off the generations-old nasty sore about the federal government's response to poverty, especially in our community. But "infrastructure" encompasses more than poverty and levies. It's a crumbling health-care network. It's a crumbling information-dissemination network that directly impacts HIV and AIDS education. It can be extended to cover homeland security.

For many Americans, Hurricane Katrina blew the roof off of our illusion of a strong federal government infrastructure that supports every American. But truth be told, it was blown off by Keith Barrow and every African American that has been affected by HIV/AIDS. It is blown off when condoms are not distributed in prisons, and when we don't allow needle-exchange programs for those who acquire the disease via intravenous drug use. We must also awaken from our illusion that there is a pill for HIV/AIDS—an illusion sparked by the welcome success of antiretroviral drugs that have added years to the lives of people living with HIV/AIDS. I encourage our HIV/AIDS advocates to continue their own roof-blowing, so that the spread of HIV/AIDS gets treated like the human rights issue it is.

As we do our respective parts to spread the word and at least slow the spread of HIV/AIDS, we also need to stay focused on the health care community's response to AIDS in the African-American community. Part of that focus includes ending health care disparities that have an impact on the overall health of our community.

In March 2001, the Institute of Medicine issued a report that revealed what many patients and health care professionals had long suspected: there was a bias in medicine. That report titled "Unequal Treatment: Confronting Racial and Ethnic Conspiracy in Health Care," is one that I am personally responsible for getting funded, and it came with several recommendations. One of these was the need for Congress to be more financially committed to creating facilities that train minority health professionals, since they are the ones who will likely end up working in minority communities. In addition, we need to promote cultural competency when training health-care professionals.

The African-American community needs culturally competent health-care professionals to adequately deal with HIV/AIDS in order to begin a comprehensive dialogue about the disease. We must also have a form of what I'll call *personal health competence*. My good friend Rae Lewis-Thornton has both full-blown AIDS and personal health competence. She was able to enroll in the right kind of health-care plan, which has allowed her to pay for the many drugs she needs in order to keep her T-cell count right. That competence also keeps her taking her medication properly, monitoring her overall health, and running Rae Lewis-Thornton, Inc., an educational organization devoted to teaching everyone about living with AIDS.

There are many people like Rae Lewis-Thornton who are victims of HIV/AIDS and are also productive citizens who contribute greatly to our society. We need to protect them with health care, but also federal and state legislation that keeps them from becoming victims of discrimination. In the 1993 film *Philadelphia,* Tom Hanks' character, an HIV-positive lawyer, enlisted the aid of a fellow attorney (played by Denzel Washington) to help him fight discrimination in his workplace. In real life, most people with AIDS often cannot afford to fight their boss and the disease. To that end, we can find ways to make important medications more affordable, and make sure that Medicaid and other programs that help underwrite necessary aspects of life for people living with HIV/AIDS— like the costs of medication—are fully funded.

For our nation to respond to HIV/AIDS in the ways I've described, we must also demand support from all levels of government. If an elected official or a political party does not share your economic and health concerns, then that official or party should not receive your vote. I believe that the lack of federal dollars for crucial health services cannot simply be explained away as a lack of funds. What is often lacking is the political will. If the government is concerned about its people, then it cannot keep, as Dr. Martin Luther King Jr. said, issuing us "a promissory note" that "has come back marked 'insufficient funds.'" The African-American community must be willing to challenge a political order that is not responsive to the toll HIV/AIDS has taken on our community, challenge itself to spread the word about this still-deadly disease, and challenge any personal behaviors we have that may place us, and those we love, at risk.

I am committed to doing what's necessary for the African-American community to triumph over HIV/AIDS. But before everything else, we must develop tolerance for those affected by this disease. Then let us stand in unity and stamp this plague of our time out of existence.

THE HONORABLE JESSE JACKSON JR. (D-IL)

Representative Jesse L. Jackson Jr. began service in the United States House of Representatives on December 12, 1995, as he was sworn in as a member of the 104th Congress, the 91st African American ever elected to Congress. He currently sits on the House Appropriations Committee, serving as the fifth-ranking Democrat on the Subcommittee on Labor, Health and Human Services, and Education, as well as the second-ranking Democrat on the Subcommittee on Foreign Operations, Export Financing, and Related Programs. His leadership created the National Institutes of Health's National Center on Minority Health and Health Disparities, which was established by the passage of the Minority Health and Health Disparities Research and Education Act of 2000, Public Law 106-525, signed by the president on November 22, 2000. This Act has been hailed by many minority health experts as the most important civil rights legislation since the 1964 Civil Rights Act. Representative Jackson also secured funding for the Institute of Medicine's 2002 report on health disparities, "Unequal Treatment: Confronting Racial and Ethnic Disparities in Health Care."

▶ *Chapter 9*

Living My Life with AIDS

I came of age during the generation of sexual freedom and rebellion of the mid- to late '70s. Parties, fun, and more fun were the objectives of life at the time, and during this period it was okay to "come out" and be whoever, and whatever, you wanted to be. Fueled by the backdrop of disco music, bright lights, bath houses, and drug binges, I allowed myself to get caught up with that lifestyle. I would subsequently discover that that freedom wasn't free. It came with a price.

Although I was never one to experiment with intravenous drug use, my sexual proclivities shifted from one-on-one intimacy with male partners to sleeping with women who very much wanted to "change me." Who I would sleep with at any given time would depend on how horny I was. People, friends, and acquaintances were dying all around me, and no conclusive cause of death was ever really identified as AIDS ... although they shared the same symptoms that were becoming evident in those who had been diagnosed with a virus called HTLV-III.

I found a certain excitement in the orgy scene, which is where I believe I contracted HIV. During that time, within that environment, and having unprotected sex, I could have gotten it from a man or a woman.

Although ignorance was, and is, rampant concerning this disease, I am fortunate that when I learned I had contracted HIV, I immediately sought medical attention. Though I was not a doctor or scientist, it made no sense to me that a disease that was affecting gay white men could not affect gay men of other ethnicities.

Because of this common-sense-based awareness, I began to do my own research.

That was more than 20 years ago, and since then, my life has changed on many levels. I have often said that on one level, contracting HIV is one of the best things that has happened to me. Let me explain ...

Although being a person with AIDS is just a fraction of who I am, having this disease has taught me so many things about life. Because of AIDS, I have faced the man in the mirror as well. All the veils have been removed from the people and things that I let into my space. Living with this disease has taught me to love myself "well" and unconditionally, and it has also shown me the way to embrace my friends, family, and most importantly, God.

I "came out" with this circle of guys who have all but disappeared. Sometimes, I truly feel like I am the last of "my kind," and I have experienced the confusion, depression, and anger at why am I am still here. The hardest part was watching them suffer as their souls departed this earthly experience. It's taken me a while to recognize that through their deaths, my friends have left me with a gift: the gift of truly understanding the dichotomy of life. We must embrace it fiercely, but just as fiercely surrender it back to the Creator. All of my deceased friends have given me the boost, the guts and determination to fight AIDS as best I can when the going gets rough.

When I think about who I am and things that I have done in my life, I think about the poet Langston Hughes. I could have been named a "Dream Deferred," I could have been named my "brother's keeper," and I could also have been named "Misunderstood." Some might say that I am insecure, troubled, angry, frightened, and empty, while others would call me a man with convictions and a friend who is strong, proud, and loving. I prefer to think of me as just who I am. My name is Jeffrey Dwayne Robertson, and I know now that I am only a child of God who has tried to be a man and has lived his life in truth and honesty.

Oh, what freedom truth brings, and I want our people to be free. The freedom I speak of begins in our minds. In the minds of our people I would like to dispel the myth that AIDS is a faggot disease. I want people to stop living in fear and to let their voices be heard. I want people to stop the denial as it relates to their reckless behavior and live their best lives. I want people to understand how alcohol, drugs, low self-esteem, the seven deadly sins, and other vices play an important role in the choices we make: choices that end in results which ultimately determine and change the shape of our lives forever.

As a result of accepting myself just as I am and not allowing the opinions of other people to sully my self-esteem, I am still here. As a result of the power of the love of my family and my faith and trust in God, I am still here. As a result of the prayers of my friends, my church, and my angels, I am still here. And I am committed to always sharing my truth.

JEFFREY D. ROBERTSON

Jeffrey D. Robertson is an AIDS activist who resides in Los Angeles.

Chapter 10

Sweet-Tea Ethics: Black Luv, Healthcare, and Cultural Mistrust

There once was a Persian cat who had a tail worthy of marvel. In arrogant displays, she would strut and fret many hours upon the stage. Suitors employed adoration, only to be rebuffed time and time again. A flawed beauty, she often pranced around the railroad tracks behind old man Johnson's corner store. That was until karma came calling. In a tragic twist of fate, her tail was cut off in a freak accident. An overzealous streetcar conductor ran over the Persian princess's tail as she attracted suitors one late southern evening. Ego crushed, and knocked from the pedestal she had carefully constructed, the former head-turner lamented her misstep. She lost her head over a little piece of tail.

"Never lose your head over a little piece of tail," snapped my southern-bred grandmother as she offered up her classic extended metaphor for sexual relations. From Samson to Kobe Bryant, many men have weathered the consequences of letting a little tail go to their heads. This fictitious "tail" narrative advanced by my late Grandma not only became classic family lore, but it also became the foundation of her "straight, no chaser" classes in sex education.

Before I hit puberty, and years before my incidences of puppy love morphed into incessant lust, my grandma had already schooled me on condom use and the prevalence of HIV/AIDS. And while many a relative chided her for being a little too frank with young folk, she was relentless with her unsanctioned safe sex lectures. You see, decades earlier, she had been the victim of misinformation.

On one such occasion, after prodding my great granddad on the whereabouts of a missing playmate, she was informed that her best friend had broken her leg. In reality, the girl had become pregnant. So she made a vow to be as open and honest about "relations" to anyone in earshot. And boy, did she burn some ears.

As is the case for many black folks, my health education rarely came from PhDs or credentialed health professionals with carefully constructed marketing campaigns or brochures highlighting empty statistics. My education happened during Friday fish fries, Sunday dinners, and other random gatherings starring Grandma Lowe and a host of uncles, aunts, "play cousins," and family friends. Wrapped in love and peppered with stern warnings—often emphasizing the consequences of unprotected sex—these informal classes would form the core of my knowledge of reproductive health.

HIV/AIDS was given a personal face when a dear co-worker of my mother's, a deeply loving art enthusiast and cultural warrior who reminded me of literary giant James Baldwin, passed away. His death rocked my spirit, and his loss resounded louder to me than any PSA or clever catchphrase ever did. Most importantly, I watched how my mother and her collection of supporters rallied around their ailing friend, filling his last days with more food, laughter, and good times than he could stand.

My story is not an isolated one, but rather a reflection of the humanistic ethos of African Americans anchored in reciprocity and strong ties to family and social support systems (church, community groups, hair salons, barbershops, etc.). Effective strategies for combating the spread of HIV must take into consideration how the African-American way of being is directly influenced by the permanence of racism, and how cultural mistrust informs the help-seeking behaviors of our people. The innate creativity of black folks can be directly linked to the dire necessity of developing coping mechanisms and adaptive strategies to eke out survival in an American society preoccupied with forecasting our demise.

Since its emergence, HIV/AIDS has always been viewed as an "other-people" affliction, as it was often associated with homosexuality, an orientation perceived by some to be a morally reprehensible lifestyle. As HIV/AIDS began to disproportionately affect the African-American community, theorists dusted off age-old notions of white supremacy couched in cultural pathology frameworks. Quite conveniently, these theories that associate immorality, free will, and inherent inferiority with African-American culture frequently become scapegoats for larger forces like poverty, persistent racism, and unchecked discrimination that inhibit life chances and deeply affect quality of life. .

Health care is often an impersonal affair regularly divorced from an African-centered worldview, but delivery of health-care services absent social context misses the mark. Therefore, it is imperative that health professionals understand black construction of social reality. In their groundbreaking work *The Psychology of Blacks: An African- American Perspective,* Dr. Joseph White and Dr. Thomas Parham clearly delineate the five major characteristics that define African-American psychology: improvisation, resilience, connectedness to others, the value of direct experience, and spirituality.

Improvisation

Black life is often full of more remixes than a song by Sean "Diddy" Combs. Outside traditional methods of Western medicine, black folks are skilled at creating alternative remedies. Making a way out of no way is a fundamental part of our existence. While HIV/ AIDS is often viewed as a death sentence, we must summon our historic impulse to maintain enthusiasm despite the bad hands we may be dealt.

Resilience

As many grapple with historical inequalities, the black experience is a constant re-humanization process. Contemporary rhetorical devices (like "hustlin'" and "grindin'," often employed by hip-hop heads) are merely updated manifestations of the vitality and fortitude exhibited by the African diaspora since the times of slavery. Magic Johnson's unprecedented fight against HIV is a stellar example of the unique capacity of blacks to transcend tragedy into personal growth. Johnson's will to live, and not medicine alone, sustains his earthly existence.

Connectedness to Others

Social institutions, including extended family, the black church, historically black colleges, community groups, and beauty/barber shops, help serve as support systems and safe spaces that ward off the negative messages of the status quo. Black folks are culturally obligated to "keep it real"—no masks or pretense—because authenticity is highly valued. Communication is marked by brutal honesty, and critiques are wrapped in love. Close-knit inner circles and family members, not doctors or health professionals, are normally the first source of information disseminated on health attitudes and practices.

The Value of Direct Experience

The truth will set you free, and trust in the black community is won only through working in the trenches on issues involving freedom and civil rights. Elders are deeply respected for their infinite wisdom, and they often pass on coping strategies and rays of hope to future generations. Slavery and the adversarial relationship between blacks and whites—that inhumane treatment created—has informed a healthy skepticism of Western institutions, practices, and values.

Spirituality

While Western medicine puts its faith in the pill, black folks employ the spirit to heal. The spiritual essence of black folk is deeply rooted in a soul force greater than ourselves. Spirituality is the unifying theme of African-American psychology, and it permeates black culture.

A little white supremacy can go a long way. Multi-million-dollar facilities and their wonder drugs are moot points if the facilities' health professionals do not have genuine love and respect for the humanity of black folk. Service-delivery models without cultural context make for nice theories without practical application. If health-care providers do not understand how the Tuskegee Experiment directly affects the help-seeking behaviors of blacks, their prized degrees are not even worth the paper they are printed on. The Experiment, a 40-year U.S. Public Health Service (PHS)–sanctioned study, used poor black men afflicted with syphilis as laboratory animals; doctors withheld the nature of their ailments from the patients and failed to administer proper treatment under the guise of research. If we are not serious about healing the wounded psyches of black folk, alleviating the angst of social trauma, challenging institutional racism, or trading stories of empowerment over sweet tea, then HIV and AIDS are the least of our worries.

EDWARD M. GARNES JR.

Edward M. Garnes Jr. is an author/journalist who lives in Atlanta, GA. A graduate of Depauw University, he launched the *State of Black Men National Tour* with fellow journalist Kevin Powell in 2004. He is also the founder of http://www.afrostoshelltoes.com.

Chapter 11

I Remember

It was a cold and dreary day outside when I first learned of a disease that could completely remove you from your faculties. My mother and stepfather were in the living room, and they had a couple of friends over. They were all ranting and raving about it. My stepfather, Jerry, a soft-spoken, 6'8" former professional athlete, blared uncharacteristically, "That shit'll make you slap yo' mama!"

I first thought of his mother, an eighty-something-year-old woman, who'd taken to me as if I were her own, and then my own mother, who made a conscious effort each and every day to ensure that I had a nice hot bowl of oatmeal in the morning before my trek to school, and I responded under my breath, "Not me." I thought to myself that there was nothing on God's green earth that would drive me to such an extreme. They were speaking, of course, about crack.

The influx of base rocks had flooded the Bay Area like the rampant disease that crack was, and I stayed a couple of blocks away from the dope track and promised my mother (and, more importantly, myself) that I'd never use it. Though the track was a stone's throw away and could easily fulfill my own materialistic desires with the fast money that I soon learned it could bring, I wouldn't sell it either. I wouldn't want anyone slapping his mama because of me.

The next, and perhaps most frightening, disease I would learn about was one that would sweep the Bay Area, the nation, and the world in one fell swoop. I was at my high school prom when a female friend of mine ran up to me with the bewildered look I'd always imagined comes across a person's face just before he slaps his mama, only she didn't slap me literally. It was the words that spewed from her mouth that sent shivers down my spine.

"Ali, did you hear?" she asked, to which I responded, "Hear what?"

"Magic got AIDS," she said, her breathing erratic.

I cursed her. I mean, who was she to tell me that my hoop hero was about to die? The man I'd patterned my game after ... the man who drew me to the game and all but made me an eternal Los Angeles Lakers fanatic from the first time I saw him execute a cross-court bounce pass ... the man that had it all ... was about to keel over because of Acquired Immune Deficiency Syndrome. Needless to say, it was a bad day.

Magic's announcement on television only made it worse, because it confirmed what I dreaded was the truth. Beyond that, it woke me, and a multitude of other kids just like me, from a deep slumber. I/we were always aware that AIDS existed. We recognized its pitiless and unforgiving ways, but had reduced it to something that only gay white men or dope fiends who caught it from bad needles suffered from. Before that fateful day in 1991, just before the NBA season started, we were all sleeping babies: high school seniors and college freshmen-to-be. We thought we were invincible, but Magic changed that. I remember it like it was yesterday.

At that point I began to use protective practices religiously when it came to intercourse. My girlfriend at the time was against it, and deep down I was too, but at the end of the day, I thought that if it could happen to the greatest point guard in NBA history, how could I be immune to HIV/AIDS?

I didn't want to have sex for an extended period of time and used basketball as an outlet to occupy my time and energy. I had no interest in having multiple partners, nor did I want to explore what my fellow frolicking "Frosh" were up to. I finished up my first year at Morehouse and moved back to the Bay Area with a renewed sense of urgency, as I had plans to enroll at Contra Costa College and earn a basketball scholarship. Then ...

It seemed like the damn thing was following me. No sooner than I'd touched down on my home soil, I learned that Jerry's brother Bernard was suffering from pneumonia. When Moms told me that it was necessary that we see him, as he was bedridden, I knew better. Even though I felt I'd matured to the point where my elders could talk to me without restraint, they still felt a need to protect me. It didn't matter though. The second I walked in there and saw his once-athletic 6'5" frame doubled over on one side of the bed, struggling to compose himself, and his pencil-thin arms, I was convinced. He had that shit.

So I've discovered my own feelings for AIDS through other people. I hate it. I don't use the "H" word too often, but in this instance, it's perfectly appropriate. It's taken people away from me that I care about, inside and outside of my personal sphere, and for that, I'll bear a lifelong contempt for it. In a similar sense, I respect it because I have to. It's taught me self-control, patience, and understanding. Moreover, it's given me another reason to be responsible. I don't feel as invincible as I once did, for obvious reasons, and as much as I don't want to acknowledge it, it's hard to act like I don't know. It's impossible for me to not remember.

There is a lot of talk among our elders of what my generation isn't, loose jargon about what we don't do and chatter about trials that we haven't faced. I'm of the opinion that we've endured as many battles as they have, if not more. Considering that we have grown up in the trenches of perhaps the most devastating drug dilemma of all time and concurrently found ourselves imperiled by the disease of the century (with little to no hope for a cure), we've done good to survive in any capacity.

N. ALI EARLY

A journalism graduate of Clark Atlanta, N. Ali Early is a hip-hop music editor.

Chapter 12

The Way Forward

It's hard to imagine, but I will be 50 years old this year!

Who would have ever thought it? By all accounts, I should have been dead years ago. I have been living with HIV for half my life. I hardly remember what it was like not to have HIV. I've lost literally hundreds of friends, loved ones, and colleagues to the disease.

Twenty-five years ago, Dr. Michael Gottlieb diagnosed a strange illness among six of his white gay patients at UCLA. Around the same time, halfway across the country, my doctor found that my partner and I both had abnormally swollen lymph nodes—a symptom of what would turn out to be the same disease that killed Michael Gottlieb's patients. A month later, Fernando, a member of our softball team, went into the hospital with pneumonia. Two weeks later, he was dead. In the intervening years, that illness, AIDS, has become the defining health issue of our time, killing 20 million people worldwide. Those six white gay men have morphed into more than 26 million black people as well worldwide, most of them heterosexual, and many of them children.

The last 25 years have not been easy. In 1996, my doctors called my mother to inform her that I was in the intensive care unit at Kaiser Permanente Hospital. I was not expected to survive. My mother flew to Los Angeles and found me in a coma. She left a note on a large piece of cardboard and taped it on the wall in front of my bed. In the event that I woke up, she wanted me to know that she was there and everything was going to be all right, because she wasn't going to give up.

When friends ask me what I want for my birthday, it is a no-brainer: I want the AIDS epidemic to be over. A lot of people think it already is. Unfortunately, even with the advances we've made, AIDS is far from being over, especially in Black America.

No matter how you look at it, black people bear the brunt of the AIDS epidemic in our country. Over 60 American black people contract HIV every day. Of the estimated 1.2 million Americans currently living with HIV/AIDS, nearly half of them are black. Among the young, black youth represent over 56 percent of the new AIDS cases. And black women represent nearly 70 percent of the new AIDS cases among women.

In the decade since effective drug treatments for AIDS dramatically cut death rates across the country, black Americans continue to get infected and die at alarming rates. According to a 2005 article in *The New York Times*, one in five black men in New York City between 40 and 49 has HIV or AIDS. Black men die at a rate six times that of white men.

Statistics gathered in 2005 show an AIDS epidemic among black gay and bisexual men that outstrips anything seen in the worst-hit parts of sub-Saharan Africa. Nearly 50 percent of black gay and bisexual men in some of our nation's cities are estimated to be infected with HIV. That's a pandemic of catastrophic proportions, and each of us must rise to the occasion.

There is also a tsunami-like epidemic growing among Southern blacks, where we see rising case loads, a health-care system already in tatters, and stifling stigma and silence.

Black America has suffered tremendous losses in the last year. With the recent passing of C. DeLores Tucker, Rosa Parks, and Coretta Scott King, the ranks of brave leaders who put themselves on the line during the dangerous, heady days of the late fifties and early sixties have become desperately thin.

It's been 43 years since Dr. Martin Luther King Jr. had that dream, and 38 years since he stood on that mountaintop and saw our destiny. Now, we are faced with a devastating disease that runs rampant through our communities and threatens not only to prevent us from getting to the mountaintop, but to roll back much of the progress Dr. and Mrs. King fought for.

"AIDS is a human crisis, no matter where you live," Mrs. King once said while addressing the Southern Christian Leadership Conference. "Anyone who sincerely cares about the future of Black America had better be speaking out about AIDS, calling for preventive measures and increased funding for research and treatment."

Those words have never rung more true. 2006 presents an extraordinary opportunity for us to change the trajectory of the HIV/AIDS pandemic in Black America. Against a backdrop of a number of historic commemorations—the 25th anniversary of the first diagnosed AIDS cases; the 10th anniversary of Highly Active Antiretroviral Therapy (HAART), the drug cocktails that have cut death rates and extended lives around the world; the first time in a decade that the International AIDS Conference will be held in North America; and the fifth anniversary of UNGASS, the United Nations General Assembly Special Session on HIV/AIDS—we have a chance to do the one and only thing that can end the AIDS epidemic in Black America and America as a whole: build a massive black response to this deadly epidemic. If America cannot be mobilized against this backdrop, it cannot ever be mobilized. I believe Black America is finally positioned to act, and there is no time to waste.

America's ability to defeat the AIDS epidemic will be determined by our ability to stop it in Black America. The only way to stop AIDS in black communities is for there to be strong institutions with the infrastructure and capacity to make it happen.

We must call on leaders to lead. The AIDS story in America is mostly one of a failure to lead. Black leaders—from traditional ministers and civil-rights leaders to hip-hop artists and Hollywood celebrities—must join in a national call to action and declaration of commitment to end the AIDS epidemic in our communities immediately.

We must call for a lifting of the federal ban on funding for needle-exchange programs. These programs have shown time and again that they reduce HIV infection while not increasing the incidence of drug use. We must stop the war on poor people with addiction and start a *real* war on drugs that looks at root causes and focuses on prevention and treatment—instead of mass incarceration. We have spent billions of dollars incarcerating young black men, and as a result, black communities are destabilized, and there are still no signs of making any progress toward stopping drug addiction.

We must call for the expansion of comprehensive, age-appropriate, culturally competent AIDS prevention efforts—with messages inclusive of abstinence, delayed sexual activity, sexual responsibility, proper condom use, and negotiated safety—that give young people the tools to protect themselves.

We must call for a massive effort to address the disproportionate impact this epidemic is having on black men who have sex with men and a rejection of stigma based on sexual orientation—real or perceived.

Finally, we must call on all black Americans to raise our collective HIV literacy and find out our HIV status. Knowledge is a powerful weapon in the war against AIDS. There are an estimated 1.3 million Americans living with AIDS today. Nearly half of them are black. A quarter of them don't know they are infected, and people who don't know they're infected are less likely to protect their partners and unable to receive treatment. Knowing your HIV status early can save your life and your partner's life.

I have always believed the AIDS epidemic would end someday, but I never thought I would be around to witness it. Now I believe it's possible that I will live to see the end of AIDS. After all, we have the tools to end the AIDS epidemic today. The question is, do we have the political and moral will to use those tools effectively and compassionately?

AIDS is not just a health issue. It is a human rights issue. It is an urban renewal issue. It is an economic justice issue. I remember Craig Harris, Reggie Williams, Michael Callen, Belynda Dunn, Vitto Russo, Marlon Riggs, Essex Hemphill, and all of my friends, loved ones, and colleagues who have died from AIDS. I honor the 20 million people who have died from AIDS-related complications worldwide, including my late lover, Chris Brownlie. I was not supposed to still be here, but I am. AIDS is also still here. And so are you.

As we grieve our losses and envision our future, we must commit not just to "keep the dream alive" but to fulfill the vision. To do so, we must push toward the mountaintop while always reaching back to anyone who might be left behind, regardless of race, gender, sexual orientation, or HIV status. I still have that note my mom wrote for me 10 years ago. And, like her, I'm not going to give up until this epidemic is over. We can stop AIDS.

PHILL WILSON

Phill Wilson is the founder and executive director of the Black AIDS Institute in Los Angeles. He has participated in numerous international conferences on AIDS and was selected by the Ford Foundation in 2001 as one of its "Twenty Leaders for a Changing World."

▶ *Chapter 13*

Coping with the Loss of My Father

I moved away from my hometown when I was about 10 years old. My mom felt that she had finally found "the one," who turned out to be my stepfather, and they soon married. He was in the military, so we moved around a lot. Because of that, I wasn't able to see the rest of my family often, including my biological father. It seemed that as each year passed, we grew further and further apart.

In August of 2002, I also found "the one" and got married. Around that same time, my biological father began trying to contact me. When I finally talked to him, he seemed forgetful and "out of it," as if something was wrong with his mind. He repeatedly told me that he was my father, and I shouldn't forget that. He also said, "You better come and see me before it's too late." He never elaborated. Then, I found out that he was repeatedly in and out of the hospital. When I questioned family members, some would say, "he has a spot on his liver ... he drinks too much."

I felt that it had to be more than that, something that could be terminal, like HIV or cancer.

I asked one of my aunts to find out more information from a cousin. Maybe because of my constant probing, my mom finally broke the news to me. My father was HIV positive.

I felt like the entire world had stopped turning. How? When? Where? Why?

When my head and heart could no longer handle my constant thoughts and unanswered questions, I shut down completely and cried for weeks. Then, one day in December 2003, I received a phone call from my brother's mother. She told me that " ...it didn't look too good, and the hospital is calling all of your dad's family to come." I flew home right away.

My aunt broke the silence during our ride to the hospital by telling me that my father had HIV. I pretended that it was my first time hearing the news, mainly because it still hadn't fully hit me. She went on to tell me that he was "extremely thin, with very dark skin, so don't be surprised."

When we finally reached his hospital bed, I was shocked. The man who I remember as being on the chubby side was now one-third of the size he had been. He looked brittle and fragile and lost in the mass of tubes that were attached to him.

I hated seeing him like that. I hated crying my eyes out after every visit. So, after visiting him for almost a week straight, I took off two days to pull myself together. On that last night, I prayed, "If there's no chance of him getting any better, please call him home because I hate seeing him suffer like this ... it's killing our family." At 5:20 the next morning, we received a call to come to the hospital. I already knew. I saw the doctor solemnly nod his head when my aunt asked if had passed.

I felt tightness in my chest, as if I was about to burst. I screamed.

I couldn't understand why ... why, after six years of not seeing my father, he would just be taken away like this. We didn't get the chance to rekindle our father-daughter relationship. It was so unfair.

As it turns out, my father had had HIV for ten years without even knowing it. He found out about a year before the rest of the family did, but was ashamed and feared that everyone would disown him. I guess I could understand, but I was his daughter ... his only daughter. Why couldn't he talk to me?

The questions will always be there ... but my father won't.

TONI NELSON

A caregiver at a child-development center in Havelock, North Carolina, Toni Nelson is a native of Valdosta, Georgia.

▶ *Chapter 14*

AIDS: You Better Ask Somebody!

For a long time, AIDS didn't have a face. Black America didn't know anybody with that shit in '85. The only one we knew was Rock Hudson, and he didn't mean anything to us. We just thought he was a freak, fucking everybody in Hollywood, and look what happened to him.

Then, we started to put a face to it, and we knew the people who were affected. It was our mothers, sisters, cousins, best friends, and lovers. We knew that they weren't horrible people that did anything bad. So we became conflicted that the shit they had been telling us wasn't true.

I've known so many people who have lived with and eventually died from this disease. Years ago, we were told that people who got this disease were irresponsible, gay, or promiscuous. I knew some people that were gay, but they weren't promiscuous. My girlfriend wasn't promiscuous; she got it from someone she trusted. It's not fair.

Even after all these years, AIDS is still considered a shameful disease. My best girlfriend was with someone for three years. She lived with him and was in love with him. She thought that she knew every move he made. She got pregnant, and while she was pregnant, she got really sick. She went to find out what was going on and was told that she was HIV positive. There was nothing "irresponsible" about her behavior.

The same goes for the husband or wife who tests positive after a 15-year marriage. Sure, there are some people who are irresponsible, but that's true with any and every thing. They are not only irresponsible with sex; they're irresponsible with their lives. That is one of the elements that help the disease spread.

I remember my girlfriend told me that when a person is diagnosed, he or she faces two possible deaths—social and physical. "*Oh God, please don't touch my soda can ... You borrowed my sweater? I've got to get it to the cleaners, quickly!*"

The family can play an important role. My uncle Donald died of AIDS. Until the day she died, my grandmother said that he had kidney problems. *Grandma, he didn't have kidney problems, baby, he died of AIDS. Because you were so ashamed of it, everyone else was ashamed of it.* My grandmother was once talking to one of her friends and said, "Baby, you know Donald had kidney problems." Her girlfriend said, "My daughter had leukemia." Both of their children had died of AIDS.

Putting my friend in the ground taught me to be non-judgmental. I dared anyone to say some shit about her. I knew she would give her heart to anybody who asked for it. So I couldn't let anyone discredit her and say she was whoring around—we're not going to play that game. My uncle Donald was sweet as pie, baby. You are not going to make him out to be crazy, mean, and bad.

We are not a stupid, ignorant people. We get it, but we don't know where all of these statistics come from. All of a sudden, AIDS has become a black disease. "*'It came from Africa.'*" Well, Africa is full of black people! We really don't know. We only know what they tell us.

How do we get control of it? We talk about it in front of a group of people. You just bust out with it. We can talk about a basketball game or the fine nigga that we saw at a club. Well, let's talk about AIDS.

When I first became a spokesperson for HIV/AIDS, someone wrote a script for me that said, "Unfortunately, there are a lot of men that are being dishonest and transferring the disease to women." I refused to say that. That makes it look like a gay disease, and people might say, "See, he was on the down-low. I can't believe he did that to her." We don't know. Hey, maybe she was shooting up with him! Maybe she gave it to him. But we don't think about it like that.

I have some male friends that are bisexual and are in relationships with both men and women. Well, all of them should get AIDS tests together. If you say, "I love you, and you love me," then you shouldn't have anything to hide. My response would be, "We're going to walk in this door together. Whatever you do when you are not with me, brother or sister, love me enough to protect me. I'm not trying to stop your happiness—as long as you say sister, listen, this is what I'm into." Give sistas an option. You might be surprised at the answer.

Our society says that if you are a girl, you gotta like a boy, and if you're a boy, you gotta like a girl. And then it says that God said so. God ain't said that shit. Please show me in the Bible where God said that. His name ain't signed nowhere. You can't show me that, I promise you can't. Some other niggas wrote it, and you're trying to convince me.

I'm not trying to get caught up in all that. You should do what makes you happy, as long as no one is getting hurt. You might go with both of them, if they both make you happy in their own separate time and space. Give them that option. Communication is key. *"Listen, sista, I like women—millions of them."*

Guys who like both men and women need to step up and say "Listen, Pam, I like Chuck. I like you, too." Pam might say, "Well, when you're with Chuck, protect us, because I'm going to protect us." We are often so caught up in what people think and say about us that we fail to do what makes us happy. I'm not that type of girl.

Some churches teach hatred and then turn around and say, "God loves everybody." Well, wait a minute! Can someone get some deaf and dumb people in here to preach, because these people clearly can't give it to me straight. "Adam and Eve, not Adam and Steve"—there's where they are in conflict. First, they tell me that God is all-knowing because He's the Creator, the Maker, and the Almighty, right? Then they say that what I am doing is wrong and that I am going to hell because God condemns it. Well, they should make up their minds! Who is He, and who am I? Some of these pastors are not only telling a lie, they're living one. They are trying to push off what they say as cashmere, but it's damn polyester. They know it, and that makes me angry; they are spewing hatred in a place where you are supposed to get nothing but love.

If these pastors who don't practice what they preach want to talk to me about God, then they should have their "God-tapes" on. Don't come to me thinking that I am vulnerable and weak, and that you can feed me any line you want. When church is over, and you decide to be with a man, then say, "I like men, and I love God." That's when I'll come to your church. Until then, I won't waste my time to get up on Sunday morning and come listen to shit that you know is cheap.

As I speak to schools around the country, some principals have gotten angry with me ... that is, until they heard the end of my message. I tell the kids, "Once you start having sex, you are not going to stop. I promise you this, because it feels great. If you are sexually active and you enjoy it, put on a condom. He's not that fine, nor is she that cute. If you don't, please tell me what your favorite color is, because I'll wear it to your funeral. Bottom line. We're not up in here playing patty-cake. If you're screwing, cover it up."

In the beginning, we were uneducated. We thought that if we were in the same room with someone that had AIDS, we could catch it by breathing the same air.

We need to learn to say, "You're still worthy." Instead, now we say, "You can take 10,000 pills, seven days a week, and that will give you maybe four more years. If you stay in bed with the covers up on you, maybe it won't be that painful." We don't say, "Baby, you got it, but the sun will keep coming up. What do you want to do about it? Let's keep on getting up." That's not what we're teaching.

We're often too afraid to be honest and say what we've really gotta say out of fears that it might be taken wrong, or that someone might question us. *"Got-dang-it, question me, so I can tell you just where I'm at. Let's get it out in the open. That's right, I said that about the church, I did—so come on and bring me the questions. Get mad. You should get mad; that way, you'll do something about it."*

MO' NIQUE

A Baltimore, Maryland, native, Mo' Nique is an internationally acclaimed comedian. She resides with her family in Los Angeles.

Chapter 15

A Message to My Straight Brothers: It's Time to Talk About Our Homophobia

I am an AIDS activist. I am an African-American man. I am hetero-sexual. And, consequently, I am often profoundly frustrated. With all the progress we've made, we—straight black men—still allow ho-mophobia to cripple our thinking and our actions, and it's time that we deal with it.

I've learned we can't talk about getting straight brothers in-volved with the fight against HIV/AIDS unless we also discuss the issues surrounding black male sexuality and homophobia. Attend any panel discussion featuring straight brothers talking about AIDS and clock how fast the conversation turns to homosexual-ity. You can set your watch to it.

For the record, I still struggle with this issue myself. I am not a finished project by any stretch. The process for me involved tak-ing an honest look at the roots of my homophobia. I know I didn't drop out of my mother's womb that way. No, it came from a vari-ety or sources. I, like most African-American men, grew up being fed regular doses of black-manhood training, and one of the most important lessons was that "real" black men weren't gay.

As I grew up in Plainfield, NJ, no one ever openly discussed sexu-ality with me. Like most, I received my miseducation on the streets. My dad and the other significant men (relatives, coaches, teachers, etc.) in my world shared their life lessons more by example than with heartfelt talks. But, for the most part, they helped me grow into a decent man, so this is not a complaint.

However, no one ever, and I mean EVER, taught me how to respect my gay brothers. I heard words like *faggot, queer* and *punk* daily while growing up—not so much in my home, but in the barber shops, playgrounds, and on the streets, for sure. The older guys on the corner, whom I admired and wanted to be like, used those terms (and worse) all the time.

The dominant media of that era also played a role. I grew up worshipping heroes of "blaxploitation" films like *Shaft, The Mack, Dolemite,* and *Black Belt Jones.* These films depicted "real" black men with severe cases of manhood overload, and any references to homosexuals were purely for comic relief.

Then there was television. I can still remember characters like Fred Sanford, Archie Bunker, and George Jefferson using disparaging comments about gays as comic fodder. These images, and many more, played a role in framing my young attitude about the world around me.

It was, however, in my beer-drinking, skirt-chasing days at Howard University in the early '80s that the tenets of homophobia were set in stone. In my circles, one of the greatest fears was being labeled gay. My friends and I would say things like, "I'm cool with fags, as long as they don't bring that mess over here," or "All they want to do is turn a straight brother out," and so on.

But what was the real fear? Did we think we could really get "turned out"? How was it that we could hide behind a wall of homophobia by day and try to sleep with as many sisters as possible by night? How could we lie to our sisters, have unprotected sex with them, and then leave them? Did being a real man mean doing and being anything you wanted—as long as you weren't gay?

The years following college didn't change things much. I got a number of jobs, dated lots of women, and generally lived with my homophobia. As I got older, I'd pretend I was beyond such feelings. But when pressed, such as being in an overwhelmingly gay setting, I'd retreat into the familiar "us vs. them" mentality.

It was not until I became involved with the HIV/AIDS issue that I began to ask myself the difficult questions.

I tried to place the black male sexuality issue into a group context. My own background aside, how was the collective black male psyche formed? What are the lingering effects of slavery and discrimination? How has the continuing devastation of miseducation and self-hatred impacted how we view ourselves as men in this society? Have we been conditioned to believe that heterosexual conquests, athletic ability, income, and a willingness to kick ass if disrespected, among other things, define our strength as black men?

While I can't accurately answer the broad questions, I know what we have to do now. We have to overcome society's influences and find the courage to re-define our sexuality with, among other things, an emphasis on compassion, understanding, and commitment. As straight black men, our first responsibility is to take a hard look at ourselves and not condemn the actions and lifestyles of others.

My work on the HIV/AIDS issue has helped me better cope with my own continuing growth process. By making me deal with folk from various backgrounds and orientations, I've realized that being comfortable with my own sexuality is not a straight or gay thing. It's a human thing. It's something I control.

Ours is a war on two fronts. We have to destroy HIV/AIDS as well as homophobia. We must reach out to our gay brothers. We must embrace them and talk with them about such thorny topics as same-sex marriage, the elusive "undercover brother," and the impact these and many other issues are having in our community.

The international HIV/AIDS crisis demands our full involvement. Our people are dying, our communities worldwide are being destroyed, and our government has proven time and time again that it is impotent in the face of this tragedy. We need our brothers, all our brothers, straight and gay, to get involved.

As strong, straight black men, many things define our sexuality; homophobia can no longer be one of them.

CHRISTOPHER CATHCART

Christopher Cathcart is a media consultant and AIDS activist who lives in Los Angeles with his wife.

Chapter 16

Acceptance Is a Good Thing

I knew a couple of people who were trying to find out what the symptoms were so they could make sure they didn't have them. For me, it was a very personal thing. There were a couple of people I'd seen experience the obvious signs, like weight loss and those kinds of things. As I am a gospel artist known to be very friendly, nurturing, and easy to talk to, fans and people naturally reach out to me.

Early on, I became aware that a few people I knew had possibly been exposed to the virus. My hairdresser had come down with a lot of the symptoms. I was very fond of him, because early on in my career he was the first one who could get my natural hair to look really good. I was born with very thin hair, and this man was gifted. He did hair for the stars and was always on the cusp of whatever styles were new. I ended up losing my hairdresser to AIDS, and I was devastated by the loss. He was a kind person and a really good friend. I have also lost a producer, the gentleman who co-wrote and co-produced my song "Fall Down."

I'll say this—I believed that AIDS was primarily connected to a homosexual lifestyle. People are comfortable staying in the dark about a lot of things. They want to hide and say, "It's everyone but me, it's not here, and I'm not like that." As a society, we hide a lot of things that we don't want to look at. It's unfortunate that we'd rather hide from homosexuality than embrace it . . . I know ministers with homosexual family members, but they just don't speak of it. Many folks feel that homosexuality goes against the word of God, against Scripture. For some Christians, people who I've grown up with who have been a part of the church all of their lives, there are certain things that are still somewhat taboo. Often, it's fear (responding out of fear instead of love, that is) that's been the issue for our people. We're afraid to be different. Fear causes you to do a lot of things.

There's a lot of denial, especially among those of us in the gospel industry that have had connections and real relationships with men who are on the "down low." I think that it's prevalent even in the church and in our community—I believe that it is particularly evident among African Americans. We have a lot of prejudices. But all of us are dealing with something, and all of us are sinners saved by grace. As for those who are not yet saved, we know that the Bible tells us to love and reach out to them. That's just calling a spade a spade, or so they say.

I think everyone has some type of responsibility. When it comes to this sort of thing, sure, we need leadership for guidance, but it's also an individual thing, and I think that is what is so unfortunate. Perhaps that is why God has allowed it to hit home, so to speak. If it isn't at your front door, you can ignore it, but when it comes to your door, there's no way to ignore it.

I admit that at first I was afraid, but I had a greater love for my friends who had AIDS and couldn't ignore them. The Bible says, "Blessed are the pure in heart, for those shall see God," and I want to see God. So I'm not so concerned about what can happen to me. I believe that these folks living with AIDS have the weight of the world on them, and they need someone to say, "I love you, brother. How are you doing? I'm praying for you." I did that early on.

What I've done is reach out to anyone that I know who is afflicted by this disease. A personal assistant of mine contracted the disease, and he had been my right hand—he'd do anything that I needed done before I'd even thought of it. When he got really ill, I made sure that I spent time with him, showed him love, and let him know how much his dedication and friendship meant to me throughout the years. I tried to ease the pain of moving on by sharing the word of God with him, and letting him know that this is not our home. We are pilgrims just traveling through this earth. All of this will go back to our Creator. And that is a place that we can only imagine: the joy, the peace, and the awesomeness of Heaven.

If God chooses to call us home before we think we're ready, then we should accept that he made us, and he knows what's best. The soul lives on after the flesh dies. One day, I'll see that soul again, and that's how I deal with the thought of my friends and family who have passed on from AIDS: I know that I'll see them again.

TRAMAINE HAWKINS

Tramaine Hawkins is a multiple Grammy Award winner and gospel music icon.

Chapter 17

AIDS Has No Tribe

Almost half of all people currently living with AIDS in the United States are African Americans. This is remarkable, considering that African Americans make up only 13 percent of the total population of United States. What does this really mean, and how does do these statistics compare to the ones regarding our cousins in Africa? There are no mysteries here, and there are no differences. If you are an African, whether in the United States or elsewhere, AIDS is your disease. You know it, you have heard about it, you know someone who has gotten it, and you may get it, if you don't have it already. But here is the mystery ... so many people contract it every day, and it is 100 percent preventable.

Compared to their cousins in Africa, African Americans in the United States have all the means to fight AIDS. Why, then, are they being wiped out just the same? This is the United States, a superpower and the richest nation on earth. Why, then, are African Americans over-represented when it comes to AIDS cases?

The answers are not different whether you are an African living in America, Europe, or Brazil. Most of us treat sex as a casual thing we can simply indulge in without caution or regard to our bodies. We always think, "If you can get it, go ahead and get it; it will make you happy, and you will have a sense of acceptance and accomplishment." We forget the potential outcomes of this act ... the diseases that may follow, the pregnancies, and the disappointment afterwards ... we forget all that for a temporary pleasure.

Go to any club where African Americans gather in a major city on a Friday night, and you will be surprised. Most people are hunting for the next score. It is a Friday night, after all. The success of the night is determined by how many people you can sleep with.

This is socially acceptable in this culture. The movies that we see featuring our heroes treat sex the same way. The famous rap stars we idolize preach the same gospel: sex, sex, and more sex. So, the majority of African Americans are not alarmed by this pandemic: after all, rappers say it is the way things are, and you are a nobody if you don't get it or participate in it. Life goes on as usual. Forget the possibility of disease ... forget the possibility of pregnancy ... just enjoy the moment ... even if it may be your last moment.

From this point of view, why should anyone be surprised by the fact that half of all people living with AIDS in this country are African Americans?

This is no different from Africans in Africa. Despite the fact that there are many warnings around, despite the fact that brothers, neighbors, sisters and other relatives have all succumbed to the disease—this is not enough to change behaviors. People will go out of their way to believe rumors and baseless information, such as the tale that having sex with a woman in her sleep will prevent a man from getting AIDS, or that having sex with a virgin will prevent you from contracting AIDS.

You see, there are no differences in the attitudes. We are all lost, and we are not aware of the dangers that surround us.

What is needed is a continued effort to educate our current and future generations about individual respect and individual responsibility. Kids and adults alike need to be taught to respect their bodies.

Do not cry foul or look for excuses for this self-inflicted wound. Do not blame anyone. Take charge. Make a pact with yourself that you are the master of your own destiny, and that you will not heed the messages from music videos that try to intoxicate you with sexual innuendos. First, start to respect yourself and your body, for it is the only body you have. Once it is violated by AIDS, no one can fix it.

The Swahili have a saying that an "ear that is about to die cannot feel the medicine," and therefore, it cannot be cured. Maybe this is true ... maybe we are all dying ears ... maybe we are tired of the message about AIDS ... but we cannot all give up, for our future, our bodies, and our race are all at stake!

JOSIAH KIBIRA

A native of Tanzania, Josiah Kibira is a director and screenwriter who currently lives in Minneapolis, Minnesota.

Chapter 18

A Stitch of Faith

Journal entry: December 20, 1991

This particular diary entry is very important, because today is the worst day of my life so far and the last day of my old life. I found out today that I am HIV positive. That is the virus that causes AIDS. I'm not sure what my thoughts are on the information right now, but I have a lot of them, for sure.

I went to take the test last week after a month of debating. My best friend told me that Shawn* had AIDS and had gotten sick in jail. One girl he had been with messing around with found out she was HIV positive and said he was the one who gave it to her. A lot of thoughts went through my head after he told me that. I tried to reason out every option why I couldn't or didn't have it. But all the facts conflicted with one another, and my current boyfriend informed me that if he ever found out he was HIV positive, he would kill me. Afterward, he left for California, and I thought I would set both his mind and mine at ease by taking the test and getting a negative result.

Well, now I know that I'm HIV positive and that I have a whole lot to think about. The doctor was very sensitive and helpful when she told me that I was HIV positive. I really don't remember much of the conversation, but all in all, she was a great help. I told her about dating Shawn a few years back, and how I'd figured he was the one who'd given me HIV—me and about a hundred other women.

But then again, it could have been anyone. After a few years of unprotected sex with multiple partners, there is hardly any way to really tell. I completely blame myself, but the doctor said that it's the man's fault for not wearing a condom. She also explained that during the late '80s, AIDS wasn't thought to be prevalent among heterosexuals, especially teenagers. But the bottom line is that I should not have participated in unsafe behavior. The harder part is before me: telling others, coming to grips with the knowledge myself and acknowledging that my time on this earth is limited. That I don't know how long I have makes me crazy. The doctor says that now, most HIV-positive patients live up to 10 years. But that only puts me at 31 years old. What about marriage and kids? Now I can't have that?

I have to reprioritize my life, and start putting family and friends in the spotlight instead of myself. I also have to get through telling my family and friends. But I am going to think more about that after the holidays because although my life has been ruined, I don't have to do that to anyone else. Not right now. I did tell my friends Nella and Tamara. Nella took it harder than I did. She hung up on me.

* "Shawn" is a pseudonym.

Like the threads on a quilt that weave patches of different textures, colors, and patterns together, so has my faith connected me from one experience to another, and held me together no matter what—even if some of the patches don't fit the rest of the quilt.

And so it happened one day that the thread of my faith strengthened as it bonded me forever to a patch that I would never have picked out myself. That was the day I found out I was HIV positive. It was the phone call that changed everything. The revelation brought me closer to the source of my faith than I'd ever been before, and I was able to marvel at the beauty I discovered in the intricate designs of life and at the omnipotent, omnipresent hands of the quilt's Designer.

I discovered that my experiences as an African-American woman living with HIV, and my life's journey itself, both mirror the process of stitching together a quilt. Just as our enslaved ancestors used connected patches of fabric to communicate a path to freedom, my experiences are linked to one another, threaded gingerly together by my faith and belief that something greater exists and that that greater wisdom keeps pointing me toward freedom.

Over the years, I have come to understand that one patch cannot and does not exist without being connected to another. My path to faith, and the discovery of the magnificent design of my life, began the day that HIV became a part my personal reality.

Journal entry: November 1991
"Girl, I heard he has AIDS," my college friend said to me over the phone. She was talking about Shawn, a guy I had dated a few years earlier, who was spending his winter break in the Harris County Jail.

I met Shawn in 1989 after completing my freshman year in college. As a young woman, I was fascinated with the privileges of independence—experiencing new things, meeting new friends, and, of course, meeting new men. Shawn was one of the first guys I'd met upon my return to Houston for summer break. Wearing his "in the game" status like a badge of honor, Shawn strolled Houston's streets with his partners in tow and cash in hand. He made his presence known and didn't have any trouble getting what he wanted, including this young, wide-eyed freshman who'd spotted him at a LL Cool J concert.

Shawn was a typical tall, dark, and handsome brother. That was all that mattered to me at the time. But what would really matter to me about Shawn was not revealed until later. He would come to represent the first patch on the quilt of my new life, and point the supposed path of my life in a new direction.

"How could he have AIDS? He's not gay! And he just *sells* drugs, he doesn't *do* them," was the only response that I had to my friend's revelation.

HIV was not something that was discussed among my small circle of friends. We were young, black, and had plenty of challenges to face within our own small circle—and no desire to add more. Besides, at the time, HIV seemed to be a disease that only affected gay white men. How could people think that a man like Shawn would have it? It was a rumor, I thought. Someone was trying to hurt him. It would not have been the first time. Shawn was always starting or ending trouble.

But as I tried to recall the few tidbits of information that I had heard about AIDS, an inner fear started to rise, making me question what this meant to me.

"It's probably not true," she said. "You know how people talk." I agreed, and in silence I prayed that her second statement was truer than her first.

Two months later, at the age of 21, I was diagnosed with HIV. During the two weeks that it took for me to take the test and receive the results, I found myself sinking into places that I had never been to before. Thoughts of death, of leaving my family and not being able to marry or have children, overwhelmed me daily. I felt completely hopeless. I was afraid of every movement that I made—I was even afraid to touch other people. I had absolutely no concrete information on this disease, and didn't know what to do. I quickly reached the conclusion that I was going to die, still confused and scared.

Back then, HIV had a stigma attached to it that could be compared to leprosy in Biblical times. Entire communities and subcultures were both victim and assailant in this deadly and unknown war. The gay community was condemned for spreading this vile poison through sex, and people struggling with addictions also spread the epidemic through needle-sharing. The rest of us thought, "We don't do those things, so HIV will not touch us." A new world of disenfranchisement, blame, and discrimination permeated the landscape of that time. It had always been a peripheral part of my world—that is, it was until I received the phone call about my test result.

At that moment, the patches on the quilt of my former life had come undone; the images of my past, present, and future were scattered about in my head, and there didn't seem to be any purpose for my life. My existence seemed random and arbitrary.

I was consumed with feelings of abandonment and rejection, and guilt flooded my world. The evening news took on new meaning to me. Now, when I heard of the trials, obstacles, and loss suffered by people with this disease and saw their faces, their problems suddenly became my problems. Their ridicule became my ridicule. Their faces mirrored my face. I wasn't alone, although I felt like it.

The only sense of consolation that I wasn't alone came from

the whispered rumors about other women facing the same fate at the hand of Shawn's promiscuity, and from the gracious courage of Magic Johnson, who had announced his HIV status a month before.

Looking back, I see that getting tested and working honestly, truthfully, and diligently to come to terms with my diagnosis were the first steps toward building my faith and a stronger personal relationship with God. After spending a few years trying to ignore the new direction of my life, I took those first steps toward freedom, whether I wanted to or not, and walked out of the bondage of ignorance into the freedom that truth brings.

After living and working in the HIV community for the past 15 years, I can look back and see that the quilt of my life was not created by random patches of fate, but through God's wonderful and intentional design, made whole through faith.

Coming out about having this disease no longer generates the same shock among the general public that it once did; society has lived with the knowledge of AIDS through a whole generation. And considering the current rate of infection among African-American women, I am no longer a surprise, but a statistic.

Journal entry: January 22, 1992
I'm in Beaumont tonight, and it has been a rather long day. We went to church, and at first, I didn't think I was going to make it through, but I did. I got choked up a couple of times, but managed to swallow it down. All I have been able to think about today is how to tell my family of this situation. I'm sure how they will react, but it is so hard. The other day, Mom asked me about the Band-Aid I had on my arm and I told her that I had some lab work done. She told me that if anything was wrong, she wanted to be the first to know. How can I tell her that her daughter will be dead in five years? In the final analysis, I had to rush everything ... and now, soon I'll be dead. I had fun drinking, smoking, and having sex. There is no one else to blame. If I hadn't been so busy trying to be a part of the fast crowd, I would have listened to my mom and aunts, and I wouldn't be worried about who else I might have infected. What was my hurry—or joy—in doing the things that I did? How much of what I have in terms of relationships

will remain after people find out about the HIV? I never wanted to hurt anyone, but that is all I seem to have done.

I am still cold, because I haven't been able to talk since I found out. I haven't been alone to talk. I was going to talk to Nella, but was unable to. Dr. Smith wants me to get into an AIDS counseling group, but I don't know about that yet. I don't know anything, except that I want to live. I keep thinking that having HIV is the reason I could never picture myself old, or with a family of my own. I can't see any future. I don't believe I have one.

The struggles that I faced during the early years are still indescribable to me. Looking back over my journal entries from when I first learned I had the disease, I can see the disconnect between the words I wrote on the page and the emotions that I felt. Although I frankly chronicled the events of my life, I failed to disclose the overwhelming sense of fear, sadness, and alienation that gripped me ever so tightly.

Thank God for freedom and healing. I can now write with my heart on my sleeve—and it's a heart full of courage, wisdom, community, and hope.

Although I didn't know it at the time, journaling served as the beginning of my relationship with God and the development of my faith. I soon discovered that it was He who was the architect of life, not me. And if I allowed him to use me, the end product would be well worth the effort.

My conversations with God led me in many different directions; my faith that everything would work in accordance with a plan that only He knew grew bit-by-bit everyday. With each patch that I gathered and laid down for the quilt, God was there to help me from one thread to another, and to create stability in my world.

The statistics on HIV/AIDS in the United States and around the globe are continuing to rise. Today, over 1 million persons in the United States have been diagnosed with HIV/AIDS. Over 75 percent of the women living with the disease in the U.S. are African American. These alarming statistics continue to overwhelm our health-care system and religious and social-service outlets; they cause ongoing suffering, confusion, and silence. It's true that the number of deaths has decreased, and that people are living longer thanks to advances in medication and prevention programs, but there is more to living with HIV/AIDS than just pills or pamphlets.

Today, 15 years after my diagnosis, I serve as a proud and privileged advocate for the HIV-positive community. I have used the abilities that God has revealed to me to improve not only my life, but also the lives of others struggling to understand the snag of AIDS in the fabric of their existence.

The experience of developing faith led me to new people, new information, and new concepts and ideas that have continued to shape and bind my own quilt. The questions I've written in my journals about my life with HIV have been answered. Yet everyday, I conceive new ones. I know now that the real answers don't come from a medical textbook or from crying sessions with friends. They come from simply sitting down, gathering your patches, and allowing God to show you how they go together. Since realizing that my faith in Him allowed me to stop running and wait for his guidance, my life is not the life I predicted, but one altogether unexpected.

My belief in something greater comforts me and helps me to maintain and persevere in times of sorrow and pain. As a child, I was taught the meaning of faith, but my personal understanding of the Word did not truly resonate with me until I reached a point where surrendering to the author of faith was my only option.

Individually, we are the same people the day after our diagnoses as we were the day before. We have to find the strength, the courage, and the faith to face head-on all the challenges that spring from this epidemic.

And until my quilt is complete, I will continue to keep it all together with the threads of my faith.

DENA GRAY

Dena Gray currently serves as the administration manager for Houston's HOPWA (Housing Opportunities for People With AIDS) program.

She is also the founder of Positive Underground Productions, a collaborative of HIV-positive people who use their experiences to educate the community on the impact of HIV/AIDS. Ms. Gray lives in Houston with her 10-year old daughter, Kandace, and her cat, Vernice.

Chapter 19

The Power of Love and Honesty in a Relationship

We met on a beautiful spring morning. As D* was entering our tenement rooming house during the wee hours of dawn, I was in the kitchen making myself a cup of tea in the hope that it would ease my restless mind. The time was approximately 5 A.M., and the house was still quiet.

I said hello as D passed the kitchen, and invited him to have a cup of tea. He accepted my offer. As he looked at me, he could tell that I was with child. As the conversation progressed, he asked me if I would like to go to the movies that weekend. I gladly accepted, not believing for one minute that he would keep his word, but sure enough, that Saturday he was at my door, ready to take me out. Our second meeting was not memorable, but marked the beginning of a bond between two lost souls. Mine was lost to loneliness, and his to drugs and a lack of trust in humankind.

Ours was always a relationship of crisis. When we met, I was pregnant with my second child. My beloved D was a working drug abuser and a participant in a swinging sex life with both male and female partners. As our relationship took flight, my beloved moved out of the apartment he shared with another man (who he'd told me was his cousin), and we moved in together.

The year was 1960, and several months after we moved in together, I gave birth to a baby girl. D immediately adopted my daughter, even though we were legally not wed. I did not know about my beloved's secret life at this time. Being naïve and fresh from the rural South, I believed whatever I was told. A year later, we had a son together and were married at City Hall.

During this time, D worked as a waiter, which allowed him to provide a modest living for us—and unfortunately also funded his continued drug use. I soon entered the work force, first as a nanny for a rich Jewish family that encouraged me to pursue my dream for advancement. I graduated with a B.S. in education in 1968.

The Crisis

It was another bright spring day that our primary physician referred us to an oncologist, saying only that my beloved D's blood work showed some abnormalities that required further study. As we arrived at the oncologist's office, we were both filled with fear of his diagnosis. We were soon introduced to a young, strapping physician who towered over both of us. Although I cannot recall his name, I do remember the pleasant manner in which he directed us to sit down. He stated that after looking over my husband's chart, he suspected that he had Immune Deficiency Anemia—in short, he had the first stages of AIDS.

The year was 1983. As I sat there, my heart began to pound, and my mind began to race with determination. I searched for a way to protect my husband from both ridicule and death. After the diagnosis, I began to look for literature on the subject, and I found a doctor who was doing some pioneering work on this dreaded disease. At the time, rumors about AIDS were running rampant. In my own family and circle of friends, the disease was only spoken about in whispers. I now know that my husband had engaged in bisexual encounters all of his adult life. This is a fact that I did not admit until AIDS made it impossible to ignore. Now, I can admit to these truths.

My husband and I had always connected through crises, and our commitment to each other remained steadfast. Through it all, we were soul mates. That was the one characteristic that always bound us together. We respected each other and loved one another despite our personal demons. Throughout our 34 years together, we remained dedicated to our family and certain values that we held dear.

The Journey

The dread of telling our family about our well-kept secret was overwhelming, but because of the nature of this disease, we had to share certain information with our immediate family members in order to protect them. My husband succumbed to AIDS in 1990. He fought valiantly against the disease, and he died as he lived his life, with dignity.

That same year, AIDS surfaced once again in my family, this time in the next generation, when my dear nephew J* was diagnosed. As I had first-hand experience with the disease, I was ready and willing to dispel some of the myths that still existed within our family. My family had always perceived me as a rebel, so it was appropriate that my nephew felt comfortable talking to me about his private dilemma and gay lifestyle. The eldest nephew in our family, J had been aware that he was gay since he entered puberty. He was extremely gifted academically and had taken a position as a junior executive with a large corporation upon graduating from high school.

After his HIV diagnosis, J continued his swinging lifestyle, living in denial and being young and carefree. He felt that AIDS would not beat him down. However, as time passed, he began to have symptoms characteristic of the breakdown of his immune system; this forced him to resign himself to the harsh realities of his situation.

J began to take responsibility for the management of his disease. He became an advocate for himself and other young gay men who had been affected by AIDS. He sought out the best medical help and participated in many pioneering research projects. He has availed himself of the most current medications and therapies that are presently known.

J has experimented with many drugs (both legal and otherwise) in his quest to beat this disease, and he has lived with AIDS for nearly 20 years. He has kept a steadfast relationship with his demons and his God. I think of him with empathy, and I sincerely believe that through all of his pain and suffering, he has managed to feed and nurture his soul and remember that life is still worth living. I salute him and the example he puts forth daily with all the love and respect an aunt can have. I admire him for his strength, perseverance, and commitment to life.

PETRA JOHNSON

Petra Johnson is a retired schoolteacher. A proud grandmother, she resides in St. Louis, Missouri.

J and D are pseudonyms.

Chapter 20

Sad News: A Reporter's Notes on an Epidemic

Nearly 20 years ago, I wrote what I have been told was the first article about HIV/AIDS for an ethnic publication, when I co-authored a cover story for *Essence* magazine. Recently, I dug up that piece and read it again and was struck by how much has changed during the nearly 25-year run of the AIDS epidemic. But at the same time, far too much is strikingly and tragically similar when it comes to people of color and this disease.

In 1986, I received a call from Susan L. Taylor, then the editor-in-chief of *Essence*, asking me to write a feature story about a mysterious new virus that was killing black women. She said that she had heard about it from her biology professor at Fordham University and recommended that I call her to help me sort through the complicated science of the disease. I had written a few little stories, but I was a young reporter and was excited to get such an important assignment.

I eventually talked to the professor, and we ended up writing the article together. She recommended that I call the Gay Men's Health Crisis (GMHC) and other organizations that could help me find women to talk to who also had the disease. I had a million questions, but the main one was obvious—why were black women getting a "gay" disease? Was it a lesbian disease? I had so much to learn.

Once I started reporting the story, I was fascinated and moved by it, but also very alarmed by what I was learning. A government epidemiologist explained that the AIDS virus was incurable, deadly, and most commonly struck the "four Hs": homosexuals, Haitians, hemophiliacs and heroin users. (How much everyone had yet to learn.)

GMHC sent me to the Bronx to interview a woman who had contracted the disease from her boyfriend, who was a heroin addict. Holding her 6-month-old baby daughter on her lap, she described the puzzling symptoms that had begun several months earlier. She was tired and had been losing more and more weight. Her brown skin had a grayish tint, and she could barely hold up her head. Gently, I set my notebook aside and took the baby from her as she continued to talk. The impish little girl, her hair in two fuzzy pigtails, looked at me and smiled, and I saw that her mouth was lined with something white and furry.

When I described the baby's mouth to the professor, she explained that it was a fungal infection called thrush, something common among people with the disease. At that moment, I grew quiet as I truly grasped that this virus was slowly eating away at both this woman and her daughter. By the time the story ran at the beginning of the following year, both the mother and her baby were dead.

That story propelled my career ahead and set me on a path toward serious health and medical reporting. Though I was proud of the article, I always wondered if the tone I'd used was too alarmist. The article basically said that there was a scary new disease that mostly affects gay men, but no one knew much about it, and since we end up with everything, black women must get the facts and protect themselves, or they'll all get sick and die. The headline blared, "Nobody's Safe!"

I am essentially an optimist and figured that I'd look back on that story a decade later, at a time when there was a vaccine to prevent the spread of the virus and another to cure it, and be embarrassed that I sounded hysterical, like some kind of Chicken Little.

Turns out I was more like the canary in the coal mine. Two decades later, there still is no cure for HIV and no comprehensive, viable plan to prevent the spread of the disease—or even to test for it in a widespread way. The main difference is that what I referred to as a "gay plague" in that early article has become simply a plague. And, given the mounting rates of infection among our people here, in the Caribbean, and in Africa, it is increasingly a black plague.

In fact, two years ago, the troubled face of the woman in the Bronx flashed through my mind when two of my stories ran on the front page of *The New York Times,* where I was a contributing reporter at the time. The first, "AIDS Fears Grow for Black Women," reported that even though it's now clear how to prevent HIV infection, black women are now the fastest growing group of new infections. The second, "Patients with HIV Separated by a Racial Divide," stated that even as others live with HIV/AIDS as a "manageable" illness, our people continue to die from it in disproportionate numbers. Both of these more recent stories confirmed the worst-case scenarios that I hinted at in the earlier *Essence* piece.

But then, as now, one thing remains strikingly clear: The only way we can stop the spread of the virus and keep it from further harming us is by caring for ourselves and each other enough to have sex safely and responsibly. I can only pray that in the next 10 years, 20 at most, AIDS is a memory, not a headline.

LINDA VILLAROSA

Linda Villarosa is an author/journalist who wrote the first article to cover HIV and AIDS in an African-American publication. She lives in Brooklyn, New York, with her two children and partner Jana.

▶ *Chapter 21*

Life's Ups and Downs

Life is like one long roller-coaster ride. And before HIV/AIDS came on the scene, we knew what to expect on the roller coaster. We had the familiar ups and downs and bumps and jolts, but when this disease infiltrated our lives, we suddenly hit a free fall so hard and fast that it caught everyone by surprise. We've been gripped with fear ever since—fear of the unknown, fear of the unexpected, and fear of not knowing what waits around the corner. Am I safe? Am I cool? Or have I done something in the past that will bring my world crashing down on me?

The impact HIV/AIDS has had on my life and the world around me has been as frightening for me as anybody else. My reaction to it came in phases, as I am sure it did with a lot of people. First, there was incredulity, then realization, then acceptance, and finally, adjustment. We've all had to adjust our lives in ways that we never dreamed we would have to.

We live in a time now where AIDS has become a snag in the fabric of our lives. We all know that we are going to die of something, and I know that I am not Miss Polly Perfect, who would never be touched by some kind of illness or disease. I know I'm diabetic. But I also know that I haven't done anything that would put me at risk for getting AIDS, and by the grace of God, I probably won't get it. But just as diabetes, heart disease, and cancer affect black folks disproportionately, so does this disease, and we are dropping like flies because of it. We must do something about it.

I first learned of AIDS from the people around me when I was touring back in the '80s. I don't remember exactly who told me about it or the first person I knew who died from it; I just know that when I learned of the disease, it was instantly a part of my reality. People I knew were dying of the disease before they knew what hit them. AIDS just overwhelmed them like a thief in the night.

Whenever I would perform in New York, I had a following, a group of gay guys who were always fabulously dressed and ready to party. They would hang around before, during, and after my shows. They were so kind, so supportive, and so loyal to me; I came to expect that they would always be there. They were a lot of fun, and I rather enjoyed having them as my "unofficial entourage." But after a while, they disappeared. They just stopped showing up.

I missed them. They had become a part of my New York experience, and I wanted to know why they had stopped coming to see me. So I started to ask around and I found out that two of them had died of some strange new disease. Back then, it wasn't even called AIDS, but I knew that whatever it was, it had just killed two people I knew.

And it didn't stop with them. I knew many gay men during that time and had a lot of gay buddies. A fabulous hairdresser friend of mine and another guy from whom I would buy the most beautiful shoes (I used to call him the pump queen) fell victim to AIDS. They just died. Back then, though, it was mysterious, and very scary.

Now, it's still very scary, even though we have a much better understanding of AIDS, and it is no longer a mystery disease. In the beginning, we thought we would be safe from AIDS if we were heterosexual; we have now learned that AIDS does not discriminate on the basis of sex or sexuality, but it does discriminate against ignorance and apathy. If you refuse to learn about the disease, or protect yourself sexually, or think that you can't get it because that kind of thing doesn't happen to you, then you put yourself at risk of contracting the disease. Nobody is too cute, too rich, too straight, or too good to contract it.

Initially, we all had a lot of misconceptions about AIDS and a great lack of knowledge. When we thought it was a gay disease, people were afraid of gay people, and society treated them like lepers. That was a sad time for our society, because no group of people deserves to be disenfranchised and treated unfairly for any reason. At the same time, so-called "straight" people thought they were free to do what they wanted to do, as long as they didn't do it with a gay person.

Then we found out that it's the ordinary person that can get it: the girl next door (the *nice* girl next door), your doctor, your bus driver, or the kid in your school. Anybody. It's anybody's disease, and everybody's. This disease is not prejudiced, and it doesn't play favorites. AIDS doesn't prefer black people, or gay people, or prostitutes, or drug addicts. I believe that it has quickly gained ground in the black community because we did not have enough information about it or access to health care. As a community, we have long stayed away from hospitals and doctors for myriad reasons, but the consequences of those suspicious tendencies have made us the new victims of this disease in record numbers.

Now of course, AIDS doesn't target a group of people, but individually, we've become targets because we have put ourselves at risk. We must raise our awareness of how AIDS is ravaging the black community as a whole. We have the highest rate of HIV/AIDS infection in our society. We cannot complain about how other people treat us if we don't treat ourselves right first. We need to wake up, stop ignoring the devil that's right on our doorstep, and fight back. We have two weapons at our disposal: education and protection. We need to beef up community awareness, get treated if necessary, practice safe sex, and be responsible in our relationships.

I have five kids, and I made sure I told them that they must be careful. I told them that if they are going to have sex, they must make sure they are protected. You can't go around kissing a bunch of trolls, because you don't know who's passing it. Some people are just plain nasty; they might have something and choose to not tell you. And other people might think that they are free of the virus, but you don't know who they have been with, and what they have got. Then, there are people who carry the virus and don't care who they infect. They're like crabs in a barrel; they know they're on their way out, and they don't care who they bring down on the way out. Some people are just vicious. And that's the scary part. A person really needs to know who and what they are dealing with before jumping into bed. You have to ask yourself, "Do I want a thrill? Or do I want to live?"

The most devastating thing about this disease has been the loss of innocence. AIDS has affected our lifestyles and livelihoods, and they will never be the same. Free love is out, and one-night stands can take you out. We're jaded when it comes to romance, because now we have our guards up instead of our arms open wide. Becoming intimate with someone has changed. We used to say "no romance without finance"; now, it's "no romance without a condom and a test." It's unfortunate that now something that used to be so perfect now has the potential to be so deadly. It's been hard to reconcile those two things. Life, love, and sex were so beautiful before this disease came about. They weren't perfect, but they weren't like they are now.

I know what loss is like. I lost my mother and my three sisters over the past 10 years to cancer. I know that life is short and unpredictable. We don't know when it's going to be our time to go. But that doesn't mean that we should be afraid; instead, it means we should be prepared. If I were to be afraid of all the different things that could possibly hurt me, I would be a petrified heifer every day of my life. So I don't walk in fear, I just live my life.

AIDS has taught me that every day we have on this planet is a blessing. We should make the best of our lives, make a positive impact on other people, do the right thing by other people, and not take anything for granted.

I've lost many people in my life, and although I haven't lost any relatives to AIDS, I've lost lots of friends to the disease. The only way I have found to deal with the hurt, the pain, and the loss is to keep on living. I am not going to stop living. I am going to live my best life. I'm going to live everyday as if it were my last. That's the least that I can do in their honor. I am going to sing until my last song has been sung, and until it is my turn to get off of this roller coaster.

PATTI LABELLE

Soul diva Patti LaBelle has enjoyed one of the longest-lived careers in contemporary music, notching hits in a variety of sounds ranging from girl-group pop to space-age funk to lush ballads.

Chapter 22

Celebrity Sex Crave in the Age of AIDS

In 1994, I read a fascinating article by the great writer Norman Mailer in *Esquire*. The piece was on the sex, fortune, and fame of the one-and-only superstar diva Madonna. Her career as a superstar was well into its second decade, and she was expanding her wings in London, a place she grew to adore toward the end of the '90s. Later, she moved there for good.

During their conversation, Mailer got Madonna to speak very frankly about her adventuresome sex life. Madonna was never one to hold back about sex, and as expected, she was pretty frank with her responses to him. She explained that she had done her thing with Tom, Dick, Hank, Dave, Joe, Walter, William, Jeffrey ... well, you get the picture. Madonna isn't exactly a bashful woman. However, she made a point to let Norman Mailer know that she always, or almost always, used protection.

That's when Mailer showed himself to be the top-notch writer, journalist and thinker that he is and has been for many years. In his response to Madonna's mention of always using protection during sex, Mailer's response was: If you crave sex as much as you do, and if you just can't do without it, and if it feels the best when it is raw and natural, then why cheat the process protecting yourself with a latex condom?

Mailer's response was along the lines of: Hell, make it an all-or-nothing deal, if you just have to have it so much. We don't kiss with bubble wrap over our lips. We don't hold hands with gloves on. We don't give hickies with plastic spit protectors over our necks. So why experience the explosiveness of sex that we just have to have with an unnatural shell over the penis?

Boy, I couldn't wait to read Madonna's answer to that. That was a real-ass interview. That's real writing. That's driving the car over the cliff with no parachute.

Madonna, brave diva that she is and has been for a long time, agreed with Mailer—in theory. She basically said that she saw his point, and that he was right. If she just had to have it, and since it feels so damn good when it's raw, then naturally she'd want to see how crazy she could get with her cravings. It made perfect sense to Madonna. Yet, in the real world of disease, AIDS, and unwanted pregnancies, it was simply more practical and sane for her to have her cake and eat it, too ... as long as a condom was protecting her.

Madonna went on to explain that her celebrity had complicated the matter. If she actually came down with something, she couldn't just go to a clinic and get it cleared up, because every gossip-spitting asshole in the world would want to know and talk about it. She explained that she couldn't have raw fun like that, even if she wanted to. She had an empire to protect. Her name, career, and brand were worth millions of dollars, and as far as her public knew, she was fucking like there was no tomorrow—on every tour ... in every hotel room ... and during every hour of the day. Madonna was smart enough to understand that she couldn't participate in that, no matter how strong her carnal desires were.

Man, I read that conversation between these two brave white folks and locked the conversation in my mind. It was an article worth remembering. In fact, even considering my own minor celebrity as an up-and-coming writer, great sex always seemed that much greater when it was on the edge. When you met that new person, in that new city, at that late hour, and you felt what you felt and wanted to go for it—that was the hottest sex in the world. But what if you didn't have a condom ready with you at the time? What were you gonna do?

I can remember those times like yesterday. And with a few of the girls, the rush of the sex crave was so spontaneous and insane that by the time I ventured out to grab a pack of condoms and make it back to the heated bedroom, the girl had thought it over and cooled off enough to change her damn mind.

"I don't wanna do this anymore. I mean, I hardly even know you."

Shit! We all know that feeling, when someone changes his or her mind on us at the last minute. It's a real heartbreaker.

Well, the more famous and sexy you are, the more insane the sexual situations get, and the more frequent they are. And I'm bold enough to say it: the majority of famous folks are on the edge anyway. Nine out of ten of them are driven to succeed at any and all costs. That's how they got to be famous in the first place. They were the ones who would break their necks to get what they wanted, and once they became successful at it, they began to expect it.

So by the time R. Kelly got into trouble with his infamous video tape, no girl alive could tell him that he couldn't have her panties, with or without a condom on. Are you kidding me? When you've sold 50 million albums, or won six NBA championship rings, or taken home three undisputed heavyweight title belts, or gotten two Oscars, or produced a billion dollars' worth of intellectual and creative property, or can ride out of your gated mansion in a Bentley to make it to your private jet for a business trip out of the country, regular, protected sex becomes boring. You start thinking about all kinds of unorthodox ways of getting your freak on, and I do mean *freak*!

Even if you do wear condoms, if you're screwing up to four and five different folks a week and enjoying a hot celebrity career that expands over several years, an accident is bound to happen. I mean, we're talking major Russian roulette here. The more sex you have, the more opportunities there are for something terrible to happen to you. But does that stop the celebrity from fucking? Hell, no! The reality is that most celebrities are willing to roll the dice on life to begin with. And if you're cautious with your passions, chances are that you're not going to have what it takes to become a celebrity.

The concept is very similar to the criminal mind. Once folks make up their minds that they're going to rob and kill people for a living, there ain't no going back. These jokers do what they do, and they get caught and arrested for it. Then they go out and do the shit again. Then they go to jail, serve time for it, get out of jail, and go do the shit again. I mean, once you make it a habit to do what you wanna do, it's hard as hell to break, especially when you've been successful at it.

Great, kinky, and raw sex with people you don't really know becomes an insane high. Why else would so many girls camp out for celebrity men, and why would so many celebrity men make themselves available to them? And we're not talking about just America here—we're talking about a worldwide acceptance of once-in-a-lifetime, on-the-edge sexuality. These women are willing to throw their sanity, health, and morals in the wind for a roll in the hay with a wanted man. Then AIDS came ... and nothing changed.

WHOA! MAGIC JOHNSON HAS WHAT? FROM DOING WHAT? WITH WHO, AND WHO, AND WHO, AND WHO?

Folks were scared straight, and everybody watched the press conference. I was in my senior year of college at Howard University at the time, staring at the small color TV in the recreation room of my dormitory with at least 25 other young college brothers. We all couldn't believe that shit. AIDS was a gay white man's disease for butt-fucking and such—not for straight, black male athletes. That shocked the shit out of all of us. So we all stopped and thought about it for a minute. Then we went right back to fucking, but only more cautiously.

I can honestly say that the Magic Johnson issue brought the facts home to a lot of folks who continued to have sex recklessly, but over time, the message wore off. The concerts were still turning out the groupies, and the ballers were still inviting anxious broads to the after-parties.

It didn't make the situation any better when Magic Johnson went on to continue living—which is not to say that we wanted to see the brother die. Magic Johnson has turned over a new leaf for African-American entrepreneurship on a major level. I'm quite proud of him, personally. But as he has survived HIV infection in a very public way, folks have found a way to convince themselves to go back to business as usual, fucking like there's no tomorrow.

By the time gangsta-rap mogul Eazy-E died of AIDS-related complications in 1995, he was no longer as popular as he was in his NWA days, so the 'hood pretty much viewed him as an unlucky dude at the time. But aside from Eazy and Magic, can the black community even name ten major black celebrities who have either died or been diagnosed with HIV or AIDS? And trust me, they are not all consistently protected as Madonna claimed to be. Nevertheless, by and large, the tragic disease continues to attack the unknown victims of unfortunate behavior and not famous people. Kanye West, on his album *Late Registration*, alluded to Magic Johnson, a wealthy athlete who has apparently survived the disease, as just another knock against poor people who can't afford the expensive medical treatments that he can.

Now I'm not saying that I wish it on myself or on anyone else, but just maybe it would be a strong and needed wake-up call for a present and popular celebrity to go down kicking, yelling, and screaming with the disease tomorrow to bring new attention to AIDS.

Africa is still suffering from it, that's for sure. And in Africa, the stories of the popularity of pure power and the men who enforce their rule on young, innocent women and infect them as they do are downright treacherous, if true. But how much can we really trust white-bread media sources to report the truth on the motherland? However, we do understand that the AIDS epidemic is widespread among the heterosexual community there.

Bill Clinton, the popular American president who had his own celebrity sex issues in and even before the White House, is ironically leading the charge to make AIDS medication less costly. Isn't that something? I guess Reverend Jesse Jackson could team back up with Slick Willie and help out.

That's just how complicated, hypocritical and intertwined the issues of sex, celebrity, and AIDS are. To this day, Jesse and Bill are considered good-looking, popular, political men who let their own sexual passions get the best of them, even while under the strongest moral scrutiny possible. And did they wear condoms to protect themselves and their families from disease in the heat of their passions? Obviously not. Jesse has a child born out of wedlock to raise, and as for I-don't-understand-the-question Bill, let's be honest here—unless you're dealing with a known prostitute, how many people do you know who actually use a condom for a blow job?

Hey, man, it's hard to say no when your vivacious spirit says yes. And here's even more honesty: I wonder how many celebrity women have had abortions in their long-standing careers. I'm absolutely sure that their public relations machines would crucify any abortion practitioners who would reveal the truth. But there is no way in hell that so many celebrity women can continue to be sexually active, not on the Pill, and not get pregnant. And if they're on any kind of birth control whatsoever, then it's almost guaranteed that they're going raw a lot more often than women who aren't on birth control at all. Using birth control is like having a platinum you-can-fuck-me-without-a-rubber card. And I'm not saying that a woman will screw as many partners as a man would, but if they're dealing with a celebrity male, or another Type-A rich go-getter (which most of them do), then what about what he's doing with other women who may be on birth control as well?

There's just no way around the conflicts of celebrity cravings. And what do they do when they're not married? They date other celebrities, who have dated other celebrities, who have dated other celebrities, who have dated other celebrities. So we ultimately end up with one giant dick and pussy being shared by all the same people. That's just plain nasty if you think about it. And you really believe that all of these rich, horny, and spoiled motherfuckers are wearing condoms? You *gots* to be out of your mind! Even the married and so-called committed celebrities sleep around, get divorced, and then marry other celebrities who have slept around and have gotten divorces. But still, more than 95 percent of these celebrities come out of all of this sleeping around with no AIDS. Herpes, maybe, but no AIDS. Crabs, maybe, but no AIDS.

So we get right back to the question that Norman Mailer posed to Madonna: Are we willing to roll the dice and indulge our sexual cravings, even in the face of the worldwide epidemic? Obviously, we are. And for those self-righteous brothers out there who are not celebrities but claim that they absolutely would never sleep around without using condoms, I give them this one last scenario to sleep or creep on:

Imagine having an opportunity to fuck Halle Berry, Meagan Good, Vivica Fox, Nia Long, Jennifer Lopez, Angelina Jolie, Carmen Electra, Tyra Banks, Pamela Anderson, Eva Longoria, Eva Mendes, Jessica Alba, and a thousand other wannabe models and starlets who look better than them (but have not gotten their breaks yet). And you know, when you deal with this kind of woman, slow decisions will definitely blow your chances. So how many of them are going to turn you down because you may not have a condom on you at the exact minute that they want your dick? Now, I'm not saying that absolutely no one can turn this temptation down, but you get the picture. That 100 percent protection shit is virtually impossible in the fast lane. Fucking under crazy circumstances and becoming a celebrity nearly go hand-in-hand.

So where does AIDS fall in that decision process? More than likely, in the heat of passion, the majority of celebrities find a way to take their chances with their lives. That's just how they live, no matter how crazy it may seem. Their craving for sex and life is just that strong. And so is mine. You can tell that by the crazy rawness of this essay. So please, wish a brother luck! And pray for us all.

OMAR TYREE

Omar Tyree is a best-selling author and recipient of the NAACP Image Award for Literary Fiction in 2001. His fourteenth novel, *What They Want*, was published by Simon & Schuster in July 2006. View more at www.OmarTyree.com.

Chapter 23

No More Debates

> If my people, which are called by my name, shall humble them-
> selves, and pray, and seek my face, and turn from their wicked
> ways; then will I hear from heaven, and will forgive their sin, and
> will heal their land.
>
> 2 CHRONICLES 7:14, KING JAMES VERSION

The virus that causes AIDS, human immunodeficiency virus (HIV), has won another battle today on the front lines of the war on AIDS.

Although this has been a 25-year fight, I am sad to say we have not come close to winning this war.

The United Nations estimates that today, more than 65 million people have been infected with HIV/AIDS, 25 million of whom have died. Yesterday, the virus killed over 5,000 people throughout the African diaspora, just as it did the day before yesterday, and just as it did one day a month ago. Today, it is projected that HIV/AIDS will kill over 700 people in Kenya and 800 in Nigeria, just as it as it did yesterday, just as it did the day before that, just as it did one day three months ago, and just as it did one day a year ago.

The experts are telling us that the armed forces of HIV have in-filtrated black communities worldwide, especially in Africa and the Caribbean islands. The islands now have the second highest rate of HIV/AIDS infection in the world—second only to the continent of Africa.

Here in the United States of America, 1 in every 50 African-American men are HIV positive, which is the same rate that has persisted for at least the past five years. In some African-American communities, one in every four individuals are living with HIV, just like in some African villages.

Every hour of every day, one American under the age of 20 becomes infected with HIV, and of those people, 70 percent are African-American youth.

Clearly, the war on AIDS is being won by the virus.

After so many years of conferencing and workshops on the issue, and increasing the services that are provided, HIV is still winning the war on the front lines.

Allow me to offer my opinion on why HIV is winning this war.

African people throughout the world have not organized themselves on the reality and casualties of this disease. The people of Zimbabwe know very little about the pandemic and how it is ravaging their country. The people in Nigeria know very little about the AIDS war in Zambia. The people of South Africa know little about the AIDS war in Tanzania. No one in Africa seems to know much about the casualties of the AIDS war in black America, or how the brothers and sisters in the islands of the Caribbean have gone unnoticed.

Thus, there is no strategic battle plan among African people to fight this war. There are pockets of success, but the information is not being shared in a systematic and practical way; this leaves the most unsophisticated people without the tools to combat this war successfully.

There is only one community within the African diaspora that can reach the masses of people—the faith community. Churches and mosques are organized institutions that have established links across borders, oceans, and mountains. You can find AME churches in Zimbabwe, New York, Nashville, Mississippi, and Jamaica. You can find Catholic churches in Nigeria, Chicago, Texas, and Trinidad. And, of course, you can find a Baptist church *anywhere*!

Furthermore, just as is true for the Christian community, you can find a mosque in every city throughout the diaspora.

Faith communities have the structure to disseminate life-saving information and services. In black communities worldwide, there is no other institution with the organizational structure and the ability to connect to blacks around the globe like the faith community.

The faith community can and must be empowered and mobilized to aggressively fight HIV/AIDS. So much time over the past 25 years has been lost to the debates on issues about lifestyles. We have debated the use of condoms and needle-exchange programs. We have had far too many discussions about homosexuality and not nearly enough on the sexual realities and alarming HIV infection rates among African-American teenagers and elderly. We, the people of the African diaspora, are losing the battle to HIV/AIDS because we refuse to leave the table of the debate and work hard, as if our lives depend on it, to stop the spread of HIV/AIDS.

Theological discussions have their place. However, clearly the discussions and debates over the past 25 years have done nothing to stop or slow down the spread of HIV/AIDS in black communities.

Our churches and mosques must become community centers of HIV/AIDS education, compassion, and services. As the epidemic rages completely out of control, we need all weapons on deck! Abstinence is an effective HIV prevention tool. So is the effective use of condoms. Faith institutions that are restricted to abstinence-only programs need to get busy teaching them.

We need your passionate response to stop the spread of HIV/AIDS through the prevention intervention of abstinence-only programs. Let's begin to teach abstinence young, between five and seven years of age, before we lose one more child to the destructive culture of sex and violence in which we live.

Faith institutions that embrace abstinence programs but also wish to save the lives of those who are sexually active need to provide condom education and make them available.

Every theological position on homosexuality should and must be respected. However, our theological positions on homosexuality will never stop the spread of HIV/AIDS within our communities. Homosexuality does not cause HIV/AIDS. The myth that HIV/AIDS is a homosexual disease is perhaps the greatest strategic weapon the virus has to destroy our people. Anyone can get the AIDS virus by sharing bodily fluids such as blood, semen, or breast milk with anyone who has the virus in their bodies—homosexual or not.

The HIV/AIDS stigma must be stopped, and our faith institutions must lead the fight in dismantling this deadly force. The stigma has killed as many people as the virus has itself.

As more faith institutions begin to open their doors to all persons living with HIV/AIDS and begin to provide HIV prevention, testing, and care services, the victims of this war will change. HIV/AIDS is 100 percent preventable.

We must aggressively stop all theological debates and begin to utilize all available weapons to stop the senseless killing of our people by the AIDS virus. Find out what prevention weapon is comfortable for you ... and use it to fight HIV/AIDS in your community.

I believe that 2 Chronicles 7:14 is a direct message to all people of faith regarding the response of our institutions to the tremendous destruction of HIV/AIDS within our community:

> If my people, which are called by my name, shall humble themselves, and pray, and seek my face, and turn from their wicked ways; then will I hear from heaven, and will forgive their sin, and will heal their land.

PERNESSA C. SEELE

Pernessa C. Seele is founder and CEO of The Balm In Gilead, Inc., a non-profit, non-governmental organization whose mission is to improve the health status of people of the African diaspora by building the capacity of faith communities to address life-threatening diseases, especially HIV/AIDS.

As founder and CEO of The Balm In Gilead, Seele has conceived and implemented several innovative programs that are being used nationally and internationally, including The Black Church Week of Prayer for the Healing of AIDS, the premier program of The Balm In Gilead and now the largest AIDS awareness program in the United States targeting the African-American faith community.

In May 2006, she was selected as one of the 100 people who "Shape Our World" by *Time*.

▶ *Chapter 24*

Generations

My mother always says that you can determine a person's age by simply asking them where they were on the day that John F. Kennedy was assassinated. I was yet to be born at that tumultuous time, and the barometer by which I determine the age of those in my peer group is a sobering representation of the sign of our times.

The year was 1991. Just days before my 22nd birthday, I had just walked into my dorm room when my friend Brett called with the news of Magic Johnson's HIV-positive status and subsequent retirement from the NBA. I thought it was all a bad joke until I turned to Channel 4 and saw the basketball legend standing at a podium. Damn. If Magic could get caught out there, weren't we all susceptible?

Where were you that afternoon? And what were you thinking?

Okay, I'll 'fess up—I'm a 34-year-old woman of color, and I'm single. I should also admit that while I'm a bit nervous about the ongoing search for my soul mate, the idea of enjoying a monogamous marriage, complete with unprotected, mind-blowing sex, is becoming more and more of a distant fantasy. I have not fully subscribed to that tired diatribe that there are no good men out here, but I am worried about the past and present lives, sexually speaking, of the men who are swimming in my dating pool. To put it bluntly, I'm not sure if I will ever feel fully confident and secure enjoying sex without the benefit of a thin protective barrier of latex. I know that it's uncommon for a husband to wear a condom when making love to his wife, but I often wonder if I can completely trust another human being with my health, well-being, and, for all intents and purposes, my life. After all, who would have imagined that you could lose your life over some good ol' fashioned loving?

Can I be straight up? Men stray. Some openly discuss their philandering, many rhyme about infidelity on radio dials and video stations, and others expect their better halves to be cool with their choice to indulge in the pleasures of extra-curricular activity—as long as it's not up in her face, of course. But in the world we live in today, what you don't know can indeed hurt you, if not kill you. Yes, I would love to be in a relationship right now, but I'm a bit blindsided by the fact that I could be putting myself at risk if my partner dishonors our commitment, even once. If my man falls into the arms of another woman, or even a fellow brother—don't sleep—can I really depend on him to wear a condom? One never knows. Quite honestly, I haven't met anyone that I trust enough to put to that test.

In all fairness, I would be remiss if I solely pointed a finger at the brothers. I have a number of single girlfriends who have admitted to feeling a bit shaken up after a careless liaison with someone who was hardly deserving of their time nor worthy of the privilege of sharing body fluids. Should I dare mention the sisters who accept cheating and otherwise-engaged partners into the walls of our bedrooms and our bodies? While I don't mean to pass judgment on how any adult chooses to live or love, I do question the allure of partaking in sexual "Russian roulette." The idea of respecting one's body as a temple has a whole new spin in these times, but there are so many of us who do not conduct ourselves accordingly.

Aside from my own trials and realities, I find myself even more concerned about the fate of my younger brothers and sisters. While popular opinion suggests that today's parents are in dire need of a refresher course in child rearing, the fact remains that our youth are continuously bombarded with overtly sexual media and entertainment that is devoid of any shred of responsibility. I recall tuning in to 106 & Park's World AIDS Day Special, which aired on BET on December 2, 2002. Along with positive, personal testimonies from the likes of Jill Scott and Ashanti, they played Salt-N-Pepa's video, "Let's Talk About AIDS," so I assumed, naïvely, that this special program was intended to shed light on the imminent dangers of unprotected sex, thus arming young viewers with education and alternatives. Ironically, between celebrity segments and PSAs, the programmers thought it appropriate to infuse the show with its usual dose of sexually-explicit, ass-shaking, pimped-out video clips. Not only did the Top-10 video countdown nullify the message of World AIDS Day, but worse yet, it made it clear that things were back to business as usual. All I could think was, "Are they *for real?*"

Back in the day, I remember being scared by the mere thought of contracting some itchy STD or getting pregnant, God forbid. Swallowing a prescribed antibiotic or having a baby—or not—is mere child's play when you consider the consequences that the next generation is faced with regarding their sexual health. We now live in a society where young men and women do not have the luxury to make the mistake of having unprotected sex. While I don't have any biological children to call my own yet, I feel a great sense of empathy for the teenagers who are left to make some sort of sense from society's bag of mixed messages. We have to do better by them, as they run the risk of being unprepared to endure the aftermath of our irresponsibility.

AIDS kills, period, yet the severity of that message continues to fall upon deaf ears. Statistics, billboards and pamphlets notwithstanding, only we can be held accountable for our own actions. While no one truly knows how the next man or woman may get down behind closed doors, the best thing we can do, individually, is protect ourselves. I'm all for folks doing their thing, but not at this high a price.

So now, when I pray to God to send me that special someone, I also make a point to ask him to help us learn to be more cautious about protecting ourselves and the lives and futures of our children. Imagine the alternative.

REGINA R. ROBERTSON

Regina R. Robertson is the West Coast editor of *Essence*. As a freelance journalist, her byline has been featured in *O, The Oprah Magazine*, the Associated Press newswire, *Honey, Savoy, Africana.com* and AOL's *BlackVoices.com*. She's also a contributing writer for the Los Angeles–based monthly *Venice*.

Chapter 25

Never Judge a Book by Its Cover

Motor City. That's ya boy up and down. I learned at an early age to represent my soil and "keep it real" at all costs. Like any other product of the most fascinating culture of the day, I am hip-hop, and hip-hop is me. I didn't choose it. I was born into it. It's a part of me. I speak it. I wear it. My gestures suggest it. Simply put, I live it.

When "My Adidas" dropped, I copped a pair—even took the shoestrings out like they do on 125th Street. When Snoop introduced "Gin and Juice" as the beverage of the moment, I concurred, and when Jay recommended we do the grown-up, I shot over to the mall and snatched up a few button-ups. Where my exterior is of discussion, there's no denying who or what I am. It's as blatant as my swagger and as obvious as my Timbos.

A deeper look, though, might suggest to some that my dialect, wardrobe, and strut are all a uniform—some sort of armor to deflect unwanted attention and criticism. The fact that I am homosexual means so much to so many people. Because of my sexual orientation, I'm supposed to defer to a straight guy, like he's somehow more hip-hop than me. Is Stevie Williams less hip-hop than Allen Iverson? Is Ice Cube less of a nigga with attitude because he made a family movie? Is Eminem less of a rapper because he's white? The answers are no, no, and no. And like them, I can't and won't run from who I am for the sake of satisfying arbitrary observers.

I was a senior in high school when I acquired HIV, but I didn't find out until after I walked the stage. Like most graduates with a promising future, I was ready to take on the world. I had begun to map out the details to career-oriented goals, was in a healthy relationship, and had every reason to think that my next phase would bring about all the success and happiness I'd ever dreamed of. But it didn't. Ironically, as I sought to move forward with my life, Acquired Immune Deficiency Syndrome was attempting to bring about the opposite.

It was about six to seven months after my big day. I had enlisted in the Air Force and underwent some basic medical examinations. Of course, they don't let you know that you're going to be tested for HIV. You just go in for a physical. I got a phone call shortly before I was about to leave for boot camp, and the person on the other end of the phone told me that I needed to come in regarding one of the tests I had taken. So I went in, and the doctor broke the bad news.

The moment I found out was like I was in some kind of movie or something. It was slow motion, like some kind of cinematic hangover. Everything was like a motion picture that day. I remember going into a deep depression as soon as the words came out of his mouth. I felt like my heart dropped all the way down to my stomach. It was really rough that day, because I had a lot of things going through my mind. "What are people going to think about me?"

Actually, it was my own perception of AIDS that caused me to question others' loyalty to me and for me. Would my grandmother still love me? Would my mother disown me? And what on earth would my partner think? Are they going to stick with me, knowing that I have something that could possibly kill them? I asked myself these questions over and over again. I thought I was going to die pretty soon, so I had all these thoughts going on in my mind and no guidance or advice about what I should do. I felt really dangerous that day.

It was a living nightmare. I contemplated suicide. For at least two hours, I pondered whether I was going to make it to the next day. I thought, "This is it for me. I might as well get it over with." I hallucinated intermittently about my chances of continuing to have a healthy social life. I thought that people wouldn't want to be around me. I thought that people would put on masks when I came into the room, or make me use plastic forks and paper plates every time I went to their house.

Fortunately, I made it through the night, and to my surprise, I was showered with all the love and support that I initially thought would evade me. It was amazing because everything I'd believed turned out to be untrue. Everything I thought was wrong. Everybody deferred to me more. My best friend, my mom, my whole family, and even my partner, were always there supporting me. They were always there to help me find the resources that I needed to go on. When I couldn't think about getting help, they were there to help me. And they still are to this day.

Being afflicted with a disease that can ultimately take you out is enough to break anyone down. Reflections are a muthafucka. You begin playing back every moment in your life, good and bad. You distance yourself from people who love you and you want to point the finger at some *one* or some *thing*! You scream, "This cannot be happening to me!!" But it is, and you have to deal with it through trial and error. Examine all the reasons why it may have happened to you, and decide what you can do to stop it from ravishing our culture permanently.

To a degree, I blame pop culture. Our mentality is a direct reflection of what we see and hear. In that vein, music is so sexual and influential that it can, and has, overwhelmed the minds of our youth. Something has to be said about this. I mean, this is still entertainment, and there is a certain responsibility that the people who entertain us should uphold. In particular, the media outlets have a duty to step up. There's no way that a nine-year-old should be able to watch a commercial that promotes sexual behavior. But it happens damn near every day on our favorite cable stations. And I'm not talking an innocent peck on the cheek. I mean tongue-down-the-throat action, followed by a show where some chick wants to win the love of Flavor Flav. In this particular case, in the midst of a competition with seven of her scandalous peers, the woman gets naked, and the cameras take the opportunity to follow her and blur out her titties. A month later, it's revealed that the whole show was a hoax. The point is, these stations are making millions and millions of dollars on the viewing public by promoting taboo behavior. They are hiring people to develop sexually driven scripts, and have absolutely no problem with the idea that it may negatively impact some unlucky child unfortunate enough to turn on the television at exactly the wrong time.

That's why I've elected to do what I can to help. Without a doubt, this life-altering experience has turned me into a more conscious, sociopolitical person. I'm a perfect candidate to speak on behalf of the disease among youth and the hip-hop generation. I've taken practically every opportunity I've gotten to do it. I've gone to local schools. I've done TV shows. I've been on BET. I've done *USA Today*. And I haven't done any of it for applause or sympathy. I felt a need to accept the responsibility of being a carrier, and an urge to do my part to clear up any misconceptions that still continue in the urban community.

I don't want other people to be denied the information I didn't have and end up in the same boat as me. So I'm out there. I'm in my community letting people know that this thing is serious, and it isn't going anywhere soon. When you're HIV positive, you have to come to terms with it, and I just want to let people know that if it could happen to me, it could happen to them.

At the end of the day, I try to be as visible as possible, and I know there's a risk in doing that. But I don't really have any other choice if I want to make a difference. If nothing else, I know that I have to show up and give people the option to hear me out. The idea that they may or may not cherish the information that I have to share is something that I live with. But I know in my heart that I've exercised accountability as someone who cares about tomorrow—for better or worse. I've accepted HIV as a part of my life, and regardless of what anybody else thinks, I'm still here and I still gotta live for me. One day at a time.

M. BROWN

M. Brown is an AIDS activist who lives in Detroit, Michigan.

Chapter 26

Knowing Something, But Needing to Know More

When I was offered the chance to submit an essay on my views regarding HIV/AIDS, I thought I had many things to say from the perspective of a 15-year-old just entering high school. But as I began to think about it, I realized that while I may have had many thoughts, I hadn't had many conversations. After many false starts, I broke it down into three parts: what I know about HIV/AIDS, how I feel about HIV/AIDS, and my family and friends.

My mom is a writer, so I started with her. We started with the interview technique, but that didn't really work because I felt like I didn't have the "right answers." So over the course of a few weeks, we just had conversations about the topic, and that's when I realized I had given the issue more thought than I had realized.

As a middle-school student at Sidwell Friends School in Washington, DC, I had the opportunity to hear my teachers speak on many topics of human sexuality. My memory of what I really learned during that time is vague. It was not so far in the past, but crunched in with math, junior-varsity basketball, mini-mester and other things, I just can't place what and how much I really learned. When you add that to things I heard on the court, in the school-yard, and on boy-girl trips to McDonald's, it still wasn't much. I think that much of the information that came to me as a middle schooler was from people talking at me and not with me. I don't remember many questions being asked or answered. They talked, we listened, and we left.

When my mom asked me about testing, I thought, "Well, that's easy. We'd all like to be positive, don't we?" Positive is good in everything else. Why not with HIV/AIDS? I was a little shocked when she explained to me that "positive" means that the sickness is in your body, and that you have been exposed to the virus that causes AIDS. I can't speak for all 15-year-olds, but I did not have that kind of detailed information. I wondered, "This thing is like a huge puzzle to me, and if I missed that important detail, others who knew that fact may not know something else important, and that's just as bad."

I hear many news reports about HIV/AIDS and Africa, HIV/AIDS and African Americans, and HIV/AIDS and poor people. Then I hear about how much money is needed to fight this disease. They make it sound like a poor people's disease. Then you hear about the disease in the context of the gay community. Almost every school has a club for gay students, but I don't know much about what is said between them about HIV/AIDS. The link is made sometimes, but never openly. Is that always true? I don't know. But I know it does not help that we never talk about it.

As an African African American (Senegalese father and African-American mother), I listen closely when I hear about HIV/AIDS in Africa. I admit that in my younger years when we took family vacations to Senegal, I never thought about HIV/AIDS. But now, when I think about what is said about the money we spend in the U.S. and in other countries on HIV/AIDS programs, there may be some racism or discrimination involved. I am not saying that there is with certainty, but if the richest country in the world is constantly accused of not spending enough money on a disease that hits Africans, residents of Caribbean nations, and the U.S. black community the hardest, then we need to ask why.

I am afraid of HIV/AIDS. I am afraid because I don't think I know much about it. Having to think about it for this essay makes me think about it differently, and that is good. I look back on other events in my life, and I think about how I feel. When I was in the fifth grade, a close relative died. I saw my mom and grandmother cry so hard that people had to help them in and out of chairs. I saw my father and other relatives try to calm my mom. I have never seen such pain. I later learned (when writing this essay) that AIDS was the killer.

Unfortunately, I didn't associate the HIV/AIDS issue with this tragedy because I did not know at the time. I do know that I was sad and hurt because someone I'd loved and who had taken care of me was gone. My mom cried all the time. I did too, but only once did anyone see me. If that is what HIV/AIDS does to families, then we need to find a cure and learn how to treat it. So far AIDS has no cure, but with all the money the U.S. has, it shouldn't take forever to find. My mom asked me what I thought about stereotypes and the stigma about family members dying of AIDS. I couldn't answer her. I wanted to say something really smart, but I couldn't answer. The one victim I knew made it a lot more painful and personal for me than most social commentary (a new phrase I learned for this essay!).

Among my friends, teammates, and schoolmates, we do not talk about HIV/AIDS. I had a hard time writing this because I had to think about, talk about, and then write about a topic that is dangerous and deadly. I do think more about my own behavior and if nothing else, that is a good thing. Maybe in school we should talk about important things instead of just listening to teachers tell us about important things. I am not sure they know what we know or understand what they have told us. Again, I can't speak for all 15-year-olds. Many may know a lot more than I do. But many of them may not.

DIAMAAN SAMBA GUÈYE

———————————————————————————————

Diamaan Samba Guèye is a 15-year-old high-school sophomore who resides with his mother in Silver Springs, Maryland.

► *Chapter 27*

From the Front Lines, and Why We Are All There

To this project I owe a debt of gratitude. I was humbled by the experience, as it provoked candid and sincere discussion with my 15-year-old son. We had discussions which I am certain would have taken too long to develop otherwise, and could have come about far too late to help him. It was humbling because in spite of my professional, academic, and life experience, I discovered that I have not properly guided him through a maze of misinformation and—more importantly—"missing information." I thought I was doing a good—no, great—job teaching my son about the dangers of certain behavior. I thought I was providing him the tools for survival in the context of the 21st century and its dangers. Nothing could be farther from the truth.

As a parent and, more specifically, as a mother, I have become accustomed to the process of letting go. Since giving birth to my son, my mission has been to give him the strength and stamina to make it without me. I've been tremendously dedicated to providing him with the necessary tools to make our separation possible. Although I know there are cases where he may choose to ignore my preparation and act as though he's fallen "out of a tree" or "off a turnip truck," I know in my heart that I have done my duty.

However, when it comes to the HIV/AIDS epidemic, I am not so sure. After reading my 15-year-old's views and comments on the crisis of this disease in the black community (from the preceding essay), I felt both inadequate and incompetent at the same time.

As a mother, I fear that my inadequacies and incompetence could cost my child his life. I am fearful that our society is leaving our sons and daughters to fend for themselves through a maze of misinformation and missing information.

Let's take a look at the numbers and impact analyses of this crisis.

The HIV/AIDS epidemic has become the single most horrific agent of change on the familial landscape perhaps since the plagues of the 14th century. With almost 40 million people worldwide living with HIV/AIDS and over 25 million lives already lost to this dreaded disease, it will continue to have a reverberating effect on families. Of the nearly 40 million cases of HIV/AIDS globally, the first, second and third highest incidences by region are in sub-Saharan Africa, southeast Asia, and in Latin America and the Caribbean. These areas account for almost 35 million of HIV/AIDS cases, and over 4 million of the 4.9 million newly infected persons in 2004. While they represent only 12 percent of the United States' population, African Americans account for approximately half of all AIDS cases in the US. The statistic for African-American women is particularly staggering: They make up 60 percent of all infections among American women.

These statistics are our community. They are our sons and daughters. Clearly, we are not doing our job to the best of our abilities, or we would have made a difference by now. When a 15-year-old says that he is not sure what he knows, we are destined to have these kinds of statistics—and worse ones yet to come.

I am not trying to sound a false alarm. I am a mother whose eyes have been opened by an epiphany surrounding what I thought I was doing. As a parent, I am alarmed. I am connected to each child who combats this dreaded disease, because I always assumed someone else was educating them about HIV/AIDS. These statistics could very well become our legacy.

These statistics represent a shocking and devastating impact on our global village. The economic impact of HIV/AIDS pierces through nations like the spear of a gladiator. The natural order of family progression is dramatically altered when parents bury their children and must assume responsibility for their children's children, becoming both grandparents and parents at the same time. International organizations cite figures as high as 143 million for the number of children across the developing world who have lost one or both parents to AIDS.

As an African-American mother, sister, daughter, friend, and cousin (you get my drift), I recognize that the burden of this disease is one of extraordinary weight, scope, and omnipotence. Its impact is not at all invisible. Women are often the pillars of their families and communities, and as they are particularly vulnerable to the disease, their families and communities are devastated as they sicken and die. Impoverished and economically disadvantaged women are already struggling to survive in developing nations. Imagine the impact of such a pervasive destabilizing force on the salaries and resources of families impacted by AIDS. Those who assume the responsibility for AIDS-orphaned children are usually women related to the victims by either blood or marriage.

Equally important is the emotional toll of watching this disease ravage our families, communities, and world. I have provided the staggering statistics that are publicly available to all who care to review them. What those statistics do not tell us is the anguish and anxiety of a mother of a young and promising 15-year-old basketball player. Have we really done our duty? Have we made our children cognizant of the role they must play in their own survival? Are we on the stump of HIV/AIDS awareness in the same numbers in which we march for abortion rights? Are we talking to our youth—and more importantly, are we listening to their responses (if we get any) so we know we are connecting? I have given my son life and tried to teach him how to survive, but have I succeeded at one of those goals only to fail at the other? Have I over-loved him while under-preparing him for the real challenges of survival? The letting-go syndrome is meant to be traumatic, painful, and challenging throughout the mother-child relationship. From the beginning of time, mothers have let their children go. Are we making potentially fatal assumptions about what is and is not common behavior among our precious offspring?

More importantly, have we left the task of explanation and comprehension to the basketball court, club, or mall benches? We must recognize that the real enemy is aided and abetted by our divisiveness. The AIDS scourge is the single greatest beneficiary of a paralyzed response filled with blame and discord. This is a most formidable opponent that knows no boundaries or demarcations. HIV/AIDS is like an intruder in the family home, and we must treat HIV/AIDS with the same response we would any other violator: Punishment must be swift and complete. As a mother, I have anxieties that can only be expressed by the intensity with which I approach this crisis. As a parent, I am on the front line and in the trenches, because that is where the battle is fought. I am frightened by the prospect that for the first time in the letting-go cycle, I may not have given him all that he needs, but I am destined to let go anyway, because he will demand it—as well he should.

Socially, politically, and personally, I am letting my son go. It is the natural progression. Over 25 years ago, my parents had to let me go. I went to college, and that phase of the letting-go process was (for them) not without similar anxieties. My parents feared that the freedom of dorm life would ruin my life. I am sure they believed that an unwanted pregnancy in school would ruin my life. They were right, to a degree, but it would not have killed me! HIV/AIDS has changed the landscape. My anxieties now extend not only to his behavior, but also the behavior of those closest to my son and in whom he places his heart, trust, and vital body parts.

I am passionate because for me, this is personal. I must ask these questions, but more importantly, I must be a willing and persistent member of the loyal opposition. As an African-American woman and a citizen of the world, I am both in the trenches and on the front lines! I am impacted every time someone falls victim to this slow and deliberate killer. I am personally offended when we—as a family, community, nation, and world—miss out on an opportunity (big or small) to attack this disease. Unless and until we make it personal for each and every one of us, this enemy has the upper hand.

I will go out on a limb, step off of the curb, walk the plank, and do what I do to bring the message home: We can and will oust this intruder from our family! I am not modest, embarrassed, timid, or shy about my personal commitment to fighting this disease. I am a mother. I have fears for the safety of my son, as well as aspirations for his future. I wonder, have I given him the tools to survive or have I thrust him out into the world of the living with only the ammunition of the condemned? We are engaged in a war here, and I for one am willing to launch an all-out offensive with information, information and still more information. Academic minds may disagree on the value of abstinence education versus safe-sex education to stop the spread of HIV/AIDS; governments bicker over dollars for treatment, research, and prevention to eradicate HIV/AIDS; and the international community struggles with its varied approaches to combat HIV/AIDS. To all of them, I suggest we borrow the motto of a more experienced soldier and commit to beating this scourge " ... by any means necessary!"

MELVENIA JEFFERSON GUÈYE

Melvenia Jefferson Guèye, legislative director for the Hon. Stephanie Tubbs Jones, is a health-policy analyst and international-affairs expert. She is based in New York and Washington, D.C. She is also the mother of budding essayist Diamaan Samba Guèye.

Chapter 28

I Have HIV Myself

I have HIV myself. I've found that I have a lot of families. I have a church family, a school family, a work family, a family of friends, a cultural family, an ethnic family, a middle-Tennessee family, a national family, a traditional, nuclear family, and since I was raised on so much media, I guess I have a media family too!

When I was a teenager, all of these families took part in raising me. They gave me information and formed my values, beliefs, hopes, and desires. They're what I built my dreams on and around. My family was me, and I was my family, myself.

It is horrible, but HIV is also a marvelous teacher. It has taught me a lot about the families that raised me. HIV taught me a lot about what love is not. It taught me that unplanned pregnancy is okay in many contexts. HIV taught me that sex isn't simply for making babies. It taught me responsibility when I didn't want to accept any. It taught me what ignorance really is. It taught me about stigma and discrimination. HIV taught me there are mistakes I can make and never get a second chance to correct. It taught me the truth about my families. It taught me who I can truly rely upon: myself.

With so many families and so much information, how could there be so much confusion among so many confident teenagers? With so much death, disease, and despair, how can there be so few choices for us?

My church family condemned me for my mistakes, and HIV was the proof. But, if God worked that way, what wrongs have so many women done to get breast cancer?

My school family ensured that I did not have information that could have helped me make a better choice. AIDS was a skinny, gay white man in my health book.

My work family is where I've found some refuge.

My family of friends has shrunk to one.

HIV taught me the meaning of friendship.

My cultural and ethnic families are dying around me. African Americans make up about 13 percent of the entire population and represent one out of two HIV-infected people in America. Their families must be a lot like mine.

My family educated me only about abstinence. Some think sex is only for making babies, but in reality, most people in my families have sex even when they don't want a child. So, I guess sex is okay if nothing bad happens to you, even if you don't follow these rules and values and morals. Some think information and discussions about sex make teens more comfortable and apt to do it. I guess you could follow the same logic and say that if more of us carried umbrellas, it would rain more often. Abstinence would have been a good choice. But even if my Prince Charming found me worthy enough and good-looking enough to marry, he still would have given me HIV. The only difference is that I would have had a ring around my finger as he gave it to me.

I love my life, myself. My self-confidence grows every day. Life is full and long, and we all have different roads to travel, things to learn, and relationships to nurture. I have a lot of families. They all have their beliefs and values about HIV.

HIV is a great teacher. I know, because I've learned a lot of truth since it became my mentor. I know how you get it and how you don't.

My name is Marvelyn Brown, and I hope my families can learn these things before HIV decides to teach them. Who will teach them? Will they listen? Do they care?

I have HIV myself.

MARVELYN BROWN

A native of Nashville, Tennessee, 22-year-old Marvelyn Brown is an AIDS activist.

Chapter 29

AIDS in the Black Community and Me

Maybe I have taken AIDS more seriously than other black people I've met over the years because of where I learned about it. (My first real knowledge of the disease came in New York City in 1989 on Columbia University's campus, where efforts to fight it are extremely concentrated.) It is not because I have personally known anyone afflicted with it. And I've never visited AIDS wards or treatment centers.

I can't explain why I have encountered such ambivalence towards the disease in my travels to the South and to Los Angeles, given the numbers of us who are afflicted. Throughout the South, there is particular reason for alarm. During a recent trip I took to Mobile, Alabama, I was surprised to see a huge billboard along a main street that addressed the HIV epidemic among African Americans. If there was no need to be concerned, I am certain that the billboard would not be there.

But one listen to a number of popular Southern hip-hop songs tells a different story. One recent hit even emphasized using "no rubbers" whenever the lead rapper referenced having sex with his girl. This appears to be in direct contrast to a number of New York rappers (Ol' Dirty Bastard's "I Like It Raw" is a notable exception) who frequently refer to using condoms in their recorded sexual exploits. New York rapper Fabolous, for example, even rhymes of an "empty magnum wrapper" in his radio-friendly tale of infidelity titled "Can't Let You Go." I bring up music because it is one of the primary outlets for addressing young black people's sexual attitudes. If it weren't, I am certain BET's *Rap It Up* campaign would not feature artists such as Ashanti and Ja Rule.

The music industry is a prime outlet not only because of its influence within our community but also because of our culture's conservative attitudes towards sex. Oh, we are having plenty of sex at all ages, but discussion about it is rare. Just because the teenage pregnancy rate has dropped doesn't mean that we practice safe sex with condoms. Early pregnancy is only one of our many obstacles. More and more often, we hear reports that AIDS is one of the top three causes of death for young black men and women. I even heard a news report once that a blood drive at a historically black college was unsuccessful because it was found that a third of those who had donated blood were HIV positive.

At the University of Mississippi (Oxford), I learned that one of my friends had worked in an AIDS ward in New Orleans. My friend spoke of a young female patient there who had much in common with her. She was academically accomplished, appeared very conservative and even belonged to a leading sorority. She was also HIV positive. That shook up my friend because, like many of us, she had previously believed that the disease struck mainly homosexuals and drug users. In theory, she knew this was not so, but it was quite an emotional experience to have living proof right in front of her.

I've never looked into the face of someone with AIDS to my knowledge, but I believe the Centers for Disease Control and their statistics. As for my own sexual activity, I more often favor celibacy. It seems easier to me.

Perhaps celibacy appeals to me because I am terrified by all the stories I hear. In Atlanta, where I currently live, there is a large black homosexual population. While there is nothing wrong with that, I do take issue with the numbers of men, in particular, who I hear lead double lives. Those stories seem to be everywhere I go. In the beauty salon, it is not uncommon to overhear another woman speak of herself or a girlfriend discovering that their lover also sleeps with men.

Or listen to the radio—I've heard more than a few gay men call in who are uncomfortable about the relationships they are having with other men who also have wives or live-in girlfriends.

I can't even pick up a magazine without reading an article like the one E. Lynn Harris penned recently for *Savoy*. In the article, Harris alleged that many professional athletes are lying about their sexual orientation. According to Harris, these men are professing to the women with whom they sleep that they are not homosexual, but they are secretly indulging in encounters with other men nonetheless.

Infidelity is bad enough, but if a person knows that he or she is in a committed relationship and breaks the rules anyway, why add insult to injury by not using protection? At least care enough for the person in your life to prevent transmitting a disease to him or her. It is impossible to tell by looking at a person if he or she has HIV/AIDS. A cheater should put as much effort into protecting him- or herself during each illicit sexual encounter as he or she puts into concealing the encounter.

These are frightening things.

Fortunately, I've encountered few arguments over condom use. The majority of guys with whom I've slept proudly carried fresh ones in their wallets.

In my early 20s, I tolerated such nonsense. Today, any man I'd have to ask to wear a condom is a man I wouldn't want to sleep with. It's probably never gotten that far because I have no qualms about asking about a man's sexual practices before we hit the bedroom. Therefore, any guy who tells me he regularly sleeps with random women without a condom is not a candidate. To me, that kind of behavior is unsanitary, unconscionable, and irresponsible. To me, sex is not casual.

At the fundamental root of this disease's debilitating effect on our community is a lack of communication. Young women should be taught to demand that their sexual partners use condoms. They should not have to trick them. Their lovers should want to use them. It should be clear that there is no sex without protection. Oral sex counts as well. I am impressed with Nas, the rapper, who tells in "Second Childhood" about a woman contracting herpes through oral sex. He makes it clear that oral sex should not be practiced without a condom. I've pointed these lyrics out to men who are rap junkies, and somehow they've managed to skip over that line. While that is bothersome, it is comforting to know that there are other people like me who take heed, because contracting any disease puts your body at greater risk. It further weakens your immune system. Furthermore, diseases like herpes and HIV/AIDS are incurable. It is no one else's responsibility to protect you. At that moment, it is up to you to choose protecting your life over a few moments of pleasure.

We cannot hide under the cloak of racism either. We cannot blame racism for the fact that we are contracting this disease at disturbing rates. We can be assured, however, that racism will prevent us from being properly treated. Yes, HIV-positive people like Magic Johnson are living longer with the disease, but he is wealthy and a beloved superstar. The average black American, however, has little financial recourse for minor health problems.

Even worse, in spite of the disease's epidemic proportions, testing is not free; in some areas, $100 or more is the going price. This is really ridiculous. How can you fight a disease like this without offering free testing? A major disease almost always signals death for most of us. Condoms are available in ample supply almost everywhere. They are also affordable. Using them should be no problem. Losing your life should be.

I know losing mine to anything other than natural causes is unacceptable.

RONDA RACHA PENRICE

A Chicago native with Mississippi roots, Ronda Racha Penrice received her B.A. in English and history from Columbia College of Columbia University in New York and attended graduate school at New York University and the University of Mississippi. The former associate editor of *Rap Pages* and *Upscale* magazines, Penrice has also published work in *Essence, Vibe,* the *Quarterly Black Review of Books, Honey, The Source, Urban Network, Africana.com, Blackvoices.com* and *Creative Loafing,* among others.

Chapter 30

Something's Gotta Give

In 1994, I made the life-altering decision to become a porn star. There was an article in *LA Weekly* that made reference to an adult-film expo in Las Vegas. I was intrigued. When I got there, I was asked if I was in the porn industry, to which I replied, "No." The very next question was, "Do you want to be?"

Amazingly, it's been over ten years now, and I'm still here. Since 1990, we've survived the death of Eazy-E, a startling press conference courtesy of Earvin "Magic" Johnson, and loads of other tragedies worth acknowledging; through all that, I've continued a promiscuous path that some call reckless, selfish, and even worse. AIDS, after all, is the number one killer of African-American men ages 25 to 44, and I fall smack dab in the middle of that bunch. In a world dominated by sex, money, and drugs, I am wedged in a place where all the alleged perpetrators have direct access to me. I can't say that it really truly bothers me, though, because when it comes down to it, I enjoy what I do. Besides, there are so many things that people can die from other than sex.

I'm actually comfortable with the way that I am. Sex is something that I was exposed to at an early age, and maybe I've spent my whole life trying to understand and appreciate it more. My outlook on sex is that it's positive and healthy. When you are young, you don't know, and eventually when you do come to a place where you have achieved some sort of satisfaction with sex, you find comfort in that. I've had my share of days when I've thought, "Whoa, I did too much today." But overall, I believe that adult film is an artistic expression that I've been blessed to share with the world.

As one of the most popular African-American men in the porn industry, I am revered. It's funny, because people are always downplaying the business, but if sex is such a bad thing, then why is it a constant tool of motivation and marketability? Why is it so desirable? Why do people want it all the time? There are countless souls that my peers and I have unwittingly taught how to perform. Bottom line: Sex is a good thing, and I'm not ashamed to say it. Moreover, there isn't anything on God's green earth that's going to prevent me from doing what I need to do in order to provide for my family. I have a wife and children to provide for; it is my duty to take care of them.

Understanding the horror of HIV/AIDS is something that I am confronted with daily, which probably makes me more conscious of it than the average person. I can't hide from it. Every day that I go to work, it's there, right in front of me. Even though I don't always use condoms in my movies, I make sure that everyone I work with is tested before they take part in any scene that I am in. In the porn industry, we are also required to take regular tests for sexually transmitted diseases, which means that I am able to stay up-to-date about my status.

On the flip side, if I walk, talk, and act with disease on my mind every day, there is no way that I can perform my job to the best of my ability. For that reason, I've formed an invisible block that allows me to separate my private life from my professional identity. I have learned to turn on and off what I do and who I am in order to get the job done. People in other professions do it all the time; it's done by police officers, doctors, mathematicians, accountants, and even strippers. Anyone whose job requires them to remain focused learns how to compartmentalize and keep separate who they are at work and who they are at home.

If I have to go to a function at my daughter's school at 5:00 P.M. and I have a sex scene to shoot at 1:00 p.m., then I have to think about what I have to do ... and usually that requires me to think as a sex addict. For those two or three hours that it takes to do that, I am that guy. The tricks that you can play with your mind are amazing, and I find comfort in that. But it's a challenge. Luckily,

I have a job that supports my outlook on sex. For me, that's a real blessing.

The irony is that I've chosen a career that is very much a part of everyone's reality. In that sense, I am compassionate and concerned. In a professional sense, though, I act with caution, as would a doctor who has to perform a triple bypass or a police officer walking up to a car with tinted windows during a traffic stop. A life in the porn industry is like that of a racecar driver who knows that every time he goes out on the track could be his last. But you just do what you have to do. Maybe I'm fearless. Maybe I'm stubborn, or maybe I just love the thrill.

I've seen some crazy shit over the past decade, and I have been very lucky. I don't mean the type of luck that comes from carrying a rabbit's foot in your front pocket. What I mean is being a healthy, HIV-negative man, despite living with the risk of being exposed to a disease that is a death sentence almost every day.

When a national news story alluded to an AIDS outbreak in the porn industry, I was one of the people mentioned as a suspected source of the outbreak. Given my status as one of the industry's most popular stars, I was a target, even though I hadn't tested positive. However, I was able to use the situation to take action. I organized a series of meetings with other performers in the adult-film industry in which we've explored ways to better protect ourselves. A lot of key people in the industry attended these meetings, and I arranged for medical advisors to attend these sessions to explain how porn performers can protect themselves from sexually transmitted diseases.

Realistically speaking, my craving for sex is just like everyone else's. I just happen to get paid to do something that every man in every city across America is in search of every night. In that sense, sex is something that I committed to a long time ago, even before I became a part of this business. I admit that I've always had some sort of fixation with it. But that didn't come without questions, and even multiple insecurities.

It's like a basketball player who goes for 30 points in a night. When he's on he's on. He's making the three. He's dropping dimes (passes), and (no pun intended) he's "penetrating to the hole" with reckless abandon. But when he's off, he doubts himself to no end. *"Should I perform for the camera?" "Should I just enjoy this?" "Am I doing this right?" "Is the viewer going to appreciate this, or does this look awkward?"* Contrary to what some may think, when I perform, I actually have to get over the sex part of it. If I couldn't detach myself when I showed up for work, my confidence would suffer. If I am not in a positive frame of mind, it is very hard to perform.

To me, intimacy and lovemaking only exist between the sheets, in the bedroom, and with the lights off. What I do professionally is different. From my pubescent years to now, I've watched girls go from guy to guy, and vice versa.

I once did a movie with 101 women called *The World's Luckiest Black Man*. When I began shooting the film, I thought I was the king of the hill. As shooting progressed, I discovered that in order to perform, I had to stimulate myself by looking at different body parts of the women. I had to wear a different condom with each girl, but I just didn't have the ability to connect with each one. I did connect with some, of course, but if I had an urgent desire to deal with one of them specifically, well, then it would have been a different fuck.

During the times when it's been just three or four girls that I have to fuck in one session, I can disassociate myself very easily, but some of the girls I work with want more. They are looking for some kind of mental connection. That's not even a remote possibility, because I have to move on. I just can't get caught up in all of that.

My grandpa once told me this story about the men in our family being used as studs during slavery times. They would take the men in our family to a plantation and have them impregnate the women to make strong babies. Given what I do for a living, it didn't take much for me to believe him, because I work as a stud every day. After I heard that story, however, I understood that it is something that I was born to do.

Even if I want to do this forever, I know that I can't. It's not physically possible. I was with a girl recently who was doing all this different stuff with her body, but it didn't do anything for me. Now, had I been younger, it may have been a whole lotta fun, but I wasn't really into it.

In some respects, it's almost as if I have no other choice. I have a friend who recently found out that he has been infected with HIV; the news made me think, "What if that were me?" Although the industry has made significant strides where testing is concerned, the possibility still exists that some producer may not be minding his Ps and Qs, or someone may have a false-negative test. In a worst-case scenario, my rubber might break. Then what?

There's still a huge part of me that is completely infatuated with my occupation. I feel privileged knowing that I have been successful as a black man in the porn industry. As I've watched some people leave my side of the camera to make significant strides behind the scenes, I am hopeful. When all is said and done, I want to grow in other areas in this industry. I really have a lot of respect for men like Larry Flynt and Hugh Hefner. They built their empires based on their—and society's—obsessions with sex. So why can't I? I think somewhere, some way, somehow, I will do the same thing. I want to create something that keeps my legacy alive.

The sex industry keeps growing. It's a driving force in pop culture; music videos, billboards, print ads, and live performers take their cues from it. I've even heard that the video camera and the still camera were created as means of documenting pornography. All naysayers should note that sales of porn tapes and DVDs are going through the roof. Why? The sales represent just how much people are consumed by pornography.

I acknowledge the fact that I have, in some way, turned myself into a reliable icon with the performances that I've turned in over the years. With tremendous respect to the industry, I always come back to the notion that my status today comes from what I was able to do yesterday. I have the unique opportunity of welcoming others to borrow from me, just as I borrowed from those who came before me.

Still, I often wonder if this is something to aspire to. There is a certain recklessness about having to dodge a disease every day I go to work. Moreover, the thought of having to restrict my emotions or thought processes in order to work is drudgery to me. I know that I've been exceptionally lucky, and I'm thankful, but the clock is ticking ... I can't do this forever. Something's gotta give.

MR. MARCUS

Mr. Marcus is an adult film icon who resides in Los Angeles with his family.

▶ *Chapter 31*

Sometimes I Cry*

I am an endangered species, but I sing no victim's song. I am woman. I am an artist, and I know where my voice belongs. I am an endangered species, but I sing no victim's song. I am woman, an artist, but I know where my voice belongs. I am sorry. I am sorry that we have a day like today. I am sorry that you are all sitting here so we can address a brand new day of awareness of HIV/AIDS as it pertains to women and children. I am sorry because I know it did not have to be like this. I know in my heart of hearts that HIV/AIDS is going to be the greatest moral test for all of us as human beings around the globe.

I remember when I first stormed the stage in "Dreamgirls" 25 years ago. Around that time, a lot of Broadway's men—gay men—started dropping dead from some mystery disease that had no name. Back then, it was called GRID: Gay Related Immunodeficiency Disease. I remember it as an ugly time in America, when good people dropped their children off in hospital driveways because they did not want to have anything to do with them. I remember that it was a time in America when people disposed of other people. You'd search for friends in the hospital only to find that they were on gurneys up against some wall in a hallway because the doctors and nurses did not want to touch them.

I remember that time in America because I witnessed it with my own eyes. Back then, when I tried to speak up about this disease, I received hate mail from people who threatened my livelihood. They told me to shut up! But I was raised to believe that if one of us suffers, we all suffer. I had to summon my courage and use my

■ *149*

voice to speak out and bring about awareness of this disease. There but for the grace of God go I, so my hope is that sooner or later the good people, the good people who know better, the good people who are not looking for votes, the good people who are not looking to make any money from this disease, will do the right thing.

I am committed to helping others find their voice and speak out, because there is nothing pretty or nice about this disease. It is time that we do more than have nice conversations about HIV/AIDS, because there are a lot of people right now in need of some real action.

I am a mother with two children who sooner or later will come into their sexual awakening. I know that at some point, they are going to have sex, and it's my hope that when they have it, it will not be deadly. These are the new facts of life that you can't run or hide from. If some of you think your children probably aren't thinking about sex, think again. As parents, we need to get educated and enlightened about HIV/AIDS. We need to get the proper information and share it with our children. If you haven't talked to your daughters and sons about HIV/AIDS, then you have not given them an essential part of their education.

Women of color, especially those of us who are black and brown, must do everything we can to give voice to what is happening to us right before our very eyes. We can't afford to remain silent any longer. If any other group in America were in such danger of dropping dead from a disease, you'd better believe that somebody would be saying something. But they are not. They are not, because we have remained silent.

That is why I have written a one-woman show called "Sometimes I Cry," which is based upon the real stories of women infected and affected by HIV/AIDS. I wrote it because the rebel voices that I heard rumbling back in the '80s are now silent as it pertains to women with this disease. Through this show, I hope to motivate and empower other women to get out there, stand up, and let their voices and stories be heard.

I am every woman, and I feel every woman's joy and pain. When she smiles, I smile. She cries, I cry. Sojourner Truth said, "Life for me ain't been no crystal stair." Mother Maya has mused, "I know why the caged bird sings." They were all just words then, but now I understand. I understand that life is a roller-coaster ride, and you'd better be strapped in. I understand that you must have a good relationship with the Great Spirit—the god or goddess who speaks to you—and you'd better hold it close, because when you hit those lows (and you will hit those lows) you'd better have a strong foundation. I understand that HIV/AIDS is an equal opportunity disease. It doesn't care if you're young, old, black, white, yellow, gay, straight, transgender, male, female, adult, child, or anything in between.

And if you do not protect yourself always, in all ways possible, each time, every time, it can get you. And as hard as it is for me to understand why I am not where I thought I would be, I must be where I am supposed to be, because I am still alive. I thank God every day for the strength to get an HIV test, so I could know my status. I thank God for giving me the good sense to seek the help I needed to combat this disease, and for the courage to continue to live my life. I thank God for embracing me, keeping me safe from harm, protecting my children, and granting me the serenity to accept the things I cannot change, the power to change the things I can, and the wisdom to know the difference. And I thank God for you, because I need you. I need all of you to speak up for me.

Speak up for me, and for the struggles I endure daily. Speak up for me, because you know how hard it is just to be. Speak up for me, for being a pillar of the strength I didn't know I had. Speak up for me, because I choose to live and not die. Speak up for me, for being a rebel with a cause I did not know was my own. Speak up for me, for loving myself enough to fight for myself. Speak up for me, for being able to look in the mirror and love what I see. Speak up for me, because I am HIV positive and I need you. Speak up for me, because I am your sister, your mother, your daughter, you grandmother, your auntie, your niece, your lover, your friend, your parent, your patient, your provider, your cook, your confidant, your teacher, and your motivator. Speak up for me. Love me. Respect me. Help me. Lift me up. Accept me. Love me. Speak up for me because I am HIV positive, and sometimes I cry.

This is only one woman's story, but it could be any one of us. So we must speak up for our sisters who may not be able to speak for themselves. I stand here now, but there are so many others who you can't see. You've got to speak up for them.

SHERYL LEE RALPH

Sheryl Lee Ralph is an accomplished stage, film, and TV actress. At age 19, she became the youngest female graduate of Rutgers College in the institution's history. An original "Dreamgirl" and a very active AIDS activist, Ms. Ralph is mother to two children and married to Pennsylvania State Senator Vincent Hughes.

Notes

*Excerpt from a speech given at the Women and Girls' HIV/AIDS Awareness Day, March 10, 2006.

Chapter 32

A Crisis in a Community

For the past two decades, many in the African-American community have been reluctant to address the severe crisis of human immunodeficiency virus (HIV) and acquired immune deficiency syndrome (AIDS) for two reasons: First, because they are afraid of elevating the stereotype of sexual promiscuity and intravenous drug use (IVDU) in the community, and second, to deny the presence of homosexuality and bisexuality in the community.

It is no secret that the African-American community is locked in a deep crisis, a crisis of survival. Even though blacks represent less than 30 percent (28.4 percent) of the state of Georgia's population, we represent over 50 percent of this state's reported AIDS cases, according to the most recent statistics from the Centers for Disease Control (CDC). Even more alarming is that over 70 percent of the reported pediatric AIDS cases in Georgia are black children. From 2000 through 2003, HIV/AIDS infection rates for African-American females were almost 20 times the rates for white females, and the infection rates for African-American males were seven times those for white males.

These numbers represent more than some "piggyback" epidemic. This is a threat of annihilation. Such attempts at annihilation are not new in black America. These attempts have been present since the first African stepped onto this country's soil in 1619. What is new about today's crisis is that it is self-inflicted for some, and in other cases caused by an unfortunate event (i.e., blood and blood-product transfusion, needle-stick injuries, and sexual contact with a partner unaware of his/her HIV infection).

The majority of HIV cases in the U.S. remain in the homosexual/bisexual male population; however, in the black community, an increasing number of the infections are being transmitted heterosexually. Most of these cases arise from intravenous drug use, sexual promiscuity, bisexuality, and/or sexual partners of individuals from these groups.

It appears that some of our souls have been ruptured and are in dire need of repair. Like all Americans, blacks are influenced by the images of violence, comfort, sexuality, and extravagance. These images have constructed our way of life while suppressing basic human values and emotions such as love, honesty, character, hope, and service to others. Instead, we have allowed our souls to leak out their instinctively good values and replace the resulting emptiness with self-destructive behaviors and pleasure-seeking activities. As such, we have exposed ourselves to this virus in disproportionate numbers.

I recently saw a television report about an HIV-positive 17-year-old who became pregnant so she could have a child; she wanted to have someone in her life who would give her unconditional love. This is a sad and unfortunate commentary on the depth of darkness and emptiness that some of us confront on a daily basis. I think most of us can understand that our souls can become compromised if we try to obtain such love in this matter. However, we must not place the life of an infant at such significant risk in order to get such love.

The genius of our foremothers and forefathers was to establish a barrier between them and the racist society in which they lived. This barrier was their faith in God. This was an impenetrable barrier to self-hatred designed to help defeat the demons of hopelessness and meaninglessness. Through their dreams and spirit, they were able to withstand the viciousness of slavery and segregation.

Today, we are engulfed with ruptured souls that spill out our spirituality and belief in God. In many cases, we are losing hope and meaning as a people. There has been a constant, logarithmic erosion of morality in the community, and many of us have lost the ability to resist the magnitude of deviant temptations and distractions in our lives. We are drowning in a sea of despair because we have not been able to maintain our belief systems. We have become disillusioned by the pervasive use of illicit drugs, proliferation of violence, and racism.

And now this malignant virus, HIV, has shaken some of our belief systems. Recently, I heard a minister state that God's laws are fixed in the universe, and anyone who goes against them will suffer the consequences. The implication from his statement in this setting was that HIV may be the result of some violation of God's law. Some in the community believe this distorted view of damnation, while others believe that no God would allow something so terrible to occur; therefore, to them, there must not be a God. Suffice it to say, God exists in every walk of life, and I do not believe that the presence of HIV is some inevitable damnation toward any particular group or humankind in general.

Upper-middle and upper-class African Americans should not become too comfortable with the pervasive misperception that HIV/AIDS is isolated to a certain segment of our community. All of us are connected by race, culture, or religion. This has been the case since we were all kicked off the spiritual playground (Garden of Eden). Therefore, all of us are at risk to be burdened with this disease through personal contacts, loved ones, or associates.

What can be done? Is there really any hope, given our shattered civil society? If one begins with the premise that AIDS and HIV are preventable, then it becomes obvious that something can be done. It is not an easy task, but it is an achievable one. First, we must educate the community as a whole, including fathers, mothers, children, grandparents, ministers, social workers, and yes, some health-care providers. We need to explain in vivid detail how this virus is transmitted.

In short, there are essentially three ways in which transmission occurs: (1) sexually, (2) parentally, and (3) parenterally (blood-to-blood contact). This virus is not transmitted through casual contact such as hand shaking, embracing, or even superficial kissing.

Since 1985, the transfusion of blood and blood products has been safer because all donated blood is tested for the virus antibody.

We need to explain to the community that blacks are no more susceptible to this virus than any other ethnic group; however, blacks are disproportionately represented in this disease process because they may be more likely to engage in high-risk behavior.

At the risk of seeming pious, we should encourage everyone to abstain from sexual activity of any kind until they are married. However, we live in a real world where some people will be involved in such activities, and these individuals should be instructed to practice safer sex, with a constant reminder that abstinence is the safest of all measures. Sexual promiscuity must be rejected, and individuals who engage in this activity must be reminded that this act is not only morally wrong, but that it can be deadly wrong.

The illegal use of drugs should be strongly denounced, and blacks must closely examine their ability to manage the pain, agony, and frustration of living in this historically racist and immoral society without suppressing these feelings through substance abuse or other destructive behaviors. We need to discuss the ways that living more simply may be necessary for us to recapture our escaping souls. We simply need a spiritual renaissance. We need to espouse the values that enrich the human experience, like honesty, integrity, respect, and love.

The reader should note that the above discussion was not about treatment options, nor was it a social commentary on those who are HIV positive or who have AIDS. This is not the intent of this discussion. The sole purpose of this article is to comment on the issues surrounding the prevention of HIV disease.

I would trust that all Americans should give compassion, hope, understanding, and support to those who have been afflicted with this dreaded disease, and that all treatment options which have demonstrated efficacy against the disease should be available for widespread use.

JAMES BENTON, MD

James Benton, MD, is a graduate of the Morehouse School of Medicine. A radiation oncologist, Benton is now in private practice in Atlanta, Georgia.

▶ *Chapter 33*

HIV/AIDS and African Americans: Reflections of a Congresswoman, a Physician, and a Mother

HIV/AIDS is the plague of our time, and its statistics paint a ghastly picture of a crisis in our midst. In 2005, the total number of people living with HIV throughout the world reached an all-time high of 40.3 million people.[1] Of these, 38 million were adults, 17.5 million were women, and 2.3 million were children under the age of 15.[2] In 2005, 3.1 million people worldwide died of an AIDS-related illness.[3] Of these deaths, 2.6 million were among adults and nearly 600,000 were among children under the age of fifteen.[4] Moreover, approximately 5 million people throughout the world were newly infected with HIV in 2005.[5] Of these, over 4 million were adults and 700,000 were children under the age of 15.[6]

These statistics are both sobering and agonizing. We are not only losing men, women, and children—many of whom are grandparents, mothers, fathers, sons and daughters, and brothers and sisters—but also the communal and institutional fabric of communities and families. This loss has far-reaching implications, including the potential to destabilize the economic, social, political, and health-care infrastructure of communities and countries already overburdened with poverty, disease, inequality, and political unrest.

This issue is very personal to me. As a physician and health administrator with 29 years of service in the Virgin Islands community, I have treated those with HIV/AIDS and have personally seen their daily struggles. I have nursed them though their HIV-related illnesses and held their hands as they entered the final stages of AIDS. I have seen the human toll on their families and the voids created in the community by their deaths. I speak of this experience not as a congresswoman and chair of the Congressional Black Caucus Health Braintrust, but as a mother, wife, friend, and grandmother concerned about the kind of world my grandchildren will face.

Those who are left behind are also the victims of this hideous epidemic. We must rally our collective voices so another child is not orphaned, another HIV/AIDS patient is not left without health care, and another mother or father is not left to bury a child whose future has been stolen.

HIV/AIDS in Sub-Saharan Africa, the Caribbean, and the U.S. Virgin Islands

HIV/AIDS is now the leading cause of death in sub-Saharan Africa.

While only 10 percent of the world's population lives in sub-Saharan Africa, two-thirds of all people living with HIV (or 25.8 million) are in sub-Saharan Africa.[7] In 2005, about 2.4 million died from HIV-related illnesses, and there were 3.2 million new HIV infections.[8] Moreover, more than three in every four women (77 percent) around the globe with HIV live in sub-Saharan Africa.[9]

In the Caribbean, the second most affected region of the world, the numbers are also disheartening. In 2005, 300,000 people were living with HIV.[10] That same year, 30,000 adults and children were newly infected with HIV, and 24,000 adults and children in the Caribbean died of an AIDS-related illness.[11] Moreover, the number of women living with HIV was 140,000.[12]

Despite having a relatively small geographic size and population, the U.S. Virgin Islands, my beloved home, has one of the ten highest AIDS case rates in the United States. Nearly two in every three reported AIDS cases in the Virgin Islands are African Americans, and one in four is a Hispanic person.

As I mentioned before, the insidiousness of this epidemic is not only its human toll, but also its destabilizing impact. HIV/AIDS is robbing some regions of their current and future workforce, because skilled workers are sick and dying. This erodes an already tenuous health-care infrastructure, because public health systems are overwhelmed and health-care workers themselves are infected and dying. Health-care workers are leached from the professional workforce because they either migrate from their countries in search of better opportunities or die from the epidemic, thus widening the brain-drain divide.

HIV/AIDS in the United States

Since its inception, the HIV/AIDS epidemic in the United States has had a disproportionate impact on African Americans. African Americans account for more than half of all AIDS deaths, despite only representing 13 percent of the total U.S. population.[13] Nearly half of all people living with HIV/AIDS in the United States are African American, and the AIDS case rate for African Americans is nearly 10 times that of whites.[14] In 2002, HIV was the third leading cause of death for African Americans ages 25 to 34[15] and the *leading* cause of death among African-American women in the same age group.[16]

This epidemic is ravishing African-American women. In 2004, African-American women accounted for 67 percent of estimated female AIDS cases, but only 13 percent of the U.S. female population.[17] Moreover, HIV rates among African-American women are 23 times higher than those of white women.[18]

African-American women are the backbone of the African-American family and community. However, this foundation is eroding as far too many of these mothers, sisters, wives, and friends are infected with HIV and eventually die from AIDS. Many of these young women never even get the opportunity to become mothers, because they are dying during their reproductive years. Since many African-American households are headed by single black women, their loss weakens the family structure not only for this generation, but for generations to come. Worldwide, over 6,000 children are orphaned by AIDS every day. In the United States, an estimated 70,000 children have been orphaned by AIDS. A generation gap exists as many of these children must grow up without their mothers and fathers and are instead raised by grandparents, aunts, uncles, siblings or family friends. This is unacceptable and unforgivable.

Legislative Remedies

The unconscionable tragedy of the HIV/AIDS epidemic is not only measured by the lives that have been needlessly lost, but also by the persistent lack of political will to end this living human catastrophe. The Bush administration has drastically cut Medicaid and has proposed budget cuts to essential health programs designed for the underserved and poor—many of whom are HIV positive—while providing tax cuts to the richest in our nation. We must remain vigilant in this fight. There are things that we can do as a country to eradicate this deadly killer and to provide assistance for victims and their loved ones, who are on the battle lines everyday—especially in the communities of color that have been the hardest hit and the most neglected.

Before speaking of legislative remedies, it would be wholly remiss to disregard the impact of the social determinants of health on access to quality, equitable, and affordable health care, and the resulting impact on the health of individuals and the communities where they reside, especially for those living with HIV and AIDS. The social determinants of health refer to the economic, social, political, and environmental structures that ultimately affect health care by perpetuating racial and ethnic health disparities. In order to eliminate racial and ethnic disparities in health, the economic, social, and environmental inequities that exist must be eliminated. Poverty is a social determinant of health. Those who are poor, and many who have HIV and AIDS, do not have the means to access or to obtain life-saving health care. However, there is legislation that will attack these inequities at their root and provide the necessary health and health care to those with the least.

The Health Empowerment Zone Act of 2005 (HEZ 2005) directly addresses the issues surrounding the social determinants of health, because it is a substantial step in breaking the connection between poverty and health. This vital legislation will empower communities and provide them with the tools to access, improve, and coordinate affordable, equitable, and quality health care. This is an undeniable necessity for those living with HIV and AIDS, many of whom live in underserved communities with limited resources.

Specifically, HEZ 2005 proposes using existing programs and resources to assess health care needs and improve the overall health of a particular community. It will establish HEZ programs in communities that disproportionately experience disparities in health status and health care. To be eligible for HEZ status, communities must demonstrate that they experience disproportionate disparities in health status and in health care. They also must establish a strategic plan and create a partnership between individuals, businesses, schools, minority health associations, nonprofit organizations, community-based organizations, hospitals, health-care clinics, and foundations. The HEZ designation provides communities with the ability to effectively access existing federal programs to improve the health or environment of minority individuals in the community and to coordinate efforts to eliminate racial and ethnic disparities in health status and health care. Communities with proven cultural and linguistic competence in responsive services will be given special consideration.

In 1998, the Clinton administration's Department of Health and Human Services, in collaboration with the Congressional Black Caucus, realized that HIV/AIDS was a health crisis in communities of color and responded by creating the Minority AIDS Initiative (MAI). MAI targets communities of color by providing technical assistance and infrastructure support, increasing prevention and care, and developing linkages for communities to access health services and care for those who are impacted. We must ensure the MAI continues to receive the funding necessary to provide these vital life-saving resources to the communities of color that are being decimated by this epidemic.

The Ryan White CARE Act, passed into law on August 18, 1990, was designed to improve the quality of care and expand access to it for people living with HIV/AIDS and their families. Specifically, the CARE Act provides grants to metropolitan regions that are most severely affected by HIV/AIDS; funding for AIDS Drug Assistance Programs (ADAP); early intervention services grants for planning and capacity building; competitive grants to programs that provide services to women, children, and their families; funding for AIDS Education and Training Centers; and funding for programs that provide outreach to communities of color to increase access to prevention and care, such as the Minority AIDS Initiative. On September 30, 2005, the CARE Act expired, and it remains that way today. The CARE Act must be reauthorized and should receive at least $3.2 billion in funding, rather than the proposed $2.1 billion, to ensure that the health and health care needs of people living with HIV/AIDS and their families are adequately and consistently met.

In July 2005, the Congressional Black Caucus, the Congressional Hispanic Caucus and the Congressional Asian/Pacific Islander Caucus introduced the Healthcare Equality and Accountability Act of 2005 (HEAL 2005). This legislation has been developed as a comprehensive effort to eliminate racial and ethnic disparities in health and health care for communities of color. As statistics show, ethnic and racial minorities are disproportionately affected by HIV/AIDS, and this legislation will be a substantial step in eliminating this and other disparities. HEAL 2005 will expand health coverage to some of the more than 45 million Americans without health insurance; remove language and cultural barriers; improve workforce diversity; support and expand programs to reduce health disparities in conditions and diseases, such as diabetes, obesity, heart disease, asthma, and HIV/AIDS, that disproportionately impact racial and ethnic minorities; and improve data collection.

Conclusion

In these uncertain times, we must remain diligent in our resolve to be the voice of the voiceless and end HIV/AIDS during our time. As we look toward the future, we must remain hopeful and not despair. Those who have HIV/AIDS have been the tireless warriors on the forefront of this battle and we, along with them, must continue the fight. We have the resources through legislation to support these individuals and their families to provide adequate and essential health care. Now we must embody the political will as well and translate it into political action.

THE HONORABLE DONNA CHRISTENSEN (D-US V.I.)

Notes

1. *UNAIDS Epidemic Update 2005.* http://www.unaids.org/epi/2005/doc/EPIupdate2005_pdf_en/epi-update2005_en.pdf (accessed April 8, 2006).

2. ibid.

3. ibid.

4. ibid.

5. ibid.

6. ibid.

7. De Santis, Dominique, Sub-Saharan Africa Fact Sheet [online], Geneva: *UNAIDS Epidemic Update 2005.* http://data.unaids.org/Publications/Fact-Sheets04/FS_SubSaharanAfrica_Nov05_en.pdf (accessed April 8, 2006).

8. *UNAIDS Epidemic Update 2005.* http://www.unaids.org/epi/2005/doc/EPIupdate2005_pdf_en/epi-update2005_en.pdf (accessed April8, 2006).

9. ibid.

10. ibid.

11. ibid.

12. ibid.

13. Kates, Jennifer and Carbaugh, Alicia. African Americans and HIV/AIDS in the United States. [online]. Washington, DC. Kaiser Family Foundation, 2006 [cited 08, April 2006]. http://www.kff.org/hivaids/upload/6092-03.pdf (accessed April 8, 2006).

14. ibid.

15. ibid.

16. ibid.

17. ibid.

18. ibid.

The Honorable Donna M. Christensen continues to distinguish herself as a leader in the United States Congress. As a member serving her fifth term, she is the first female physician elected to the U.S. Congress in its history, the first woman to represent an offshore territory in Congress, and the first woman delegate from the United States Virgin Islands. She serves on the Committee on Resources, which oversees territorial and public land issues; the Committee on Small Business, which oversees entrepreneurship and business activities; and the Homeland Security Committee, which oversees preparing the nation to prevent and withstand attacks and disasters.

Christensen is a member of the Congressional Black Caucus and chairs the Congressional Black Caucus Health Braintrust, which oversees and advocates minority health issues nationally and internationally. She is also a member of the Congressional Caucus for Women's Issues.

Chapter 34

i can't stand the rain

a difficult question—would i date a man with hiv? the answer comes with a shocking swiftness—shocking in its immediacy, shocking in its urgency.

i would not now knowingly date a man with hiv, not because a man with hiv is unlovable, or that i don't believe that any moment of love is preferred to one without, but because i have had my sunshine, and i "can't stand the rain."

that is david's legacy.

sunshine on my shoulder ...

i met david almost 17 years ago. it was love at first sight. he was a flamboyant hairdresser wearing tight jeans and muscle shirts. i was a fledgling lawyer wearing blue suits and spectator pumps. locks of golden curls hung adroitly from his head, and drew your attention to his beautifully-sculpted shoulders and ever-present tan. i teased him unmercifully about his vanity, as well as his black man's booty, which he kept in marvelous shape through routine workouts.

he called me his "cool little lawyer." while i handled his legal matters, he handled my hair—both matters of prime and equal import in our minds. he professed to understand the nuances of my self-coined "trailer-park jheri curl" hair by claiming that we had the same "roots"—literally!

david was funny, femme, and fantastic, and our friendship was "rooted" in mutual adoration and trust. we were like mutt and jeff: a caucasian gay man and an african-american female lawyer as buddies, both out of place in our environment, yet completely at home with each other.

makes me happy ...

when we met, david was working at a high-end hair salon in the city. he later moved to a salon to the suburbs. the move served to strengthen our bond. by that time, i was the only african american in a judicial position in a predominantly wasp-y suburban community. although it was only a part-time position, my mere presence proved to be too much for some of the residents. david blithely dismissed the ignorance that sought to consume us and continued to embrace me without pause.

i regaled him with hilarious and horrific stories of my time on the bench, including the one where a woman pulled out her deceased dog's teeth for examination as evidence. when i failed to rule in her favor, she called my court a "nigger court" as her mother stood in the back of the room crying tears of shame and humiliation.

it was a difficult time and path for me. i was graced with the opportunity to sit in that high seat, although the weight of a thousand years of oppression on my shoulders compelled me to accept the opportunity even though it was not right for me. that compromise would later cost me and make my road a little rocky. the public saw a black judge, and to them, that was the problem. i was an artist with a law degree wearing a black robe and banging a gavel. that was a problem for me.

david and i later learned that he would venture down a lonely and separate path himself; his was not because of the pigmentation of his skin. being gay and comfortable in his skin would later prove to be his rocky road. his sexual preference would hinder and, later, bar his way.

by night, he was sunshine (his stage name); he performed as marilyn monroe in drag, dancing madly and merrily in a cage at a local nightclub.

by day, he brought sunshine. one day each week, he traveled to a nursing home outside the city to do roller sets on little gray-haired southern belles and flirt with them insouciantly.

david didn't care what people thought of him. he was living his life on his terms, and he seemed completely unfettered by judgments and hate. i admired his moxie as i buttoned myself up into ill-fitting suits in an effort to conform, please, and be accepted. but i would soon come undone, and mutt and jeff (david and i) would have the last laugh. in a fit of rebellion, we dyed my hair blond, and i laughed all the way to the bank. there was a new judge in town, and those who ventured to judge me were actually paying my salary. touché!

sunshine almost always makes me cry ...

funny how david and i seemed to live parallel lives; we even started losing weight around the same time. as i denied the artist in me freedom of expression, i also denied myself the freedom to be happy with my success. my body followed suit. i didn't eat or sleep because i was unhappy. i denied the fact that i wanted to do something creative with life instead of sitting on a bench judging people. i didn't consider myself a grand success because i wasn't following my passion. my outward appearance became a reflection of my inner starvation. it is amazing how denying yourself one good thing can lead to a progressive denial of all good things. all joy becomes at risk.

david's weight loss resulted from something that couldn't be cured by freeing oneself and following one's passion. instead, his uninhibited freedom of self-expression, and the passionate pursuit of it, led to a diagnosis that doesn't have a cure, and all of his joy would be at risk.

as the arc of his private life paralleled my professional one, our paths diverged when it came to our reputations in these regards. where i was reserved, careful, and selective, david was a serial lover and proud of it; he was wild in his ways and wanton with his liaisons. he was the best of boys—and "girls." he was sunshine to everyone.

he loved well and he loved hard; he also lived well and he lived hard. i lived vicariously through him. i was fortunate to know him, to be loved by him, and to love him in return.

then, there were the signs. he was losing weight rapidly and could no longer claim that he was trying to diet. his perpetual tan could not be revived. it was that beautiful skin of his that offered one of the most telling betrayals. i was not surprised when he told me that he was hiv positive. i was glad that he trusted me because there was much stigma attached to the disease at the time. he knew that i was involved with a minority-affiliated aids organization, and the fact that i was well-informed probably eased any shame he may have had about disclosing his personal health crisis to me.

despite the depth of our friendship, i don't know that he would have confided in me had he not been compelled to do so. he wanted someone to make decisions for him when the time came: life or death decisions. i agreed to help him without hesitation, unaware that one "yes" would lead to another. in the end, i knew that the final "yes" would tilt my world and taint my ability to fully and freely love for a very long time. david's life was soon overflowing with secrets. it was not an indicator of the man he was, but of the disease he was hiding.

love changes

i was surprised to discover that david's last and most ardent lover veiled himself as heterosexual. he was a musician in a band that had some success in the industry. while david wore his sexuality like a badge of courage, his lover refused to introduce david to his bandmates and friends. it hurt me to watch david be hurt by such calculated rejection, and by someone whom he loved beyond measure.

he was dying. to my shock and dismay, david did not tell his lover about his status. i struggled with the deception, but tried to reconcile my concern with the thought that each deception begot the other.

he loved the man he was deceiving, and as much as he loved his work. hair was his passion. it should not have surprised me that he also refused to tell his clients. we had difficult discussions over the right to know versus his right to earn a living. david was certain that he would be ostracized. he needed to work to be able to pay for his medications—to live. he assured me that he was careful and that he was being safe.

sunshine almost always makes me cry

eventually, david's body deceived him. his former scrupulously sculpted frame became an emaciated silhouette. his beautiful skin became marred by lesions. his spirit was broken by his image in the mirror.

the road was long, but the end was near. when the end came, it came quickly—all in a series of ones:

one ominous call
one frantic trip
one whispered question
one screaming family member
one painful "yes"
one hand held
one last breath
one love lost
one life remembered

would i date a man with hiv? right now, today? i would love a man with hiv; i would love him desperately and fiercely, and with all my heart. but if i knew that he had hiv, i couldn't fall for him. i couldn't/wouldn't want to watch him/help him/let him go. for me to love fully and freely, i need options, like the option to give him my entire heart, to live and love forever, and to grow old together.

hiv itself does not limit options for me today. i am able to experience true intimacy across the board, with all men. i am not talking about sexual intimacy. i would limit myself with a man with hiv in that i would always be waiting for the first symptom, and the next, and the next. i would live in fear. who among us can love fully when afraid?

i don't have hiv, but i do not want to specifically join other "non-hiv-positive" people or characterize myself as such. i don't want to wear my "non" status like a badge of honor. it could happen to any of us.

i don't believe that every day with a loved one with hiv brings heartbreak. i do believe that my experience with david would be a constant reminder of that singular heartbreak, and i would always (in any subsequent scenario) be expecting that familiar heartache.

however, as i share my thoughts, i don't want to limit the hopes of anyone loving someone with hiv or living with hiv themselves. i want to be responsible about this and not perpetuate any of the prejudice that uninformed people fall back on due to fear. i just want to say that the shadow cast on my life by watching my beautiful friend die loomed long after he was gone.

ain't no sunshine when he's gone

i will love and do love men with hiv, but i know i will catch myself before i fall in love, and i will catch myself every time.

i can't stand the rain.

IVORY T. BROWN

---

ivory t. brown is a lawyer turned literary and a blonde turned serial shades of metallic. depending on the day, you will find the shade of metal matches her mood and mettle.

► *Chapter 35*

Not in My Family, Not in My House

"I have AIDS," were the first and only words I remember hearing when my best friend first informed me about his condition. I remember my first thoughts were, "Oh, God, not in my family, not in my house!" I was afraid of how he would be treated by society and also how I would treat him myself, now that I knew his deep, dark secret.

As a friend, you want to be supportive of your loved ones and a rock to them. There are times when that rock may be shifted, but not broken. That is what happened to me on this occasion: I was shifted, but not broken. I had to overcome my fears of the unknown in order to provide strong, genuine, loving support to my friend, for I knew he desperately needed it. I had to overcome the fear of the unknown and learn to see through his eyes how society treats HIV/AIDS patients.

When you are 22, the last thing on your mind is dying at a young age because of HIV or AIDS. At that age, you believe you're invincible. You talk about the future and tease one another about who is going to get married or have children first, or you're trying to get your money together for the next trip or party coming up. Well, all that changed for me when my friend was diagnosed with AIDS. When he told me that he had AIDS, I felt like my world had come to a halt. I felt as though he was just issued a death sentence that could not be overturned. The jury had rendered its decision. Although I comforted my friend and told him everything was going to be all right, in the back of my mind, I was afraid not only for him, but for myself as well.

I was afraid that I might treat him differently because of my fear of the unknown—because I did not know the true meaning of this disease called AIDS. In the beginning, I must admit, my friend and I were afraid to do the same things we had done when we were younger, like sipping each other's sodas, eating off of each other's plates, or sharing a bar of soap—all because we were afraid of the unknown. He was afraid of passing his disease to someone he loved, and I was afraid of contracting it. As a true friend, I had to be honest with my friend and let him know that I loved him and wanted to support him. Although we both had our own fears, we had to learn more about this disease so we wouldn't allow it to control everything we cherished and loved—each other. We visited a few support groups, and I took some medical classes to help us both overcome our fears. Doing so brought much peace and balance back into our lives.

After my friend and I overcame our fears, we learned that society could be very judgmental because of its own fears. At times, society tries to place AIDS victims in particular categories. Society tends to associate AIDS with homosexuals or individuals who are promiscuous; this is so sad, because this disease is much bigger than that. I remember accompanying my friend to doctor's appointments and noticing that when the medical assistants realized my friend had AIDS, they would wear gloves even to carry his chart or give him a gown. They, too, were afraid they would contract the disease. Going to the laboratory was no different. Lab assistants would try to get others to draw his blood when they learned he had AIDS.

I remember visiting his family's house for dinner. Before they found out about his condition, we would eat in the house with plates and forks. Once they found out, every get-together took place at a restaurant or at a park where everyone had to use paper plates and plastic forks—all because of their fear of the unknown. I couldn't understand their logic—they were afraid to use their own family member's plate or fork, but they had no problem sipping from a cup or using a plate or piece of silverware that many strangers had used time and again at a restaurant.

I remember that some people were afraid to even give him a hug. Seeing that through my friend's eyes made my heart cry. Through those experiences, I knew I did what I had to do to change my fears. It's just a shame that everyone doesn't take the initiative to stop the fear of the unknown.

As time passed, I felt that our bond was unbreakable. By learning more about AIDS, my friend and I overcame our fears of the unknown. This knowledge provided us with the ability to become each other's rock. I learned how to comfort him about my fears of losing him and how to be there for him in the way that he needed someone to be there for him. He learned how to comfort me and be honest with me about his fears as well. We were always each other's rock. As that rock shifted, we gained more understanding, and our rock became too strong to be moved.

By learning and gaining more knowledge, we as a people can overcome our fears of the unknown.

NICOLE JOSEPH

Nicole Joseph is a 30-year-old account representative for MHN, a comprehensive mental and behavioral health services company, and a phlebotomist at Kaiser Hospital. She resides in San Pablo, California with her daughter, Ajani. She dreams of one day opening a nonprofit organization to provide housing and education for young adults who have been recently released from the foster-care system.

Chapter 36

The Black Church: False Prophets and Wandering Sheep

In 2004, Bishop Eddie Long, flanked by the Rev. Bernice King, led a strange and misguided demonstration that left many in the Atlanta area shocked, angered, and mystified. Using the King Center as his launching pad, Long, the flamboyant leader of New Birth Missionary Baptist Church, led thousands in a march against the civil rights of gays and lesbians.

Long characterized the march as a demonstration in support of family values. But it may well stand as the first time in memory that black people, marching under the banner of civil rights, have essentially campaigned against themselves.

In a very real way, homophobia—disguised as a so-called "moral agenda"—could actually endanger black people's lives.

Despite swift and strong criticism from civil-rights leaders, Long has insisted that he will not be "silenced" on the issue. That may be a good thing, since his public spectacle raises more questions than answers. The primary question that Long's crusade raises is this: What about the monumental problems facing blacks? More than ever, those problems require a show of unity. So why would Long choose to focus upon such a divisive issue? Why now?

Long casts his homophobia as an element of his Christian faith. Anyone tempted to accept this position should be reminded that Ku Klux Klan members, along with a host of other crackpots and demagogues, also insist they are led by God.

The civil rights of gays and lesbians do not, as Long suggests, threaten to destabilize our communities. Our communities are at grave risk because of an array of other factors: drugs; unemployment; police profiling, which results in high incarceration rates; and the pandemic of AIDS, which disproportionately affects African-American women. Further, our communities are at risk because of a low regard for higher education among our youth, the pervasiveness of sexism, and the glamorization of violence. The list of real threats to black survival goes on and on.

So why, in the midst of all this wrenching madness, would a black preacher who claims to lead a flock of 25,000 choose to target gays and lesbians?

If his motivations are murky, it is quite clear that Long's crusade may undermine our communities' efforts to ward off some of our most serious threats. As a result of public demonstrations like his, people with AIDS will be less likely to come forward for help, and even more lives may be lost to the disease.

Homophobia and denial about homosexuality are already major challenges among African-Americans. This was demonstrated at Morehouse College in 2002, when one baseball-bat-wielding student brutally beat a fellow student. The fellow student's crime? He was suspected to be gay.

It is unlikely that a preacher from Lithonia, GA, would be quite so eager to grab the public limelight to accept responsibility for the acts of anti-gay violence that could extend from his reckless holy war.

Another disturbing aspect of Long's demonstration was the participation of the Rev. Bernice King. An assistant at Long's church, she referred in a speech to the bishop as a "prophet." The word itself, along with her association with him, ascribed to Long an almost cult-like status and symbolically anointed him as the heir apparent to her father's leadership mantle.

King's stance placed her in direct conflict with her mother, Coretta Scott King, who worked hard to ensure that her husband's legacy is not misappropriated. For decades, Mrs. King expressed support for the civil rights of gays and lesbians.

To their credit, members of Atlanta's civil-rights establishment, including U.S. Rep. John Lewis (D-GA) and the Rev. Joseph Lowery, denounced Long's actions. If they are to prove themselves consistent in the fight for justice, other leaders, including Andrew Young, may now be required to campaign against a black preacher. They should do so with all the fervor with which they fought the Klan.

As the march began, Long sought to establish his civil-rights credentials by lighting an Olympic-style torch from the eternal flame at the King Center. The action leads one to wonder what King, winner of the Nobel Prize for Peace, might have said about the bishop's hate crusade.

A study of King's writings makes it clear that Long's mission to target gays and lesbians is antithetical to the civil-rights legend's vision of the beloved community, where all men and women, regardless of difference, constitute one community.

"Now we have got to get this thing right," King said during a famous 1967 speech. "What is needed is a realization that power without love is reckless and abusive, and that love without power is sentimental and anemic. Power at its best is love implementing the demands of justice, and justice at its best is love correcting everything that stands against love. And this is what we must see as we move on."

NATHAN MCCALL AND RUDOLPH BYRD

Rudolph Byrd is an associate professor of liberal studies at Emory University. Nathan McCall is a visiting lecturer in journalism at Emory.

▶ *Chapter 37*

Shedding Secrets

When my mother was diagnosed in the late '80s, AIDS was still considered a "gay" disease. She was a single woman with two young children. She wasn't a drug user or a gay man, so how did *she* end up with this disease? At the time, my mother had no time to worry about the past. She had to figure out how to live for the future. She had to figure out how to continue to be the strong and caring woman that we had all grown so dependent on. Rather than burden others or shame herself, she kept her HIV status a secret from us, her family, for over 10 years. She only shared this information with her doctors and partners.

As kids, my brother and I never saw the signs. But now as adults looking back, they are clear as day. When she would get sick and go to the hospital, we were told that Mommy had the stomach flu. When the doctor once told me that my white blood count was low, a look of concern crossed her face, and she and my doctors left the room. Later, they would return to draw more blood. I always wondered why she would freak out when I would use her razor to shave my legs. Hell, I just thought she was an overly concerned mother with a bad stomach that didn't like me touching her stuff. Never in a million years would I have thought she was HIV positive.

My mother decided to tell my grandmother, brother, and me that she was HIV positive in the winter of 1998. She told each of us separately, and of course, I am always the last to find out everything. When the words came out of her mouth, it was like a fight scene from the film *The Matrix*—it was in slow motion, and I couldn't believe what was happening. Several different emotions hit me all at once: hurt, betrayal, sadness, and disappointment. In the end, I chose to stick with just one: denial. How could this be? She is the smartest woman I know, my best friend, the wind beneath my wings, all that. How could she have this disease that has *killed millions*? Was she going to die too?

I asked my mommy all those questions and more. She answered them truthfully and honestly. When I asked her who else knew she said, "My brother and your granny." She also said that she was afraid of what her family and friends would think of her. She didn't want to lose them. That really confused me. We were talking about our family: the people she lives for and would die for. What would they say except, "You are my sister/daughter/aunt/best friend, and I love you"? Back then, the stereotypes attached to HIV were still considered truths. Even though the black community was strongly affected by this epidemic, it was still uneducated and misinformed about the disease. Who was to say that our family was any different? We could hope so, but she wasn't ready to take that risk.

Well, in 2003, my mother said, "To hell with what people think." She had begun speaking to small groups and even did a radio interview with me on my college radio station. She had begun to feel more secure and was ready to talk about it. So when she was asked to participate in a special episode of the UPN show *Girlfriends*, she proudly said yes. On May 12, 2003, the rest of our family and the world found out that my mother, Julaun Lewis, was *living* with HIV. During her appearance, she was beautiful, strong, and most importantly, forever free of the burden of this secret. I had never been more proud of both her and my family. Like we'd hoped, everyone had the same response, "We love you and always will." See, I told you, Mommy ... you had nothing to worry about.

I truly feel that the key to stopping this disease is education and acceptance. Once we as a community educate ourselves about the disease, and our own personal status, we will open our hearts and minds and finally accept how HIV/AIDS has affected our community. I know first-hand that HIV/AIDS is not a death sentence. People with it can live long, full, and healthy lives. Our brothers and sisters must move past their stereotypes so no one will have to keep being HIV positive a secret.

JENEANE LEWIS

Jeneane Lewis is a 27-year-old graduate of Morgan State University in Baltimore, Maryland. She enjoys talking to youth groups and mentoring young women. She currently lives in Los Angeles, California, with her fiancé and five-year-old stepson.

Chapter 38

As It Stands

Back in the day (pre-AIDS), people would hook up casually just for fun. Today, a decision like that could ultimately land you in the grave. HIV ended the whole free-love thing, and it brought back dating.

If you think about it, we were heading toward a very wanton society. There was a sense that things were out of control. This also led to paranoia about the disease and some people denying its relevance to them. That's why I dealt with AIDS in an episode of my show, *One on One*.

At that time, the show's star, Flex Alexander, had just lost a brother to AIDS. I've now had three dear friends—two men and one woman—die from AIDS. I felt compelled to do something in their memory, while simultaneously making an effort to raise awareness and get the information out.

Most African-American women think that it is necessary to their existence to have a gay friend, and as a result, most of us do. My friend Arnaz was the first person I knew who openly talked about the bathhouses and what he did in them. He described the gay lifestyle as a promiscuous one. I think those of us who are able to should keep getting the message out about AIDS. One 2004 episode of *One on One* dealt with safe sex as a way to avoid conception, AIDS, and STDs. I think that's very important, since the rate of infection is up dramatically for black adult women and teenagers alike.

There is a misconception that AIDS is not a problem anymore. I think we must seize every opportunity we have to show the black community that this is untrue. Until music videos start preaching safer sex, however, problems will continue.

The hip-hop community has got to take some responsibility. The constant message of hip-hop videos is clear—have sex have sex have sex, hit it hit it hit it, smack it, flip it, rub it down, and don't put on a condom. I think it's very hard to think about safer sex when a big ass is in your face bouncing up and down and you only want to "hit it." In movies and sitcoms (especially those where women have been involved at a high level, like as creator, writer, or producer), we've seen a bit of progress.

If we cannot bring this epidemic under control in our community ourselves, we may have to rely on the government to reel us in. If the government demanded that every American get tested, we would have no choice. Of course, I understand why people don't get tested. Nobody wants to be labeled as a victim and walk around with a scarlet letter. I totally get that. The black church doesn't accept the fact that there are people of the same sex who are attracted to each other sexually, nor that those people are a part of its congregations. There are also people in the church's congregation who are sexually active and sexually irresponsible. What is the church's message to them? If a minister hands out condoms during his service, what is he saying? He's saying it's okay to have sex even though the church's policy is abstinence.

To forget that HIV/AIDS is ravaging black communities and affecting a staggering number of African-American women would be a critical mistake. I honestly believe that every part of the black community must make the prevention of HIV/AIDS its number-one concern—including parents, schools, and churches. By doing so, we'll make sure awareness of the disease is high. It's up to us to decide when, and how, we are going to eliminate HIV/AIDS.

EUNETTA T. BOONE

Eunetta T. Boone is a successful television writer, producer, and director. She is the creator of the popular sitcoms *One on One* and *CUTS*.

Chapter 39

A Revolutionary Act

This essay is a commemoration and appreciation that I can celebrate reaching the cusp of my 20th year of life with HIV. Feeling as healthy as I do and having AIDS is a mixed blessing, of course. I love being as healthy as I am. I have not yet lost the thrill of living that many of us lose long before we die. I feel fully immersed in the stream and flow of life. In particular, I love the physicality—the carnal aspect of living.

I love being in my body. I am learning to worship my body without shame or apology. It is not just a mere vessel for me. While it is not my essence, it is certainly an essential part of me. I have got to love it. Every day, the HIV that lives within me threatens to slowly and imperceptibly nest and divide to weaken and kill this body of mine. I will not let that happen.

And if viruses possess some form of intelligence, as some admiring virologists suggest, then I suspect that this virus, my virus, understands that. We have at least reached an agreement, if not an impasse. I cannot get rid of it, and it can't get rid of me. We have a very dysfunctional mutual respect for each other.

But because I have been spared many of the severe manifestations of this disease, I still have to remind myself to remain vigilant—to get my blood work done, to call and find out what my viral load and T-cell counts are, to continue to set up appointments with my case manager. My long-term wellness has made such precautions seem less urgent, but I know better. I know that the insurgent force that lives within my territories is clever, with inexhaustible patience and stealth as its greatest weapon. I must not fall asleep on my own watch. I do things to ensure my survival, informed by both intelligence and, far more frequently as of late, instinct.

For instance, I love my body quite tenaciously. Remember Baby Suggs's soul-stirring sermon on the mount from Toni Morrison's *Beloved*, in which she admonished black people to never ignore their flesh? "Love it," she commanded. "Yonder," she warned, "they do not love your flesh."

Well, I have a new understanding for this these days. I indulge my body in certain disciplines and certain pleasures. To eat dessert, to sleep late, to run, to exercise, to stretch, to feel the weight that I push against or pull upon, to inhale, to drink, to lick, to suck, to sweat, to smell, to exhale, to touch, to feel ... this is to Live. This is life in the body. Each body is as divine and as unique as the color Purple, and I think it "pisses God off" for us to dwell in our body all the live-long day and not see this. I find myself sometimes smelling myself between my own legs. I taste the salt of my own tears. I touch the viscous tissue of my own pungent cum. I listen to the sound and hug the abrupt quake of my own laughter. This is what I will recall when those angels ask me about the beauty of it all. What was it like down here, below.

If my focus is highly erotic, it is because the erotic, like nothing else, reminds me of the animal that I am. I am still discovering the differences between the erotic and the sexual. During a recent men's retreat, I met a kind and honest brother who asked to spend the night with me without having sex. I agreed, but as there was a mutual attraction, I was afraid that I would not be able to resist the temptation of his body laid up next to mine. How fortunate then that I managed to refrain from any sexual touch and still hold and be held by him in a manner that left me more naked than many of my sexual encounters. I felt safe and loved in the warm blanket of his body. I felt no lack or regret, and even though I was excited by his touch, I felt no need to do anything other than be touched. I never felt more alive or fully open.

I once believed that the erotic and the sexual were one and the same, and that anything considered erotic must serve as a prelude, an invitation, to the inevitable sexual act. I believed that without the all-important consummation, anything erotic was in and of itself a worthless tease, a ruse not worth getting hot and bothered about. In this line of thinking, erotic things, after all, are the appetizers that whet our appetites for the main course, sex. And sex, then, means intercourse; in the homosexual world, it specifically means anal penetration. Anything else would then be foreplay, and sex must culminate in ejaculation. Somebody has to come, or the deed will be left undone.

My first boyfriend and I often enjoyed hours of delicious sex, sometimes without penetration or climax; when I shared this with friends, several of them claimed that this was not "real sex." Our culture, true to its Judeo-Christian roots, enforces a thick, dark line between sexuality and spirituality. It also reduces the erotic to serve the singular agenda of intercourse.

I believe that one of the reasons why homosexuals are so feared and reviled is because our sexuality is often not legitimized by procreation, marriage, or monogamy. The values that define sexual pleasure outside of such constructs as base and immoral are the same values that, in these United States, frame the bodies of women, black and brown people, and gays as terrains of unbridled desire and decadence. These bodies must be covered because they are profane; sanitized because they are hopelessly dirty; punished or imprisoned because they are criminal; and lynched, raped, mutilated, or otherwise destroyed because they are evil and threaten to subvert the dominance of white men or sully the purity of white women. When the voluptuous Janet Jackson flashed her breast before millions, it was a transgression for which she was swiftly punished. When a virile, dark-skinned 17-year-old named Marcus Dixon had sex with a 16-year-old white girl in Rome, Georgia, it was a transgression for which he was speedily imprisoned. When I perform fellatio on another man and then enjoy passionate sex with him way into the midnight hour, it is a transgression for which I could be consigned to eternal damnation, or at least be dispatched from this life like our young sister, Sakia Gunn, a 15-year-old murdered because she rejected the advances of a man by declaring that she was a lesbian.

Since I am revealed as an outlaw by my skin and my sexuality, it is crucial that I celebrate my day-to-day survival in a land that rejects me as if I were an infection it has discovered and hopes to wipe out. But I know that I belong here, triple offender though I may be; despite the odds, I have managed to survive here. It is my birthright "bought and paid for" by my African ancestors and their American progeny, as well as my homosexual forebears. I am compelled to celebrate those who endured and those who perished so it would be considerably more difficult (though not impossible) for me to be killed or jailed for eyeballing a white woman or balling a man of any color.

Black men who love men tend to carry heavy loads of shame that are often masked by addictions and distorted self-images. We are usually served by well-intentioned organizations that don't have a clue about how we see ourselves and where our power and resiliency lies—that we are not merely walking pathologies to be saved by catchy messages with hip-hop soundtracks or mudcloth graphics. How do we reach the sensual salvation we seek when we are forced to love on the "minefield" described by the brilliant Charles Stephens in his contribution to the seminal anthology *Think Again*? It is, I think, an unanswerable question, and yet we must ask it.

One of the most powerful ways for me to exalt the improbable triumph of drawing breath is to fully embrace my own body, and to kiss and trace every warrior mark, whether or not it was earned or deserved. As a teenager, I often felt embarrassed by my desires and what or who—either innocently or deliberately—aroused them. I did not wait to relinquish that shame before I started having sex with men. But no paramour, however skilled or compassionate, could hope to love away the stains ingrained beneath my skin. This is my work, and I am so commissioned for life.

Shortly after I discovered that I had been infected, there came a time when sex was no longer sexy to me. After all, it was the very thing that got me into this mess. I was afraid to pee, much less have sex. I was so preoccupied with the fear of infecting someone, or someone finding out, or not being able to get hard, that the first time I tried, I found I could not perform. Well, I met this one brother who told me that he was HIV positive as well. And we did it. And it was good. It was so good that the morning after, I prepared for him an exquisite breakfast. And after he left, I took the day off so I could take time to reflect on the experience. I didn't want to let go just yet of what had just happened and act as if nothing had changed. I wanted to savor it. I was not in love. I do not even remember his name. But I do remember that he gave me something precious. He reminded me of my right to life, to a corporeal, sexual life.

My flesh. I have got to love it. "Do not forget to love your flesh. Just love it."

CRAIG WASHINGTON

Craig Washington is a self-affirming, HIV-positive black homosexual who has engaged in writing and organizing to foster progressive social change. For more information, please visit www.craigwerks.com.

Chapter 40

Dispelling the Myth

I think that HIV/AIDS is taking such a great toll in our communities largely because of the myths and misinformation surrounding it. This started back when the disease first became a presence in the United States and was labeled a white gay man's disease. This created a major barrier in the black community, where virtually no one admits to being lesbian or gay, even when we are. It kept us from paying any real attention. We chose to believe that this disease wouldn't bother us.

We didn't listen to the messages that were put forth because they were not geared to us. Other communities and people from different backgrounds and education levels were being targeted by the campaigns. This created another barrier that led us to believe that HIV/AIDS wouldn't bother us.

We continued being very indiscriminate in our sex lives. As African Americans, or blacks, or American Africans, we just felt that AIDS was something that was going on to some degree in Africa ... and it was only a little bit later that we began to learn of the widespread death tolls across sub-Saharan Africa. Unfortunately, by that time HIV/AIDS had already gained a foothold within our community as well.

The inaccurate association of this disease with homosexuality has been an enormous barrier that has prevented many black Americans from paying attention to HIV/AIDS. The denial that many of us hold on to about the prevalence of homosexuality in our community has led to many transmissions of the disease through heterosexual contact. In this regard, the black church must bear responsibility. Black Americans are very religious, and the church is one thing that most of us believe in and support. However, certain wrong messages about HIV/AIDS that we've bought into are preached to us there every Sunday. This has ultimately led to a proliferation of myths and misinformation because of which people may fall prey to HIV/AIDS.

The prevalence of HIV/AIDS within the black community is very much related to the community's overall lack of knowledge about the disease. Too many of us don't read the paper and don't pay attention to media reports about HIV/AIDS. Many of us only get a part of the messages. With incomplete educations holding them back, many in our community are open to believing and repeating myths.

We must learn the ABCs of AIDS prevention:

A. Abstinence.
B. Be truthful.
C. Wear latex condoms.
D. Do other things.

In this country, when people want to take action, things will get done. In the '80s, hemophiliacs were contracting AIDS with alarming frequency. Since hemophiliacs require frequent blood and blood-product transfusions, we quickly discovered that the disease was being transmitted through our blood supply. Tests were subsequently created to screen the virus out. Now, that problem doesn't exist anymore. When the connection was made between this disease and intravenous-drug use, educational and needle-exchange programs were instituted. As a result, new incidences of those transmissions are decreasing. As long as black Americans have the highest percentage of HIV/AIDS cases in the country, we can certainly say that not enough is getting done.

The Brazilian government has aggressively fostered educational and awareness campaigns about HIV/AIDS. Throughout the country, messages that every citizen can relate to are disseminated. Even more importantly, the country's leaders talk openly about

HIV/AIDS, which leads the general population to do the same. They talk about condoms and engage in honest dialogues about sex and sexuality. In Brazil, people are willing to acknowledge that they're sexual beings and that sex is for pleasure, but that it should be practiced with safety in mind.

I took a similar approach during my political career, but in this country, many leaders still want people to believe that sex is only for procreation. Everyone knows that's the biggest lie in the world. We all know that 99.9 percent of sex is done for pleasure, but some are unwilling to admit it. Instead, men are often permitted to not wear condoms because they say they "don't want to waste seed" or because "it doesn't feel as good," even though we know this kind of behavior can be tantamount to signing a death warrant.

Given the current corresponding AIDS statistics by geographic area, it is not a big surprise that 80 to 90 percent of all new venereal disease case incidences are in the southern United States. Historically, Southern states have had larger populations of blacks and people living below the poverty line, which in turn leads to populations that are less informed and less educated. So you have more of the myths. What's troubling about these statistics is a person who has one venereal disease is three times more likely to contract another one. Since women are at a higher risk of contracting HIV/AIDS from a single sexual encounter with a partner who has it, they must insist that their partners wear condoms. Otherwise, no one can feel truly safe having sex except for people in stable, monogamous marriages or relationships—and since you never really know how stable and monogamous they truly are, where does that leave us?

The bottom line is that women and men must stop engaging in high-risk behavior and remain constantly concerned about tomorrow.

The black community must make eradication of this disease a top priority. Every sector of our community—business, politics, entertainment, and religion—must come together and demand that our government take real action and put real muscle into this effort. The time for lip service is over.

Each and every member of the black community will have to make an individual commitment to do his or her part to fight this disease. We must stop buying into urban myths that hide the real truth about this disease, and instead direct our focus on a scientific approach to prevent and cure this disease. We need to make sure that support services and resources are available to people living with HIV/AIDS. It's very important that no- or low-cost HIV-testing opportunities are available within our communities so those who are infected will know their status. More than 42 percent of all new infections are from people who don't know they're passing the virus on to others. Finally, the black community must accept that right now, having sex without a condom is as dangerous as driving a car through a red light during rush hour.

Black America has no choice but to break its silence and talk honestly about sex, sexual identity, and all the other contributing factors connected with contracting HIV/AIDS. The time to stop pretending and ignoring this disease is long past. Now is the time for our community to change its behavior, attitudes, and beliefs, so we can wipe this disease from the face of our planet.

JOYCELYN ELDERS, MD

Joycelyn Elders, MD, was the first black U.S. Surgeon General in history. Her career also includes tenures as president of the Association of State and Territorial Health Officers and as a professor of pediatrics at the University of Arkansas Medical Center.

▶ *Chapter 41*

Love Your Brothers and Sisters*

When I think of HIV/AIDS, I think of a dreaded disease that is wreaking havoc in the global communities of people of African descent. It is a disease that is often misunderstood. Once considered a white gay plague, it is now a black female epidemic. HIV/AIDS is a disease that has divided families and aroused ancient superstitions. It is a disease that, as yet, has not been effectively checked. In order to achieve this end, we need treatment for HIV/AIDS sufferers. We need more information about HIV/AIDS and wide dissemination of that information through education. We need preventive measures like condoms and programs that discourage promiscuity and encourage clean-needle exchange. We need a cure. If these things don't happen, it could mean more devastation and, ultimately, genocide. It could mean the annihilation of black people worldwide. What may be even worse than the tragic spread of this epidemic is that we have been lulled into a sense of complacency. We have come to easily accept HIV/AIDS and what it is doing to our communities. As a result, we are not doing all that should be done in order to arrest the growth and promote the eradication of HIV/AIDS.

I have had many experiences counseling brothers and sisters suffering from HIV/AIDS. One was a young lady who served in our junior church choir named Elizabeth. Elizabeth had married a young man who was a drug user, and she contracted AIDS from him. I remember praying for Elizabeth, because she was like a daughter to me. She needed encouragement in the word of God, as she wondered what she had done to deserve this disease and

■ *191*

what sins she had committed to precipitate this death sentence. I told her that she did nothing wrong, that she didn't know that the man she had married had been a drug dealer and user, and that HIV/AIDS is not a divine punishment for anything she did. I told her, "AIDS is a disease that can be contracted like other diseases. It is not highly contagious, but there are certain ways you can contract it." I added, "Hold firm to the truth. God loves you." The fact that I sat with her, prayed with her, and was unafraid to embrace her gave Elizabeth comfort and peace.

While I would not include myself among those leaders within the black church who have been callous to members of its congregations who suffer from HIV/AIDS, I have made some errors along the way. In that way, I am no different from anyone else. Of course, as a minister and community leader, I am particularly concerned about what I say and the image I project. I remember that I once preached a sermon on the "recovery of righteousness." I thought the sermon received a great response and that people came to God through Christ as a result of the sermon. In my message, I discussed the AIDS epidemic. I talked about how unrighteousness exhibited through promiscuity was making AIDS a scourge of our community. I was not wrong in emphasizing promiscuity as a factor contributing to the spread of AIDS, but I stressed it to such a degree that it seemed like the only cause. And that was my mistake, but one that I did not realize until someone challenged me to see it.

After the service, a young man came to my office and told me that I was the reason that he came to worship at Abyssinian; he liked the preaching and what I said from the pulpit. But on that day, he said, some of the aspects of my sermon had troubled him. I had admonished the congregation that promiscuity and drug abuse were killing us by facilitating the spread of AIDS. He then offered a different perspective.

"My brother died of AIDS," he said. "My brother was not promiscuous. He was not a drug user, and he was not gay. My brother got AIDS from a blood transfusion. You didn't consider that. Your sermon was very strong on the point [of promiscuity and drugs], and it has upset me."

The young man was never angry or mean; in fact, he said, "God bless you," as he walked out. I was frozen, because I knew he was right. I hadn't told his brother's story, or any other stories that portrayed the diversity of HIV/AIDS victims. The young man never came back.

Another brother's story got to me—the story of Bishop Carl Bean. I am chairman of the National Black Leadership Commission on AIDS and one of its founding board members. Bean is the openly gay pastor of Los Angeles' Unity Fellowship Church and the founder of the Minority AIDS Project, a community-based HIV/AIDS organization.

One year, Bean visited New York to attend a gathering of preachers to discuss the AIDS pandemic. During his stay in New York, Bean told a story about how his pastor would call on him during worship service to sing specific songs. He said that he never argued with his pastor, even though on some occasions, he'd had something different in mind to sing.

He reflected, "If the service got sluggish, I would sing the church back to life. Sometimes, without any notice at all, my pastor would announce, 'Oops, we have to go across town to visit another congregation,' and if the choir could not go, I went by myself."

People loved to hear him sing, but one day when Bean called in to say that he was ill, no one came to see him.

Early on, my colleagues at the church and I visited and prayed with many sick members long before we knew they'd had AIDS. There was Benny, a brother who made delicious cakes. Benny took ill, and none of us knew what was wrong with him. It wasn't until much later that we learned he had AIDS. Benny was gay—not closeted, but openly gay. There were other gay men in the church who became ill. But we didn't know that they were sick with AIDS, and they didn't know either. As we began to find out more about AIDS and its impact on our church family, I visited more and more of our brothers and sisters.

Now we know what AIDS is. But the question remains, "What can *we* do?" The answer is that we can educate people about HIV and AIDS. We should spend more time talking about this disease, its current impact on our community, and what we can do to stop it. Magic Johnson travels the country talking about his experience living with the disease. Like Johnson, we need to be open in our conversations.

At one point, it seemed that AIDS was being discussed openly in the community more frequently. Now there are drugs that help some people to keep the disease in check, and unfortunately, this has created a false sense of security and has silenced some of the discussion. Even today, Americans tend to associate AIDS more with the Africans living across the Atlantic than the Africans living right here. This is the tragic reality of AIDS in the black community—many people are suffering because of reliance on erroneous assumptions.

I have always argued that the church should be the primary place for sex education. We should not leave teaching human sexuality to the schools. These lessons must come from the home and the church. But this is where my position becomes very problematic. If the church is going to talk about human sexuality and sex behavior, how is it going to deal with the question of homosexuality? If I think homosexuality is not a legitimate lifestyle according to the Bible, then how do I teach about it? What do we say about it? Is homosexuality a sin? Is it to be condemned? According to parts of the Bible, homosexuals are supposed to be put to death. But then Jesus said, "Love your brothers and sisters. I died for all men and women. I draw all men and women unto me." So then what is our approach? You can't finesse your way out of this question. You could say that homosexuality is wrong and that people should not live a gay lifestyle, but then what do you do with the brothers and sisters who are homosexuals and believe that it is a fundamental component of who they are?

Some ministers have been accused of insensitivity toward members who have AIDS, particularly those who embrace homosexuality. We have gay male members of our church. Some time ago, these men invited me to speak at a conference, and during the course of my presentation I mentioned homosexuality and AIDS in the same sentence. When I finished, they waited for me and said, "We don't appreciate you identifying AIDS with homosexuality. We are not the only ones dealing with this issue. Children, women, and drug abusers have all been impacted in large numbers. You didn't bring them up." When AIDS first appeared, there was a sense that it was just a white gay man's disease. While this assumption has since been proven false, many still believe that men having sex with men account for the highest incidence of AIDS cases. People have better knowledge now and understand that drug abuse is another way to spread the disease, but we still associate AIDS with homosexuality.

I think what has really made people look askance at the homosexual lifestyle in the black community is the "down-low" phenomenon. The community's response to individuals who are living on the "down low" is, "Look, brother, if you want to be gay, be gay, but don't lie about it. Don't fool us." In response to the prevalence of black men "on the down low," many heterosexual black women are choosing celibacy. I think what concerns people more than anything is the dishonesty of men who are "on the down low" and the deadly consequences that can result from this deceit when combined with sexual irresponsibility.

Our church recently held a forum on the "down-low" issue. As a result, some of our gay brothers said we are now moving in a positive direction. I'm sure it might make national headlines for someone like me to publicly recognize homosexuality. There are many white entertainers who have been public about their homosexuality and as a result have created forums of dialogue. This is not an unfamiliar conversation to me, but my position has been consistent. Several of our gay male members want me to address human sexuality in the church, and I have refused these requests. I told them, "If you're gay, you can be a member of the church like anyone else. Everyone can come to Abyssinian and worship God." But what I have not said is that I accept the gay lifestyle. And that issue is what creates tension. It's not a major source of tension, because neither I nor other heterosexual church members are protesting or trying to put homosexuals out of the church.

There is also a gap in our community. I have been criticized by some of my congregation members because at communion, I always say, "Everyone is welcome, men and women, black and white, gay and straight." "You didn't have to say all that," they say. I listen to these members as I would anyone else, but how are you going to stop someone from coming to God's table through Christ? Christ died for everybody. We are all sinners saved by grace under the blood of Jesus Christ. Why do I have to make an issue out of sexuality?

I am aware, however, that if I did make this an issue, it might allow people more freedom to be who they are. Openly addressing sexuality reduces the shame and the slipping, sliding, and hiding that contributes to the spread of AIDS in our community. I love my gay brothers and sisters, and I am working to defuse these conflicts. I also try to encourage the church to avoid being homophobic, but there are lines that I will not cross.

I will continue to pray for all of our members, because the church is a place where all of us, regardless of sexual orientation, should feel comfortable gathering. Each one of us is wrestling with issues of life and trying to find our way. A minister is supposed to provide, to the best of his or her ability, the guidance that comes from the Bible. I must help lead our congregants to live full and Godly lives.

For me, however, the challenge with homosexuality is that the Bible is very clear that relationships between men and women are expected. Even so, practicing a homosexual lifestyle does not separate you from the love of God. It does not separate you from being my brother or sister. It's just something you and the Lord are going to have to work out. As far as I can see, the church should not be in the business of condemning anyone.

My reluctance to go further is not about me taking a direct hit. What I am really concerned about in this discussion of AIDS, sexuality, and the church is whether or not my words and deeds are in keeping with what I believe. I want to save lives, and I want the gospel to be available to everyone. But what I don't want is to do what seems like the right thing to do for all the wrong reasons. My principles are tied up in what I believe about the family and the divine imperative for creation. The salvation of the black community is tied up in black male and black female relationships and our relationships with God. I have not yet come to the point of believing that God ordained men to have sex with other men and women to have sex with other women. I am just not there. However, I don't think people, gay or otherwise, should be denied their civil rights. If I saw a gay man in trouble or someone trying to injure him, I would jump to his aid. That's the kind of unity that brothers should show one another.

I am not sure where we go from here, because right now, there is not an open and honest discourse about sex and sexuality in the church. Actually, maybe I do know, but I am still wrestling with how far to go. The Lord has not moved me in the direction where some would like me to go, but I know I have come a long way. No one has expressed that they have felt threatened or persecuted by my words or deeds. That's one of the responsibilities of the church—to work against the stigma surrounding HIV/AIDS. We have to help people.

Some assume that if a man has HIV/AIDS, he must be gay. Well, that's not true. He doesn't have to be gay, and even if he was, what difference does that make? If a woman has AIDS, we assume that she must have been promiscuous. What's wrong with us?

We have to stop this kind of finger-pointing. The church is in the position to put a stop to it, and I will continue to talk about these issues. Condemnation is wrong. I'm not saying I have always seen the light, but I am trying to change.

A minister should never run from an open discussion. Some members in this church will accuse me of running. They will say that although we held a forum about being "on the down low," we did not host a similar forum about human sexuality. There is still a tug of war.

We have to educate people about this disease, and we have to love and care for those living with the disease. Love and care means lot of different things. It means supporting organizations like God's Care We Deliver in New York City and creating hospices for the sick and the dying. It means establishing family life centers and discouraging parents from disowning their children because they are gay and/or have HIV/AIDS. It means praying with people who have the disease and caring for their spiritual well-being.

These are all things the church should do for any individual. The church should never condemn people, and should instead help community members embrace one another as brothers and sisters, whether they are gay or straight.

I know that a significant portion of the black churchgoing population is poor, and that most of these poor people are women. I also know that this particular population—poor, black women—is one that has been ravaged by HIV/AIDS in America. The black church should take the lead in embracing our brothers and sisters who are fighting this disease. We have to reinforce the message that the love of God is available to all—especially those who are suffering. The stories I hear about preachers who refuse to visit sick members are terrible. The church must not allow any of its members to be alienated. We must reach them all. And we must be careful about what we say and never estrange our members.

Initiating open dialogue on this topic will not open Pandora's box. Dialogue will not lead to more gay sex. AIDS affects not only those afflicted with the disease, but their families, friends, children, husbands, wives, boyfriends, and girlfriends; it is undermining our sense of community. Having candid conversations about sex would not make us hypocrites. This is a discussion that I have had back and forth, but it's not a threat to who I am. It's about trying to gain a broader understanding of each other in order to rebuild our devastated community.

THE REV. DR. CALVIN O. BUTTS III

The Rev. Dr. Calvin O. Butts III is pastor of the nationally-known Abyssinian Baptist Church in New York City, president of SUNY College at Old Westbury, and chairman of the National Black Leadership Commission on AIDS.

Notes

* Excerpted from an interview.

Chapter 42

Back to the Basics

At first, it was something that seemed really far away. It didn't seem that it could actually affect me or anyone in my immediate circle. We thought it was something that didn't affect too many people other than the nameless gay white men.

Then, Rock Hudson brought it to the forefront, and overnight it was an epidemic.

A friend of mine, the great gospel-music writer John Askew, was diagnosed with it five or six years later. It was really hard seeing him battle the disease. He was the first person that I knew to die from the virus. When he passed, it began to sink in with me that this was something serious—you can be affected directly by it, or indirectly through people you know.

Soon, it became more prevalent in the heterosexual community, and people began to think, "Okay, I just need to practice safe sex."

I think it is a modern-day plague that will probably go down in history as one of the deadliest diseases to plague our country and our world, almost as prevalent as cancer. It is a disease that has caused hurt, but at the same time it has informed and helped us to educate ourselves.

It's caused hurt because of the many people that we've lost to it who have died painful deaths. On the other hand, it's helped us understand that we need to protect ourselves. Obviously, the best way is abstinence. Second is practicing safer sex with condoms. I think that if AIDS has done anything for our community, it has made us aware that what we thought was impossible is definitely possible. Before, we'd had a "this cannot affect me" mentality, but now we see that it can and will affect us.

Ignorance, to me, is like a drunk driver and his naïveté about being pulled over for a DUI. If a person has too much alcohol, his judgment is impaired. In the same way, ignorance about HIV/AIDS makes people play Russian roulette with their lives. It's a morbid way of looking at it, but it's true, because people really don't think it can happen to them.

I'm married, and I sympathize with single people. Today, the single life is a lot harder than it was when I was growing up. Back then, we didn't have the same kind of struggles. The scariest thing we could imagine was getting a girl pregnant or getting an STD. We never thought for a moment about the risks of getting a disease that could steal your health and, ultimately, your life. We never thought of sex as something that could literally take your life.

As a Christian black man, I believe that when you take your marital vows and promise you're going to do certain things before the sight of the Lord, you should diligently consider everything that is before you. In your heart, you have to be able to trust. When I married my wife, I trusted that she had been honest with me, just as she trusted that I had been honest with her. We operate under the covenant of our marriage that God has ordained. No matter who our partners were in the past, once we entered into the covenant of marriage, there was no deceit. Outside of Christianity, the trust factor is a game of chance, because you really never know who's telling the truth.

As far as trying to place blame or responsibility, I don't know that we can necessarily point to one person. I do think we have set a bad example for our young people. Attitudes toward sex such as viewing women as objects mean that our young people do not look at young women as the mothers of our next generation. Until we get back to that understanding of who we are as a people, I think we will continue on this roller-coaster ride.

The church is one place we look to for guidance that is without a doubt homophobic. It is unfortunate that the black church has preached for many years that AIDS is a punishment for gay people. That's just not the case. That's like saying that heart disease is a punishment for obese people who overeat. When you have knowledge that something can potentially hurt you and you learn a way to get over it, you do so. Irresponsibility comes into play only when you do not act upon the information that you have. Knowledge is power. The more you know, the more informed your decisions will be.

I think continued education is the key to solving this health crisis. As people of color, we need to continue to educate ourselves. Once we know the effects of HIV/AIDS and have seen examples, we can translate that into lessons learned. After we learn those lessons, then we move on to the next place: finding the solution. The solution in this case is that we need to literally turn our faces back to God. Our trust needs to be in Him, and we must return to the values our mothers, fathers, grandmorhers, and grandmothers taught us long ago.

BYRON CAGE

Byron Cage is the musical director of New Birth Cathedral in Atlanta, Georgia. As a solo artist, he has recorded three CDs for Gospocentric Records.

Chapter 43

21st-Century Sex Etiquette

The '70s was a time of free love, when many folks mingled sexually without a lot of fear of repercussions like STDs. Even if they were troubled by the possibility of disease, their biggest concerns were getting syphilis or gonorrhea, and penicillin was the cure. Fast-forward to today ...

I recall being at a club once with members of the Black Entertainment and Sports Lawyer Association (BESLA) conference in Mexico. We were drinking and socializing when a news flash hit the television monitors. Earvin "Magic" Johnson had held a press conference to announce that he had contracted HIV. Shock permeated the place, and we all talked about the ramifications of this news for him and for us. The talk included speculation about his promiscuous behavior with women, and then there were the whisperings, innuendo, and rumors. This wasn't Rock Hudson—it was a well-known and beloved Los Angeles Laker and a popular black man. Times had changed, and fear was running rampant. It was supposedly a new day for black folks, but was it really?

I am a single woman with a girlfriend who was infected with the HIV virus by her "down-low" husband, who has also watched several friends—mostly males—die from this dreaded disease. I am afraid. In fact, I am suspicious of brothers and was celibate for several years after ending a long-term relationship. I was terrified to embark upon an intimate sexual affair for fear of contracting *anything*. One of my friends contracted herpes while in a four-year relationship; another who spent five years with her man picked up the highly contagious human papilloma virus (HPV) and now faces a lifetime threat of cervical cancer (not to mention the possibility of passing the virus to others). Of course, these STDs are not the same as HIV/AIDS, but they were passed along during unprotected sex in what these women thought were relationships with men they could trust.

While I have slowly delved back into the dating game, it has been with trepidation. I often feel like a private eye. Now I know how to ask questions and research. I will "Google" a guy, inquire about him to girlfriends who might know him, and then directly quiz him about his past relationships. I love black men in a major way and am not engaging in man-bashing here, but the bottom line is that many brothers are not forthcoming or honest about their stuff. Ladies must be on point all the time once you consider the "down-low" syndrome, busy guys with multiple partners, and many more potential risks.

I admit to having had a heat-of-the-moment sexual episode where I took a terrible chance. In a let-my-guard-down, stupid-girl move, I had unprotected sex with someone with whom I had been using a condom for months. Nervous, I immediately ran to my doctor and got tested for HIV and everything else under the sun. I was gripped with fear while I waited for the results; only the nurse's reassurances that I was fine could release me from the anxiety.

I can't tell you how many of my savvy, well-educated, world-traveled girlfriends have shared their many experiences of unprotected sex with me. In fact, one of my married girlfriends told me that once during an extramarital affair, she discovered that her lover had not used a condom while they were having sex. That terrified her beyond belief, and she immediately ended their relationship. We spoke extensively about the risks that she may have put herself and her husband through by having a relationship with this lunatic (who was clearly marking his territory). Many women that I know, whether they are single or in committed relationships, know better and still don't demonstrate responsible action in bed.

In *Jerry Maguire*, Cuba Gooding Jr. said, "Show me the money." I say, "Show me the condom." I'm smarter, more careful, and not willing to take risks. Lots of guys say, "Just let me put it in for a minute," or "I won't come …" Yeah, right. I got your minute!

My girlfriends and I still debate the oral-sex questions. Giving head with a condom on … receiving head through a dental dam … What do you do?

I am now quick to offer my negative HIV and other STD test results to a potential partner, and I ask to see his in return. I know it doesn't sound very romantic, but it is far more pragmatic. Sex and love can be dangerous in this day and age. As my friend who contracted HIV from her husband can attest, her vow of "till death do us part" did come to pass, as he died a year after their marriage. She mentioned to me recently that women must be alert and mindful of such things as night sweats, lacerations on the tongue and genitals, plus any immune-system disorders. All of these are signs of HIV. Knowledge is power.

The rules of conduct are different now in the 21st century. Sistas need to recognize that no matter what our socioeconomic status or education level, who we know, or what experiences we've had, we need to bring our "A game" to the table and not think that HIV/AIDS is something that happens to someone else. The increasing statistics bear witness to the fact that we are in the midst of a serious epidemic. HIV does not discriminate, but we must. We cannot allow our desire to have companionship at any cost to compromise our physical and overall well-being. It's time to mix old-fashioned values with modern-day sensibilities. Let's not forget the lessons our mamas, nanas, aunties, and other female kinfolk taught us: to use our fine minds and common sense and to practice 21st-century sex etiquette.

When you feel that tingle and start hearing "Let's Get It On" and/or "Sexual Healing" in your head … take a deep breath and have that conversation with your prospective lover about being safe and using condoms.

- Stay ready … be ready. Carry either the female condom or various sizes of male condoms … one size does not fit all. Flavored condoms without spermicidal gels are great for oral sex!

- Peek in a prospective lover's medicine cabinets, makeup bag, or shaving kit to see if there are prescription drugs inside for herpes, immune diseases or HIV. Call a pharmacist if you need further explanation, or "Google" the name of the medication.
- Examine the goods, just like you inspect fruits, vegetables, and other food items. Check out the lips, tongue, and genitalia for warts, sores, or other irregularities that are signs of a potentially transmissible illness.
- Watch for night sweats. If a lover sweats profusely at night and soaks the sheets while sleeping—something just ain't right.
- Buy over-the-counter HIV tests for yourself and your potential lover. Share the results with each other and take it from there.
- "Google" your potential love interest. See what the Internet has to say (if anything) about him or her to get a better sense of who you may be dealing with
- Administer sodium thiopental or a lie-detector test to verify sexual preferences, HIV status, etc. Grill 'em detective style!
- Be mindful and careful, even after you have let your guard down. Unlike a racist, HIV doesn't discriminate.

DYANA WILLIAMS

Dyana Williams is an artist development coach, the CEO of Influence Entertainment, and the founder and president of the International Association of African American Music.

▶ *Chapter 44*

Bittersweet Memories of a Musical Legend

Death is inevitable, but it seems no one is ever prepared for it. When my brother Sylvester died, I was devastated. He was a fabulous and very special person.

I remember us as kids watching old black-and-white movies together late at night. He was beyond a classic movie buff. He used to hide me under the covers if my parents came in while we were watching the likes of Katharine Hepburn and Spencer Tracy. Sylvester adored Mae West and acquired quite a collection of her films.

As an adult, Sylvester used to like to visit Los Angeles, but he never stayed long because of his highly structured schedule. He loved to see his family and find out how everyone was doing. He would play the piano for us, have some home cooking, and journey back on the road. Even though his schedule was busy, he always made time to attend our family reunions.

He was just like the little Sylvester that always wanted to be around family when we were children. Around us, he was always happy. If there had been something going on with him, we never would have known it.

When Sylvester was diagnosed with AIDS, not very much was known about the disease. Nearly everyone in the family was oblivious to what was going on with him because the disease was so new and so little was known about it. We did know this: He had a disease, and it was killing him. It hit him fast and moved quickly. We didn't have much time with him after his diagnosis—maybe two years at the most.

I spent the last week of Sylvester's life with him. We knew that it would be the last holiday he would spend with the family. So most of the family, about 20 to 25 people, flew to San Francisco to spend his last Thanksgiving with him. We made it like a family reunion. He passed on December 16.

After his death, every family member went through his or her own private mourning. I think it impacted my mother and me most of all. She'd spent a lot of time researching HIV/AIDS. I think it was probably hardest on her because she lost a child. She and my father were never ashamed of Sylvester and were always supportive of whatever he did. My mother moved to San Francisco so she could spend every day of the final six months of his life with him.

Sylvester and I were the closest of all the siblings. When he died, I felt like the one person who understood me the best was gone. With Sylvester, I could open up and talk about any and every thing. I no longer have that person there.

Sylvester was one of the few stars that openly admitted that he was gay. All that mattered to us was that he was family, so we really didn't think twice about it. When he became ill, to us he was simply a family member who needed our support. Of course, there were a few exceptions: A couple of family members shunned him after his diagnosis.

His celebrity friends seemed to have no problem at all with Sylvester or his illness and kept in contact with him. During his last days, Patti LaBelle came to the house and cooked for him, sat with him, talked with him, and had a good time. Unlike so many others, she had educated herself about HIV/AIDS, so she had no fear.

I am very surprised to see that HIV/AIDS has hit the black community so hard. It's puzzling to me, because the information about HIV/AIDS is out there. Everywhere you turn, free information and free help to stop this disease is offered. Today, having unprotected sex is extremely irresponsible, and I think it's a sign of laziness. It's very disappointing.

If my brother were alive today, I think he would be an unstoppable advocate for HIV/AIDS education. He'd be involved in fundraisers, free concerts, and other efforts to get the correct information out to people and encourage both homosexuals and heterosexuals to practice safe sex.

To this day, when people find out that I am his sister, they tell me how proud they are of him and how much they love him for what he did. We recently accepted awards for Sylvester for the Music Hall of Fame, the Dance Hall of Fame, and the Gay Community Performers Hall of Fame. His legacy is that he was himself, no matter what.

Cherished memories, and hearing Sylvester's music, still put a big smile on my face.

BERNADETTE BROWN

Bernadette Brown is the sister of musical icon Sylvester.

Chapter 45

HIV/AIDS: The Litmus Test for Love

Amongst the drama, trauma, and hysterics surrounding the HIV/AIDS pandemic within the African-American community, there lies a hidden blessing: a forced emotional maturity and a deeper and more intense reflection of life, love, and relationships.

This phenomenon is doubly amplified within the black gay/same-gender-loving community, as our romantic relationships are often invalidated, canceled, and rendered null and void by the heterosexual black community. The black church and its religious leaders often sit proudly at the helm of such invalidation exercises.

With such entrenched societal pressures against gays/lesbians, a budding gay/same-gender-loving relationship is often burdened and complicated further with the blow of HIV/AIDS, a force so great that it could potentially disrupt and devastate the lives of individuals standing in its path.

However, a glorious truth ... a shiny pearl of wisdom ... a long-suffering root of life arises from the potential specter of HIV: It is called unconditional love. Love springs eternal, rising above the ashes of what HIV seeks to burn and what society seeks to condemn you for.

You see, HIV/AIDS is the ultimate litmus test of love, especially within the black gay community. It divides the men from the boys and the women from the girls, and it forces you to think, rethink, and think again. So are you in love with him, or just in lust with him? HIV/AIDS knows the difference, and the proof will be in your decision to stay or to walk away.

Regardless of your status, the weightiness of HIV/AIDS automatically sends you marching off into deep prayer and meditation. And from this space of self-reflection comes your power, strength, and will not only to survive but instead to thrive, despite and in spite of HIV/AIDS.

Now that HIV/AIDS is the litmus test of love, when an HIV-negative person begins to engage in a relationship with an HIV-positive person, all of the bells and whistles of fear come to the forefront of both of their psyches. If they are not careful, the fear of HIV, not love, becomes the center of their relationship.

But before a relationship between one person who is HIV negative and one person who is HIV positive can even begin, there's usually a courtship (i.e., dating), a meet-and-greet, a time to test the waters, and a time to really get to know one another.

Hence, during this dating stage, three challenges come about:

1. When to disclose HIV status.
2. Which sexual behaviors/practices to engage in.
3. How to embark on the future, should illness occur.

When to Disclose HIV Status

The topic of when to disclose is divided into two camps. The HIV-negative camp believes that HIV-positive people should always disclose their status, while the HIV-positive camp believes that the responsibility should not solely lie upon their shoulders to disclose, but that HIV-negative people should also ask and become participants in their own health and well-being.

Many HIV-negative individuals believe that if HIV-positive people engage in sex (whether protected or not) without having fully disclosing their HIV status, they've committed attempted murder. However, many HIV-positive people say that "you should ask, and don't just assume."

Understandably, when a person discloses his or her HIV-positive status, his or her world initially appears to shut down. The potential dating pool is reduced, as societal shame and stigma for being

HIV-positive is unfairly hoisted upon them. So why disclose so quickly? Why take the risk of having your business spread in the street by disclosing unless you're absolutely sure that the person you're dating is truly "the one"?

The fear of rejection, gossip, and alienation looms heavily over the head of the HIV-positive individual; however, fear and the right and responsibility to know and be informed rests with the HIV-negative individual. The question of the moment is: When should you disclose, and how?

Here's the bottom line: You should disclose and/or ask for HIV status before sex, but after you feel that you might be emotionally, not physically, falling for your potential lover. If you're not sure whether you're emotionally or physically in love with him or her, allow HIV to be your litmus test. Whether you stay or walk away based on the results will answer the question.

Even if you both disclose that you are HIV negative, continue to get tested together, use condoms for six months to a year, and remain monogamous with one another. It still takes time for the virus to become detectable, and you can become infected within that window.

If one of you discloses that he or she is HIV positive and the other discloses that he or she is HIV negative, and you decide to stay together nonetheless, remember that unconditional love rises above HIV. You can make it work and last, but it takes love, commitment, and communication. So go ahead and disclose, ask, and move forward.

Which Sexual Behaviors/Practices to Engage In

So you've disclosed and you've asked, and one of you is HIV positive and the other is HIV negative. You're now faced with the options of safe sex, safer sex, or no sex at all and instead intense intimacy or foreplay. Is anal sex really required in a gay male relationship? Can your relationship last on just oral sex, cuddling, and mutual masturbation?

And what about condoms? Will you faithfully use them each

and every time? Can you love responsibly? All of this involves communication, a deep commitment to the careful use of condoms and lube, and an understanding that love is not equal to sex. Love and sex are not the same.

When HIV is introduced into your relationship, love and sex are placed in the proper perspective, and intimacy is ushered in and revered to new heights. Actually, this is really the way it should be anyway. Once again, HIV is the litmus test for true, unconditional love. HIV teaches us how to be intimate and romantic, and to love intellectually and not just physically with our bodies.

To decide which sexual behaviors/practices to engage in is truly a mutual decision and must be regarded as such. A mixed-status couple can have an amazing sexual relationship, but it must be measured through the lens of safer sex and viewed not as a restraint but instead as part of the lovemaking process.

"I love you so much that I'm going to ensure you do not become infected," or, "I love you so much that I'm going to ensure that you never have to worry about me getting infected." You see again that the focus is on love, not on HIV. It is through this love that proper precautions are taken without fail or disruption, and with *loving care*.

How to Embark on the Future, Should Illness Occur

Probably the biggest fear about dating someone who is HIV positive is that one day, he or she will become sick and die, leaving you burdened with the primary role and responsibility of caretaker and then mourner. But if you think about it, we're all going to die one day, and if you're going to be in a long-term gay relationship, eventually one partner will bury the other.

Although HIV has the potential to accelerate the normal life cycle, so do cancer and diabetes, if not properly treated. If you've never cared for anyone other than yourself, then HIV now becomes the litmus test for both love and compassion.

If you've never assisted an elderly grandparent, an ailing parent, or a sickly brother or sister, or if you've never helped to nurse someone back to health, then caring for someone suffering from an HIV-related illness will give you a crash course in compassion and humility.

But prepare yourself. In the worst situations, caring for someone with HIV will also give you a crash course in the legal system. We've all seen or heard of situations in which a gay partner is mistreated by the family of his or her partner who is dying of AIDS.

We've seen and heard how gay partners have been kept out of hospital rooms, been physically threatened to not attend funeral services, and have had their homes invaded and seized by greedy family members who never agreed with their homosexual lives and never visited or tended to their sick family member.

In these cases, the family invalidated the gay couple's relationship in life, and now in illness and death they seek revenge upon the surviving gay partner. Hence, it is critical that gay couples seek legal advice from attorneys specializing in gay rights before an illness occurs within a relationship. This includes creating a living will, assigning power of attorney, communicating with doctors and hospital staff in advance, and seeking out other legal protections such as marriage or civil unions.

Even though all of this must be kept in mind, please do not be discouraged by these challenges of mixed-HIV-status dating. Remember that although the HIV/AIDS pandemic has suddenly become the litmus test for compassion, strength, endurance, and legal education, it also has become the standard for unconditional love. Through commitment and a continual, never-ending communication, you too can experience such love in your relationship with an HIV-positive or HIV-negative person.

HERNDON L. DAVIS

Herndon L. Davis is an author, lecturer, and host of the first black gay-oriented television talk show, *The Herndon Davis Reports*. For more information, visit http://www.herndondavis.com.

Chapter 46

Greater Lessons Learned

Farther along we'll know all about it
Farther along we'll understand why
Cheer up my brother, live in the sunshine
We'll understand it all by and by.

GOSPEL STANDARD "FARTHER ALONG"

I can remember my father often singing this song around the house. I believe he sang it when he missed his mother. I find myself singing it now, from time to time, when I'm missing him. Unfortunately, my repertoire of songs is not vast enough to fill up my days of missing him. You find comfort where you can.

My father died of AIDS on a still New York night in August 1994. His male lover of 18 years had died six months before. My father and Chip had been living with that invisible noose hovering just above their heads, in secret, for 10 years.

Theirs was a life in show business. My father had been one of the few sought-after African-American Broadway choreographers. His choreography was featured in such shows as *Bubbling Brown Sugar, Eubie,* and an all-black version of *Guys and Dolls,* among others. He also successfully straddled the ballet world, as well as that of academia.

As a result, my brother and I experienced an exciting and nontraditional upbringing. Our days and weekends were spent in and around rehearsal studios and backstage. Social gatherings were a "who's who" of black entertainers of the day. We lived in a giant melting pot of artists and interesting people. It made for a pyrotechnic reservoir of memories from which to draw.

But the most important and cherished moments were those spent with my father. Despite my struggles with our unique family unit—one with two fathers and a void where perhaps a mother should have been—I feel blessed to have had my particular family life, as well as a life in and around the theater. My father's hard work and successes also afforded us a comfortable standard of living, and we enjoyed being spoiled.

Apart from an ugly divorce and standard racism along "The Great White Way," life had been good to the Wilson clan. My father and Chip had managed to thrive for some time. And despite all of the horrific whispers of "the gay disease," they were staying healthy.

That was true until events both disappointing and heartbreaking began to tighten like jagged screws into their world. They were beginning to fall prey to the stresses they could no longer outrun. Those of us who were directly affected by HIV/AIDS's wrath in the '80s know what the scene was like in New York, as well as the globe at large. In the dance, theater, and fashion worlds, in particular, the reality of the rising toll seemed at times to be some wildly perverse joke. There were weeks when I'd attend three funerals before the weekend rolled around. The artists' bittersweet and seemingly inexhaustible attempts to play these dramas as dark comedies and "parties" were as absurd as they were valiant.

Where so much human joy and talent is concerned, how does one reckon with such pandemic loss? One answer might be, "One at a time." For me, I suppose, the answer lies in recognizing the great fortune I had to have the father I had. His example was the embodiment of years and years of physical and emotional strength, coupled with an unshakable faith in God and humanity. All of these bits of his character were parts of what went into making, in my eyes, a giant of a man. It is this perception of him that made his eventual illness and death unfathomable. He had always been my rock. He was sensitive, compassionate, imperfect, and incredibly stubborn, but he was also solid, constant, and forever there for me and my brother.

It was he, our father and the man in the marriage, who had rescued us after the divorce. It was he who had willingly and gratefully accepted custody of his children. It was he and Chip who had bathed us, clothed us, provided our schooling, shuttled us hither and yon, and sat on the cold bathroom tiles during those middle-of-the-night episodes while we retched from flu or food poisoning. He had been my god and had never steered me wrong. He had integrity and wasn't afraid to go left when everyone else was going right. He also conducted his private life with grace and tact. His unwavering love was evident to all of us, and he never suffered from a lack of pride or affection. These qualities had been my example. His strength was unmatched.

I watched as he stood by Chip's side through record-label disappointments, a witch-hunt episode in which a cast was fueled by jealousies to undo him, the devastating nervous breakdown that would soon follow, and his insidious slow death in the grip of AIDS. It was a friendship that had ripened, "stunk," and endured to arrive at the consummate hour where love is needed. All else had become secondary during this frightening time. At the moment when many families and so-called friends flee and run unabashedly for those deceivingly "safe" hills, my father was there through it all.

And like the father he had been to me, he returned naturally to that role of caretaker. He cradled the 6'2" Nubian-like Chip in his arms like an infant and kept hope alive in every imaginable effort to keep his friend and lover alive. When all was said and done, when the good fight had been fought, the tears came, and we wore our shock like heavy winter coats that did not keep us warm.

After a little bit of time came the memory of something vaguely having to do with "moving on." That might have been enough to think about, except that the loss and stress of all those months of keeping faith, trying different drugs and "better" doctors, and newer promises had unwittingly led my father to welcome in the unwanted. I never believed he could become so sick. I never believed he would be the one, six months later, to collapse alone on the sand in Aruba, or faint numerous times in the hospital as I watched his eyes roll back into his head. He would falter and shake uncontrollably as he tried to take one step.

At one time, he had flown! This man had danced and danced circles around those more than half his age. This was not supposed to happen. However, this had become our new reality. It was the continuation of a chapter not yet over. It was now my father's turn to experience his own fear and fight his own fight.

Now I had become his best hope to survive. The torch, without democracy, had been passed. There was no time to consider being up for the task or not. This was the witching hour, the time of the coup de main. I had had my lessons, seen my examples, and knew that his same Herculean blood also ran through my slender veins. I called upon that; I called upon God, the Fates, the sentries, and any other defenders against unrighteousness.

Billy Wilson died at St. Vincent's Hospital in Manhattan on the night of August 14, 1994. He will always be my knight in shining armor, and I will always miss him. It may sound clichéd, but his presence grows stronger in other ways and is not lost on any who were touched by his elegance, talent, humor, beauty, or childlike wonder. It has been his strength of character, as a man and as a father, which has led the way for my undeniable determination not only to survive but also to thrive.

My greatest desire, while in the midst of a most challenging storm, is always to ask myself: What can I learn, how can I grow and how can I be better? Human suffering takes many forms—HIV/AIDS, cancer, Hurricane Katrina, or the Holocaust—and those chosen to survive it can find the possibility for greater healing, greater enlightenment, greater forgiveness, and bigger love. It sits within each of us, waiting to be cracked wide open!

ALEXIS WILSON

Alexis Wilson is in the process of publishing a memoir about her non-traditional upbringing. She continues to stay actively involved with AIDS-related organizations, particularly in the arts. She lives in Ohio with her musician husband and their two children.

Chapter 47

Love for a Season

In the wake of my separation from my husband due to his infidelity and subsequent abandonment, I tried hard to move on with my life and distance myself from the pain. Though I still loved my husband, being with him was not an option. The betrayal was too great. I was left devastated and distraught. I had lost hope in love and lost faith in the capacity of men to be good.

Love had deserted me and ripped my heart apart. I was longing to be healed. Then, I met a man who proved to be a balm in Gilead.

A client seeking someone to ghostwrite his autobiography was referred to me. His was a tale of one man with two lives: his life before Christ, and his life after Christ. It was a Horatio Alger story— the ghetto version. He was a man whose pernicious past led him to a propitious future in a circuitous manner; his tale swung from rebellion to redemption. His life story would make a fascinating book. His story would change people's lives.

Meanwhile, my estranged husband was still caught up in a vicious cycle of addiction and infidelity. He was a young musician with "visions of sugar plums dancing in his head" perfumed with pot. Reality was a place he did not want to be, so he pickled his brain with alcohol, and dreamily candied his mind with jazz flavors, caramelized hip-hop beats, and the incense of "try Jah love." He was torn between two worlds: a world of wine, women, and song and a world of living according to the Word of God, in line with the calling of his Baptist-preacher forefathers.

The balm I needed to heal my broken heart was to see the

manifestation of what God can do to change a man—in particular, my husband. However, my husband was not the man delivered by God to provide me comfort.

His name was Malcolm, and when I compared him to my husband, with his various addictions to marijuana, alcohol, psychedelic mushrooms, and Ecstasy, my estranged husband looked like a hippie pothead. In his wilder days, Malcolm had smoked crack, shot heroin, speed balled, and chased pills with alcohol. He'd only smoked weed because he sold it to support his drug addiction and got it for free.

It was his sordid drug addiction that led him to all sorts of mayhem, including murder.

But God is a deliverer and a redeemer, and what the Devil meant for bad, God turns around for good.

Malcolm eventually served time in prison for his transgressions and completely turned his life around and over to Christ. What an awesome testimony he had! Not only did he end up clean, sober and God-fearing—he also continued to pay his debt to society by serving as an upholder of the law, and also ministered to other addicts in rehab, prisons, Narcotics Anonymous meetings, and any other opportunities where he could share his story and show others the awesome, life-changing power of God.

I reveled in his story and fell in love with how God used him. I also fell in love with the love he showed my daughter and me. He, on the other hand, fell in love with my brain and my pain, as well as my heart for the Lord. I demonstrated God's unconditional love to him, and to me, his life was a demonstration of God's unlimited grace.

At this point, I was only a few months into my separation from my husband. He filed for divorce and two weeks later got engaged. I found out because a family member saw their picture in a jewelry store where they'd purchased rings, and told me about what he had seen.

My head got light, my ears got hot, and my heart sank. I felt like someone had just punched me in the stomach.

They say divorce and the death of a loved one carry the same amount of pain. I felt like my husband had died. The man I married no longer existed for me. The pain was unfathomable.

In the midst of my humiliation and further devastation, Malcolm counseled me, consoled me, and comforted me. He was proving to be not only my client, but also my best friend. He made me laugh through my tears, gave me hope through my despair, and gave me the love I so desperately needed to feel whole again.

Neither of us wanted to fall into the sin of fornication and adultery, especially me; I did not want to be what my husband had become: an adulterer. And Malcolm wanted to be my ideal as well as his ideal. He wanted to be a man of God. He wanted to be something he had never been before: chaste.

Fortunately, our lofty ideals caused us to abstain from ever becoming physically intimate. We were fortunate not only because of the possible ramifications of our actions in the flesh, but also in the spirit.

As our relationship blossomed and the telling of his life story was coming to a close, there was one thing he wanted to share with me about his life that he did not want disclosed in the book. Because our personal relationship had progressed to a level of intense emotional intimacy, the desire for physical intimacy was weighing on us, and this thing he wanted to share was necessary information indeed.

He was HIV positive.

He told me in person, at my home, as we were working on the book. He pulled out a collection of prescription medications and asked me if I knew what all of this medicine meant. I said, "No." He hesitated, looked down, and then looked back up at me and said, "I've got HIV, the virus that causes AIDS."

Once again, my head got light, my ears got hot, and my heart sank. I felt like someone had punched me in the stomach. I felt like he'd just told me he'd died, like my ideal man just disappeared before my eyes; in fact, he never existed.

Oh, no. Not again.

The pain rushed in. I cried. He cried. I thought it was a death sentence, and that I was going to lose love again. He knew, however, that my love for him was only an illusion, and a part of him wanted to shatter that illusion by revealing the truth about himself to me.

He was just a man: a survivor, not a savior.

He contracted the virus through intravenous drug use.

But I didn't care. All I wanted to know was how did he live with the virus, and how long would he live? I didn't know much about HIV, or how it is treated, or how people manage it, but I did know that I couldn't "catch it" just from being around him or touching him. But I did want to know how one managed being in a relationship with someone with HIV. What was his life expectancy? How would that affect me? Were there other ways to be exposed to the virus without having sex? How could I protect myself? And what about my daughter? How would this affect her? It was too much. He told me he would set up a meeting for me with his physician, who would answer all of my questions. That is, if I wanted to continue in the relationship.

I don't think he expected me to accept the fact that he had HIV. But I did, at least in the moment. In that moment of acceptance, he realized he was worthy of love and worthy of life.

As he realized he was worthy of life, he knew I was worthy of life also. He let me go. He knew I had an abundant life ahead of me and that he was not meant to be a part of that equation. This was not because he was HIV positive, but because God wasn't finished with the two of us yet. God still had work to do in me. God still had work to do in him. He had still not yet forgiven himself, though God had forgiven him. I was in the midst of a divorce.

Ours was a love born out of need, not deed. I was on the rebound, and he wanted acceptance. True love would find me again, and that love would be borne out of God's purposes.

Our relationship had its purpose. It was designed for love and for healing. And it was time to move on. As 1 Peter 4:8 says, "And above all things, have fervent love for one another, for love will cover a multitude of sins."

I loved him in spite of HIV. Were it God's purpose for us to be together, we would be today. However, God had other plans for us, and we were not meant to be together, at least not forever—just for a season.

Kelley Bass Jackson is a commercial and political speechwriter currently working in the Georgia State Attorney General's office. She is the founder of *thegodchronicles.com* and WIN Ministries (Women's International Network). She can be reached at jacksonwoman@gmail.com.

► *Chapter 48*

Stand Up!

I was deeply in love with my partner. We loved each other. It almost killed me to watch him die from AIDS.

After he died, I was a complete mess. But if there was a bright side, it's that his death was part of the inspiration for my work. I fell in love with a man of high integrity, a loving, decent brother who just couldn't believe some of the things that were true about him. He figured that because he was a black homosexual male, he was not a valuable human being. I knew this was a ridiculous notion, and our mutual discovery became the impetus for the Black Men's Xchange (BMX). I had done similar work before, but meeting so many beautiful black men caught up in the mythology that they were worth less than others advanced the work that much further. This may not change completely in our lifetime, but I am convinced it will one day change.

My name is Cleo Manago. My background is in cultural anthropology, public health research, and black human-rights activism. I also manage the AmASSI Health and Cultural Centers, with projects in Atlanta, Los Angeles, Harlem, and Johannesburg. The acronym "AmASSI" stands for the African American Advocacy Support-Services and Survival Institute. AmASSI uniquely combines skill-building and educational programs regarding the prevention of HIV/AIDS and various other health threats with cultural affirmation, critical thinking, and self-concept development. Our approach confronts many of the psychosocial and mental-health factors (both contemporary and historical) that impact black health and well-being. In addition, AmASSI explicitly invites, serves, and affirms the black community's diversity. This diversity includes heterosexuals, same-gender-loving (SGL) people, and bisexuals, as well as teens, senior citizens, middle-aged adults, and children.

We aspire to improve the health of the black community by addressing the fragmentation that occurs when we don't affirm one another. This holistic philosophy must be applied to the HIV/AIDS epidemic that has disproportionately affected black people.

Given the still-high rates of HIV infection in the black community, many activists are being asked how to effectively prevent HIV and AIDS. I am pleased to be able to offer some answers—not ones with theoretical or hopeful concepts, but ones with real solutions-based empirical data from studies conducted and tested at the AmASSI Center.

Before I move on, however, I'd like to first note what has made HIV prevention a challenge among black people. People wonder why, for example, white gays are able to manage the disease successfully in their community, while the disease continues to ravage the black community. Of course black people can manage it, but it cannot be done without specific strategies, courage, and an unflinching and active commitment to the empowerment, affirmation, and focused protection of diverse cross-sections of the black community.

Because males have the capacity to inject infected semen into their partners during sexual intercourse, males are the primary transmitters of HIV. Stemming the spread of HIV/AIDS in the black community requires protection of males from HIV. Of course, in tandem, black women must also think critically and value their lives enough to take precautions against contracting the HIV virus. Still, abating the proliferation of HIV/AIDS in the black community requires actively caring about the black male.

For a few hundred years now, this concept has been a challenge for America. Since our arrival on the American shore, black males have been marginalized and under attack. Black males have always been disproportionately impacted by HIV/AIDS. As it has impacted white gay men, and more recently, black women, HIV/AIDS has garnered unparalleled media coverage. To date, there still has been no large-scale media focus on protecting black males from HIV. This only serves to keep black women and the black community at large at perpetual risk.

Myriad challenges face black men, such as police brutality, fatherlessness, disproportionate rates of murder and incarceration, false arrests, low college attendance, and unemployment. On top of it all, the struggle of black men to realize justice and parity in society—and in no uncertain terms, respect—is not addressed. Oprah Winfrey once featured a black man on her show to discuss the idea that black males were putting black women in HIV/AIDS danger. The Oprah hype, coupled with the dehumanizing depiction of black males as "down-low" predators, only re-traumatized black males and did nothing to unify black people toward collectively resolving the HIV/AIDS problem.

It appears that it's against the law to make sure that black males are healthy. As this black-male-marginalizing society dismisses the experience and perception of the black male as a man, damage is being done, and society provides no space to ameliorate it. Thus, the consequences fester like an untreated sore. The manhood and significance of the black male is under perpetual scrutiny, especially within himself. The diversity of black men—heterosexual, homosexual, light-skinned, and dark—creates even more layers for black males to sift through to discover their worth in America. This produces anxieties and struggles that must be considered when resolving HIV/AIDS (among other issues) within this neglected population.

One of the most poignant experiences I have had in my life was attending the Million Man March in 1995. The most stirring moment was when, almost in unison, a sea of black males—fathers, sons, same-gender-loving and heterosexual men of various religious sects—all fell into one another in tears. Not a word was said. We all knew the language of intergenerational black male soul-level grief and pain. On that day, probably for the first time in African-American life, we visited that pain together.

Ten years later, the Millions More Movement (MMM) March, though also powerful in many ways, was less poignant for the men there. I was the first openly SGL black man in history to speak at the MMM March, and I was invited by the Nation of Islam and its organizers. That was an amazing experience—but more on that later.

Because women were present this time, there were no tears, and there was no healing. Most of the brothers this time did what we usually do when others are around. We act powerful, while myriad unaddressed issues under the surface debilitate us into life as usual. So the black male wound is still raw. Of course, women have healing needs too. Still, women cry. Black women also have always been less of a threat to white supremacy, and thus have always had more opportunity to prosper and be present than the black male.

Women have also had more capacity to love.

When the members of the white gay community decided to address the predominantly white male HIV holocaust, they understood that empowering, affirming, and actively concentrating on protecting themselves was crucial. That protection did not consist of just a white-gay-focused HIV education campaign. Within the white collective, despite the benefit of entrenched white privilege in America, white gays also experience discrimination. As they prepared to challenge the HIV/AIDS epidemic, it was already understood that low self-esteem resulting from institutional homophobia was a potential barrier to preventing risk behavior and the disease.

Consequently, they implemented a sociopolitical and systems-change campaign in concert with their HIV/AIDS education efforts. A group called ACT UP (AIDS Coalition to Unleash Power) led that campaign with a militant spin. They were clear that preventing HIV only through education was the equivalent of resolving blindness only with prescription glasses. They realized that more intense work needed to be done.

Much of this work occurred in the middle to late 1980s. As the already disproportionate rates of HIV and AIDS soared in black communities, I, too, understood that additional work beyond education was necessary.

It was also apparent to me that African Americans were not prepared to manage a deadly disease that was linked to male homosexuality. Continuous years of oppression, stigma, and feelings of powerlessness among the black community has driven it to disassociate from the disease rather than focus on changing racist systems to ward it off. At the time, many African Americans were already living with longstanding stigmas that made black life a challenge—especially for males. Black males were America's poster children for negative behavior: They were rapists, social menaces, sexually reckless predators, hustlers, media buffoons, and, in general, violent and dangerous human threats. "Stigma phobia," or the fear of being stigmatized again, was, and is, a legitimate state of mind in black communities. How blacks were seen by others—especially powerful whites, police departments, and self-concept-conflicted blacks with authority—could severely affect the quality of life for an African American. Unemployment, disproportionate or false arrests, and premature death or disfigurement at the hands of "law enforcement" were mainstays—across class—in black communities. Remember, this was before the 1991 Rodney King incident exposed police brutality as a problem, and before gang violence reached epic proportions as well. African-American concern about the potential for a new stigma surrounding HIV/AIDS was not a helpful response, but it wasn't irrational either, given the black experience.

Despite its struggles with discrimination, the white gay and lesbian community maintained a sense of white entitlement. They felt entitled to being saved by the American government, as well as by each other. It's a state of mind many black people cannot even fathom. It is also worth remembering that white gay men can choose to not to reveal their sexuality and just be white when it is convenient for them to do so. Black men do not have the same luxury.

Before the HIV/AIDS epidemic hit, the white gay community already had, in some geographical areas, political clout and organization on its side. Understanding the danger of stigma, gay whites refused to live with the name first given to AIDS, GRID (Gay-Related Immune Deficiency). Through ACT UP and other (white) gay resistance efforts, the acronym GRID was successfully abolished. Soon after, Acquired Immune Deficiency Syndrome (AIDS) became the primary term used to describe the disease. (Later, gay whites would become the only group on earth to successfully combat HIV/AIDS in their community).

But there were HIV/AIDS stigmas and myths that did stick, and they were self-consciously noticed by the black community. Haiti was initially blamed as the place of origin for HIV/AIDS. After this was proven to be 100 percent inaccurate, the blame was transferred to an African green monkey. Though widely published as fact, this too would later be proved 100 percent false. But there was no media recant, and the stigmas persist even to this day. There was little resistance to this among African Americans, probably because HIV was never blatantly called "APRID" (African-People-Related Immune Deficiency); it is undeniable that the implication was there all the same. So was the potential for new black stigmas, self-consciousness, and inferiority complexes.

As previously stated, African Americans were not prepared to manage the spread of a deadly disease linked to male homosexuality—it was merely another opportunity to host more stigmas. Unfortunately, this was not considered when HIV prevention strategies were designed for the black community. HIV prevention strategies used in the black community were not designed by the black community, but by the white gay community. When HIV education failed the black community, it was blacks themselves who took the fall: They were accused of being homophobic and uneducated. This racist "blame game" essentially left the black community unprotected from the disease.

Nationally, HIV/AIDS prevention in African-American communities has been historically led by homosexual black men deeply involved in white gay identity politics and culture. For many years, the largest government-funded organization assigned to prevent HIV/AIDS among black men who had sex with men (MSM) was the National Task Force on AIDS Prevention (NTFAP). This agency was an offshoot of a gay community organization in San Francisco called Black and White Men Together (BWMT). BWMT was founded by a white man with a sexual appetite for black men.

Though black men were often at the helm of NTFAP's HIV prevention projects for black men, typically they were not in relationships with other black homosexual or bisexual men, and their programs were not located in black communities. Many NTFAP employees tended to be black members of BWMT (or the like) and rarely interacted in traditional black-on-black male-community social networks. NTFAP's white-male-constructed gay-empowerment approach to black HIV prevention alienated most African Americans who were at risk for HIV infection. This included black males involved in homosexual relationships, homosexual activity through incarceration, survival sex, sexual and substance abuse, and experimentation not identified as gay. Also not accounted for were young people and heterosexual black women at risk. The lack of appropriate services provided left the black community completely vulnerable to HIV. Several years later, NTFAP was stripped of its funding and closed due to a lack of effectiveness and the mismanagement of millions in government dollars.

On to solutions: In the early nineties, over 10 years into the epidemic, the overriding theme used to explain the still-escalating number of black HIV/AIDS infections was that blacks were ignorant about HIV/AIDS. At AmASSI, we found this misconception peculiar. The great majority of people we were seeing, including those who were HIV positive, were not ignorant about HIV/AIDS. To reach a clear understanding of HIV/AIDS literacy in the black community, we conducted our own survey and found a lot of basic HIV competency in the community. Many were able to make logical deductions about how the disease was sexually transmitted. There were some misconceptions, of course; however, for the most part, there was a true comprehension of how HIV/AIDS is contracted.

The Kaiser Family Foundation conducted a national African-American HIV/AIDS knowledge survey that had a similar outcome. Black people were aware of HIV/AIDS—particularly black males who were homosexual or bisexual. Still, this population continued to make up the lion's share of new infections. Concerned about the clear lack of prevention strategies in the HIV/AIDS field that were truly built around the realities of black life, sexuality, and culture, we conducted a pilot study.

Inspired by previous research on diverse groups of African-American men and the themes that showed up during interviews with them, the pilot study was called "Critical Thinking and Culture Affirmation" (CTCA). The men were enrolled in weekly individual psychotherapy sessions and tri-weekly group discussions. The programs focused on the following: the history of accomplishment, cooperation, and success among Africans and African Americans of diverse gender; sexuality; philosophy; the media and environmental literacy (deconstructing the influence of media and mainstream institutions on black self-concept, manhood, culture, and sexual prejudice); the benefits of critical thinking and self-respect; and HIV 101.

In a pre-intervention assessment, 70 percent of the participants reported being willing to put themselves and their sexual partners at risk for HIV; 75 percent reported that being a black male was "traumatic," and 90 percent reported seeing no positive value to homosexuality.

After the six-month CTCA intervention was complete, only 30 percent reported being willing to put themselves and their sexual partners at risk; 80 percent reported learning to value themselves as black males; 80 percent reported consistent use of safer sex practices; and 80 percent demonstrated increased levels of positive self-concept and proactive commitment to protecting themselves and their community from HIV. Only 20 percent, most of whom were substance users in recovery, reported that they did not fully benefit from the intervention. The CTCA HIV-prevention strategy successfully changed HIV risk behavior among the majority of participants. It was a successful intervention!

Illuminating what these men are living with is very important. Some of the men explained that being a black male alone is traumatic. Being under constant suspicion, enduring low expectations from others, and having to prove oneself all the time are all factors that weigh heavily on the black male. One guy said that he married a white woman to escape the pain of just being black. Some had experienced trauma from sexual abuse, and had never addressed it. Some were dealing with trying to keep people in the church happy and got married as a result.

These men lived an agonizing dual life of trying to keep God happy—through other people—while being unable to sexually express how they really felt. Some did not feel good about their sexuality. Some had issues with homosexuality and didn't value it. This was not always due to external homophobic attitudes; sometimes it was an issue of gay men not wanting to be a part of the gay community. These men experienced the gay lifestyle as depressing, dark, unfulfilling, isolating, and sex-obsessed—all factors that made it difficult to find a relationship. One man said, "When I look at my life, I say, 'This is my alternative? My option? It depresses me. Maybe I want HIV, so I can get the fuck out of here!'" Others agreed. Some felt isolated and distraught about racism and how they were sometimes treated—not only by whites and other races, but by other black people as well.

One young man spoke poignantly about not knowing his father, being in constant question of his masculinity, and never having talked about it in his life. Some spoke of the importance of sexually connecting with another man, and that a condom barrier defeated the whole purpose. Unaddressed depression was a central theme throughout the group, and some couldn't explain why they engaged in unsafe sexual behavior at all.

These varying perspectives were not unique to one particular economic demographic among these black men. These guys were all kinds: working class, poor, and affluent. There was a junior deacon in the group and an attorney who had mastered the art of litigation but not of self-preservation. There were clear schisms between their HIV knowledge (all were fully informed on how HIV was transmitted), their emotional states, their self-concepts, and their sexual impulse control.

Our experiences with these men and the CTCA study's findings indicate how essential it is that the black community address and resolve how racism and a disruption of both black manhood and black people leads to resistance toward HIV/AIDS prevention. The canvas of black issues addressed needs to be broadened. My invitation to speak at the Millions More Movement was a tangible first step, I believe.

We as a people must shake ourselves from the white-accommodating, black-marginalizing trauma trances we are in, and unite towards saving ourselves. This is within our grasp; it is so close. But it requires that we actively begin and re-learn how to value black people: black women, children, and men. The challenge has been valuing black men and boys when they are no longer babies. Black boys have to be raised by skilled guardians. In a hostile environment like America, specific focus must be given to nurturing black males into community-loving men with strong self-worth. The tendency not to do this—in too many cases—has put us all at risk, for HIV and so much more.

CLEO MANAGO

Cleo Manago is the founder and CEO of the Los Angeles-based AmASSI Health and Cultural Centers in Los Angeles, New York, Atlanta, and South Africa. He is also founder of Black Men's Xchange (BMX).

Chapter 49

The Blueprint My Father Left

My name is David Horton, and this is my story. My full name is David Harold Horton II, and I am the only son of my father, David Harold Horton. He is my pain and my strength all at the very same time.

My mother and father divorced when I was about eight years old. I'm no longer sure exactly when they split up, and based on that alone you can tell the date was not a significant one in my life. My father was the reason for the divorce, and he left my younger sister, Danita, and me behind in hopes of putting his life together again.

Between the ages of 8 and 12, my communication with my father was sporadic at best. Either I just became too busy to care, or my negative feelings from a particular conversation gone wrong resulted in me not ever wanting to speak to my father again after I was 12.

Time passed. I laughed, joked, played, and was generally always surrounded by friends. I lived my teenage years as most teenagers do—getting into trouble, thinking about life after high school, and chasing girls. I was a pretty good kid, too—I earned mention in "Who's Who" and received Boys' State honors and college scholarships.

College began, and I adjusted quite easily. I was on cruise control, enjoying my first real taste of freedom. Being fatherless hadn't seemed to affect my state of mind. It was a non-issue at that point. But then everything changed.

I'm not sure what month it was. It's a blur now, because time moved so fast. One day my mom called to ask me if I would like to see my father.

My answer? "Hell, no." Of course, right?

She informed me that he wasn't doing well and was on his deathbed—and that his girlfriend, the mother of my half-sister, had just died of AIDS.

My first reaction was that I didn't want to get involved. Not now. My life was just getting started. Now, here comes this dude again. I thought he should have known where I stood. I was pissed. After some thought, I decided that I'd let him know.

So I went to see him with my little sister in tow. I really didn't know what to expect. Many thoughts were going through my mind; I actually had no plan, and it didn't matter—I was just mad. I was now a man, and I had some stuff to get off of my chest.

My first impression was frightening. He was waiting for us outside. There he was. He was my father, all right, but he was definitely not the same person. At first glance, I thought he didn't look tall enough to be my father. The thought that followed was, "Man, he looks bad."

We sat down and talked briefly. After discovering his physical state, I tempered my anger some and tried to probe the last ten years of his life. When I asked, he did indeed confirm that he had AIDS. It was amazing. I had heard so much about it, especially since Magic Johnson had recently announced that he was HIV positive. But *never once* did I think it would be so closely linked to me. Talk about the real world.

It was crushing, but at the same time it wasn't. I had lost a great deal of love for my father, and from the very start, I treated our visits as a chore. I acted as though I'd been saddled with a sick man rather than taking the opportunity to get to know a man whose life had gone astray.

I had to deal with a lot of misconceptions. My father wasn't gay, and I could never verify any drug abuse (even though I suspect that there was). HIV/AIDS was no longer on a poster or billboard—it was actually in my immediate family. It wasn't hiding. It wasn't a government ploy. It was right in front of me, with migraines and slow-feeding brain tumors. AIDS now had a face, and it looked just like mine.

On our first visit, he gave my sister and me some money. It was curious, considering that I knew he couldn't have had much at all. My sister immediately accepted it and even called him Daddy. I was immediately disturbed by this and told him we couldn't take his money, but the look on my baby sister's face made me give in. I figured, "Hell, he owes us this, anyway." He had a lot of making up to do, and the disease had taken away any chance of my father sticking around to make things right.

I was young. I was only 19 when he died, and I was still pretty angry. He was in and out of the hospital. It all became normal until the last time, when I was told to come see him immediately. He was dying from brain tumors; cancer was ravaging his body. Many people still don't realize that it's not AIDS that kills a person—it just opens the door to everything else.

I didn't rush, but I went to the hospital by myself and didn't take my sister. It was something I didn't want her to see. This was between father and son.

He was lying in the bed during my last visit, a mere shell of the man I once knew. I stood and watched him try to feed himself Jell-O for five minutes. In hindsight, I understand that he was fighting to the end. After a few minutes, I finally let him know that I was there, and his face lit up. I had never really seen anything like that before. The first thing he asked about was my mother and my sister. I told him they were fine. For the first time it dawned on me that it had taken being that close to death for my father to realize what was really important to him.

We talked a little while, and then I felt that I couldn't take it anymore. I left the hospital with tears in my eyes. It was a weird feeling. I hurt for him as a human being more than as my father. The fact that his name and mine were the same, and the legacy that now represented, caused me a tremendous amount of confusion.

After the funeral, I internalized the situation. It wasn't until about two years later that I really began to think about what had taken place and tried to come to terms with it. That also involved some tears, but when the tears disappeared, they left room for acceptance.

The end result? After acquiring many bumps and bruises during a foolish yet quite accomplished and enjoyable youth, I decided to become a man—not just any man, but the man my father never could be, and the same man that he would have wanted me to be. I am at peace with my father and feel that he's looking down on me. I definitely have some angels.

When things go wrong, I think of what my father must have been going through during his downward spiral and how he must have realized that he had thrown it all away. I got a blueprint on how *not* to live my life. He is my gift and my curse.

I challenge myself every day to be better than I was the day before. With my mother's love and guidance, I have learned to give back to my community and not accept anything less than excellence from myself. It's a fight, but when it comes down to it, I get the job done. I have learned how to get ahead of the game, and I pass this same knowledge on to those who are younger than me. That's something my father probably wished he could do.

I encourage everyone to take care of his or her body and get tested. HIV/AIDS is no laughing matter. You can hear all kinds of statistics, but when it comes down to it, there's only one person that matters: You. You must protect yourself.

We shouldn't stop treating people with decency because they have HIV/AIDS. HIV/AIDS may weaken your body, but it cannot kill your spirit. I have learned to live my life intentionally, with care, while enjoying every minute of it. A man who died from AIDS—my father, David Harold Horton—taught me that.

To this day, I still haven't personally met anyone else with HIV/AIDS, but I know it's out there, and I know it is serious business.

DAVID HORTON

Best-selling author David Horton hails from Durham, North Carolina, and currently resides in Atlanta, Georgia. While working full-time at his job and on his master's thesis at the Georgia Institute of Technology, Horton maintains a strong presence in his community advocating the advancement of the young black male. You can find more information about Horton at www.negrointellect.com.

► *Chapter 50*

Giving Back: The Greatest Love of All

Invincibility: It is the mindset of our youth. It's amazing how young people think. When you're young, you think that nothing in the world can stop you. You think you're going to live forever; that can be a positive or a negative approach to life. It's positive if you take the stand that you are always going to win. In this line of thinking, no matter what the circumstances, you are bigger, stronger, and better than your adversary. But when that notion of invulnerability turns into ignorance and/or refusal, a problem arises; this is a truly negative approach to life.

The issue of invincibility is of great concern. I guess I've always had some sort of connection with the younger generation, because I can relate to the way our youth think. I was born and raised in Baton Rouge, LA. I received my undergraduate degree from Southern University. After attending medical school in Tennessee, I performed my family practice training in Dayton, OH, followed by a sports medicine fellowship at Ohio State University.

I've always worked with young adults and hip-hop music. I've found that it is a powerful influence on them, and inspirational if nothing else. Hip-hop music is my connection, my communication tool, and my link to the unreachable—our youth. I am always focusing on hip-hop beats and the needs of the kids while working with them, so the kids have subsequently labeled me the "Hip-Hop Doc."

At the parish prison in Baton Rouge, I probably diagnose, treat, or counsel someone with HIV/AIDS once a week. Seventy-five percent of the prisoners that I deal with at the prison are African

American, so when I tell a man that he is HIV positive, he's usually African American. It's obviously odd for me because I'm looking at a man who looks like me, whose father looks like mine, and whose grandparents lived through absolute terror, like mine. I am troubled that I must give these men news that translates to them as some sort of death sentence. Of course, this misconception comes from inadequate education. There are probably many more HIV-positive inmates than I am aware of, but most refuse to get tested; they are scared to ask or lack understanding about the disease.

One of the biggest contributors to this problem is substance and drug abuse. I see so much of it.

We've got to get the message out to young people to stay in tune with their bodies and find love for themselves. Most of the kids that I deal with don't think they can get HIV. They think if someone looks okay, comes from a great family, and is educated, then he or she is not at risk. That's one of the biggest misconceptions. What they don't realize is that one interaction or encounter can expose them to HIV. People are at risk due to denial, and people under the influence of drugs are not thinking about their risks. That subconsciously contributes to the idea of invincibility.

Many people are in so much denial that they refuse to get treatment or to even be tested. I once heard an HIV-positive man theorize that Magic Johnson was a poster child for HIV, and that he's really not infected. In theory, he'd convinced himself that he was okay. That's a problem.

It's a warped mindset, but there's a level of patience and understanding that I must have as a physician. I have to understand that someone living with HIV/AIDS has to deal with it on a day-to-day basis. Many people living with HIV/AIDS find themselves ostracized the minute others become aware of their condition. Ignorance, I feel, is one of the main reasons why the message is not reaching everyone.

These days, it's just not a good idea to be uneducated about HIV/AIDS. This disease has been running rampant through our community for at least 20 years. We have to make a change. As a community, we have to make the effort to educate everyone, from children barely old enough to digest vital information to the elderly, who may be stubborn and set in their ways.

I have a need to clarify why this disease has spread so rapidly, and why the message is falling on deaf ears. Many in our society have chosen lustful and greedy lifestyles and have failed to embrace the concept of devotion to just one person. Monogamy in relationships is not as sacred as it once was, and that plays an important part in our willingness to acknowledge HIV/AIDS. We prefer not to curb our sexual appetites! It's blatant disrespect, not just for the disease, but our partners as well. It's just not cool to have extramarital relationships. I think that promiscuity in the African-American community exists more in underserved areas, where the dissemination of information is hampered by the lack of resources and manpower.

One of my goals as the Hip-Hop Doc is to reach a population of young individuals who are underprivileged and lack access to information. I want to let them know what's out there and what's happening.

In the prison where I work, there was a family that will soon become extinct because of HIV. Most of their arrests and convictions were for stealing to support their intravenous drug use. The entire family shared needles together—mother, father, brothers, and sisters. I've personally seen two of the sons die. The mother, father, and two of the sisters are also already dead. There is only one son left. The family name and family tree stops with him. It's sad, and there must be a feeling of hopelessness that tortures him daily, but he has an opportunity to turn this into a positive by telling his story. Our community needs to hear it. Every time I see him, I tell him that he should write a book about his family.

As gratifying as my job is, I never thought that being a doctor would bring on such sadness in some instances. I am forced to watch my people die slowly, and it hurts. You never know what's going to happen or when. I could have the warmest interaction with a guy and then—boom! It's all gone in an instant. I've had patients not come back to see me again for a follow-up visit, and I always know why. Before I do an HIV test in my office, I sit and talk with the patient about their thoughts on the disease, what family support they have, if any, and what their plans are if they have contracted HIV. If I don't get the right answer, then I give them some information to read. It's a 20-minute test. In 20 minutes, I give them either good or bad news.

I see many different patients—white, black, male, female. Regardless of their social class and status, most tend to be in denial and think that they're not at risk by having casual relationships.

There must be significant efforts among hip-hop artists to spread the message about HIV/AIDS. Common, a rapper from Chicago who is an advocate for HIV testing, has made some good attempts to bring positive messages to the hip-hop community. That's my mission as well. I'm targeting a specific population, from 16 to 30, and trying to reach different groups to help bring the message of HIV/AIDS awareness to the young people.

We must explore all avenues of how to enlighten, educate, and explain this disease so we can work to eradicate it. A great place to initiate this process is in the church. That is and always has been a powerful place in the African-American community. I think it would really hit home if we did it collectively and with a purpose. That's how it used to be back in the day, but now, we don't have the community network that previously existed.

Business and education are also the keys. The approach we're on is the right one, but there has to be a more concerted effort. Talking to the young about disease prevention, eating right, and exercising are things that will keep us from being at risk, and allow us to live long, happy lives.

One fact, one statistic, one conversation! Just one! If every one of us enlightens, educates, and explains HIV to just one other person, then we have reached millions. It's a shame that youth is sometimes wasted on the young; they live their lives carelessly at times, not always concerned with their health—that is, until it is too late.

It's "Tha Hip-Hop Doc," they call me H_2D; come on now, and let's get "Hip-Hop Healthy." Peace, I'm out!

RANI G. WHITFIELD, MD

Rani G. Whitfield, MD, a board-certified family physician, is currently in private practice in Baton Rouge, Louisiana. He uses hip-hop music as a medium to educate teens and young adults on current health issues. He is the creator of the Hip-Hop Medical Moments, one-minute commercials that discuss pertinent medical topics affecting the black community. Visit his website at www.thahiphopdoc.com.

Chapter 51

When Love Abounds

I was introduced to HIV and AIDS as a teenager in New Haven, Connecticut. I'd seen it run rampant in my community. In the '80s, per capita, we had the highest HIV/AIDS rate (with numbers greater than New York), because it was a small city with a bustling crack cocaine trade; the prevalence of drugs led to a prevalence of HIV/AIDS, primarily in the African-American community. In my community, HIV/AIDS was something that was, unfortunately, quite normal, because crack cocaine and intravenous drug use was everywhere in New Haven. When you think of Connecticut, you often think of wealth, but there is also extreme poverty and a lack of jobs.

It literally hit home for me when I was in the tenth grade. I remember being called into the kitchen by my parents, who had an on-again, off-again tumultuous relationship. This was when I found out that my father was HIV positive. My mother had just found out after he had been diagnosed. After he exposed her to the virus, he said, "Oh, by the way ... I'm HIV positive."

When they told me, my mom did not yet know her status. I just remember standing in the kitchen with tears running down my face. They were not tears of sadness. I was angry and devastated because my father had never been a stable force in my life, but my mother was. Exposing her to the virus was incredibly selfish.

I'm an only child. Despite everything, my mother always had my back. The idea that my father could potentially steal the only thing that I really had going for me was a major devastation. I was angry, hurt, and quite frankly, not interested in his health at that time. Ultimately, he lived another 10 or 11 years and, thankfully, we were able to repair our relationship.

My mother tested negative, and I went on to become an HIV/AIDS peer counselor as a high school student. I went on to college and in my junior year, I came back home to compete in the Miss Black Connecticut pageant.

The night before the pageant, my best friend's mother died. It turns out that she had contracted the virus from her husband, who was a drug user. She didn't know he was HIV positive when he died, and she was in denial the entire time that she was sick. She became a recluse. My best friend was only able to disclose her mother's status to me because she knew that I understood the dynamics of HIV/AIDS within the family. Her mother died never talking about it.

I can remember sitting in my girlfriend's living room, surrounded by her family and laughing, crying, and comforting one another. At the end of the night, I remember saying, "I'm going to compete in this pageant for Susie. I am going to win it for her, and for my father." And I did win.

The next year, 1994, I went on to become Miss Black USA. Again, I took my platform nationwide, visiting historically black colleges and universities to talk about HIV/AIDS. It was my mission. I also became a spokesperson for the American Red Cross.

Another revelation came to me when I attended college at Howard University. I was a theater major and interned in one of the dean's offices in the Fine Arts Department. One day, a man came in from the street. He said that he was a former student, and he was clearly in the final stages of AIDS. It seemed that he had returned to the school to get closure, because he just stopped by to see some of his old professors, teachers, and administrative staff. He gave people hugs and kisses.

As soon as he left, they took out the Lysol cans and started spraying and disinfecting everything. I stood there in disbelief.

I followed him a short distance after he left the office. I watched him walk around the campus and wave at people. He waved at everyone. People were looking at him strangely, like, "Who are you? What's wrong with you?"

My heart dropped as I stood on the steps of the Fine Arts Department. I watched him from a distance with tears coming down my face. I thought at the moment, "My God, that could be my brother, my friend, or my cousin." And then it hit me—it could be my father. I had an epiphany.

That night, I called my dad, and we began to repair our relationship. All of the resentment, anger, and hurt that I had felt could finally be replaced by mutual love.

I learned so many things from my personal experiences.

I realize that denial, like that of my friend's mother, exists in our community for many reasons. There is a stigma because HIV is a virus that is associated with behavior. In so many cases, especially with black women, it's usually not negative behavior of our own, but because we have unknowingly been exposed by our partners.

As we all know, one of the ways that the disease is contracted is through sexual contact. Dealing with sex and sexual issues is always a difficult issue for us as a people. We don't talk about it. We do it, everybody does it, but we don't want to talk about it.

Members of the black leadership, whether they are coming from a traditional civil-rights, political, or religious perspective, do not want to talk about it. They often want to talk about what you shouldn't do, but they don't necessarily meet people where they are—dealing with an epidemic in their communities and homes.

An examination of the educational messages about HIV/AIDS that are most prevalent reveals that they are rarely specific and germane to the African-American community. Thus, the only way we could address HIV/AIDS early on was with statistics. But even when you approach the black community with alarming statistics, you find that we as a people do not respond to numbers and figures. We respond better to feelings and faces.

I am not infected, but I am affected.

In some of my advocacy efforts, I've just tried to begin conversations. Even at parties, I start talking about it, because I believe it is paramount that we normalize dealing with HIV/AIDS in our community.

When you find out that someone is HIV positive, don't demonize him or her. From the '80s on, many HIV-positive people were isolated and stigmatized. Many people died alone.

You don't have to agree with someone's choices in life to love him or her. In fact, you are able to reach more people if they know they will not be judged. People are fearful of the reaction they'll get, so they don't tell; they don't want to be judged. "If I don't talk about it, it's not real." However, it will come back to haunt you later on, depending on your degree of involvement.

As African Americans, we understand what it means to be discriminated against, ostracized, and marginalized. Why, in God's name, would we do this to other valuable people in our community?

We can't afford to stigmatize and ostracize, because we need every useful and viable person in our community. When some of us are down, we must have systems in place to raise them up, because we need each other.

No one dies from AIDS. It's the complications of the disease that result from their immune system being compromised. One of the major killers is depression and loneliness—people just give up. A person can live for a long time with hope. In our community, we often steal hope from our own loved ones. They often die alone because they are not able to be truthful about who they are, and because those around them are fearful of the unknown.

My motto is, "Your circumstances do not determine your destiny, but your choices do." Everyday life is about choice, and even though we don't always make the right choices, we still have the gift of continuing to live and grow and make different, and better, choices.

As my father's death was near, I realized that part of the process of moving forward was to be open and straightforward with him in the time that he had left. Because of our communication and love, we were both at peace when he died. There was closure, and I was a part of the process of helping him enjoy every moment that he had left. Everybody wants to be loved unconditionally.

Ironically, my mother also became involved in HIV/AIDS work, and to this day she is an outreach worker in New Haven,

Connecticut. Even though she and my dad weren't together before he died, she became his caretaker. She went to see him every day. When he passed away, my mother was there with him. The love was there with her, even though he did a tremendous disservice to her by hurting her physically, emotionally, and, potentially, fatally. In turn, she loved him and cared for him. I am amazed at her capacity to love. When I was younger, I resented it. I felt that she was foolish, and I was angry about it. But life teaches you some things.

Ask questions, and if you don't have peace in your spirit about the answer, then follow your gut. Have the courage to walk away and say no.

In 1998, Congresswoman Maxine Waters, the Congressional Black Caucus, and the National Minority AIDS Council called on President Clinton to declare a state of emergency in the African-American community. The disproportionate number of HIV/AIDS cases reflected the massive lack of funds in terms of prevention and health care, etc.

In response, President Clinton did not call a state of emergency. Instead, he called it an "ongoing crisis." He didn't call it a state of emergency because that would have caused him to devote certain funding to fight the disease in the African-American community. Nevertheless, there were provisions made for specific funding for African Americans with HIV/AIDS by the federal government.

Today, our local, state, and national leaders need to address HIV/AIDS as a state of emergency. In an emergency mode, the need is immediate. Black people know a lot about reacting to emergencies. But we don't have the time or the energy to lobby Congress. That's why we elect representatives.

Although we are overwhelmed by life, we still have to do more on an individual level. It is literally about saving our lives and our children's lives. Because we are in survival mode, it may not be as easy for us as those who are in better positions to be more charitable. Because we are so busy trying to work out our own lives, it's harder to have that larger world focus.

We need both personal and social responsibility. We must have more communication by our leaders. We need targeted messages and more funding for HIV/AIDS outreach in the African-American community.

We've got to talk and talk until we steal the power of the stigma. Ignorance and silence equal death. When it comes to HIV/AIDS in the black community, we need a revolution, and it starts with you and me.

DEYA SMITH

Deya Smith is an actress and AIDS activist who lives in Los Angeles, CA.

Chapter 52

Bearing Responsibility

There's a huge health crisis in this country, and I believe that black men, in particular, have to be more responsible. HIV/AIDS rates are increasing among African-American women. Yet when you look at the sexual behavior of African-American women in general, it is not any more promiscuous than other group of women. I believe that the "down-low" phenomenon is largely to blame and, in my opinion, the root of it is dishonesty. Contrary to popular belief, "down low" has different meanings. The term suggests multiple, undisclosed sexual partners, whether they are homosexual or heterosexual. And too often, such sexual encounters are unprotected.

The problem is that not enough people want to talk about their sexual behavior. Even fewer people want to be tested. One of the reasons for this is that people are afraid of being stigmatized. But we have to let them know that today, there's no need to feel stigmatized. There are confidential places where you can get tested.

Should test results come back positive, it is not the end of the world. Years ago, being diagnosed with HIV/AIDS was tantamount to receiving a death sentence. Magic Johnson used to be the exception to that rule, but today, people with HIV/AIDS are living 20, 25, and even 30 years of very productive lives. We've come a very long way in improving treatment. We must make more people aware of these advances. By conversing with each other and educating people about these advances, we can encourage our community to be more forthcoming about other sexual diseases.

Unfortunately, I think that some black men still believe that they can prove their manhood through their sexuality. Too many of them feel that sex is the only way they can have control in this society. When you are not able to control your employment status, you can feel inadequate, especially in a society where male economic power is lauded. Black men are caught up in a changing American economy. When you are a part of the group already on the bottom, globalization just pushes you further down. For black men, globalization means that they must compete for work not just with local competition, but now with the entire world. Many low- or no-skill jobs no longer exist in this country. They have now been moved to developing countries.

As a community, we have not emphasized education enough in recent years. Before the civil-rights era, it seemed that everyone stressed education. Even uneducated parents wanted to make sure their children were properly educated, so they could be better prepared for the future. Today, you must possess a solid education or skill set to qualify for the jobs that are available. If we are not serious about education, the situation facing black men will be that much more dire. They will continue to use sex as a tool of empowerment, which ultimately will perpetuate some of the unsafe sex practices that negatively impact our community. Clearly, such thinking filters up to those of us who do have economic means. Therefore we, as a community, must reexamine our overall priorities.

We also have to become more compassionate. I once heard a slogan that "we all have AIDS." If one person has it, we all have it. It is a problem for everybody, not just the person who is diagnosed with it.

As it pertains to government, however, we must increase the focus on addressing the black male population. Previously, much funding for HIV/AIDS awareness has been funneled into the homosexual community. We also have to make sure that the money is being allocated to those organizations that understand, deal with, and provide the necessary support for the population of heterosexual and homosexual African-American men and women who are also affected by this crisis.

More importantly, we have to look within our own families. My family, like so many others, has been personally affected by this pandemic. A few years ago, a very close friend of our family was diagnosed with the disease, but he didn't want people to know. It did not help that when he did confide in a member of our family, that family member acted inappropriately. We, however, were able to meet as a family, without his knowledge, and begin a conversation about HIV/AIDS wherein the entire family was educated about the disease. When we all had a better understanding of his condition, we were able to support him spiritually, verbally, and economically. We let him know that we would never ostracize him from our family, that he was loved, and that nothing had changed simply because he had contracted HIV.

So I know from personal experience that that ignorance feeds people's fears. By and large, our community still has a problem with homosexuality, and HIV/AIDS is still associated with homosexuality. Therefore, there are people who will not deal with this pandemic openly. Out of their ignorance, they fear that they can contract the disease by just being around someone diagnosed with it. It's sad, but that ignorance still exists in our community, and education is the only way we can combat it.

Most importantly, though, we have to stick to the mission of prevention. It is absolutely essential that we educate young people about responsible sexual behavior. It is absolutely critical that we practice abstinence or other means of protection. This disease can be controlled.

We can support family members infected with it. We do not have to cast them aside.

HIV/AIDS is a problem in the African-American community because our priorities are not where they should be. We must change our priorities. When you know who you are, then you will not allow anyone to treat you in any other fashion. Knowing where you come from lets you know where you must go. I am convinced that a better sense of our community will help us move beyond this tragedy.

THE HONORABLE GREGORY MEEKS (D-NY)

Representing the 6th Congressional District, Congressman Gregory Meeks currently serves on the House Financial Services Committee; the Subcommittee on Capital Markets, Insurance and Government-Sponsored Enterprises; and the Subcommittee on Financial Institutions and Consumer Credit, in which he champions the cause of home ownership and tries to eliminate predatory lending practices. He is the author of a major revision of the federal statutes governing state predatory lending abuses. He also serves on the House International Relations Committee, where he is a member of the Subcommittee on Africa and the Subcommittee on Asia and the Pacific. With an interest in the development of small economies, he has made strides toward using trade and international relations as tools of both diplomacy and development.

► *Chapter 53*

AIDS in My World

As I write about some of my closest friends who died from complications due to AIDS, I realize it has been over 20 years since their deaths. I realize I've avoided writing about them and about myself in regards to this present-day plague.

Although I've lost five friends, only three of them admitted that they had AIDS. Officially, the other two died of other causes, but I've always suspected they had AIDS as well. I guess it was too embarrassing for their families to admit as much.

There was Carlos, a man so handsome he could have easily passed for a young Harry Belafonte. Carlos was smart, flamboyant, and loud. He was an elegant dresser with a sleek, muscular, brown body and the biggest white smile you could imagine. He had a stinging wit; working with him made the job seem like play, and staff meetings often broke into roaring laughter.

Carlos clubbed all weekend long. His energy was relentless. I remember the fear we all had when his body was invaded by shingles. He could not understand why he had fallen prey to this strange illness. How could a physically majestic example of the human race break down like this? How could such bodily perfection give way to putrefaction?

Then there was Gilberto, a tall, light-skinned man who took enormous pride in the way he presented himself to the world. Gilberto was a demanding person who insisted on the attainment of perfection. Being in his presence meant I had to look top-notch, with all my clothes in place, color-coordinated, and in style for the time. My makeup, hair, and nails had to be impeccable, and the manner in which I carried myself and spoke had to be distinguished. Gilberto made me a better person.

At first, he dealt with the thrush that infested his mouth in a matter-of-fact way, but as more and more illnesses ruined his body, he withdrew. One day, he simply stopped communicating with his friends. He said that we had offended him. We tried with phone calls and letters, but none of us could get through to him. Months after his death, I found out his mother had relocated from Puerto Rico to live with him. She took care of him until his death. Now, I understand Gilberto wasn't really angry at us. He just wasn't able to deal with the idea of leaving us and this world.

Giza was the person I knew most intimately before his death from meningitis. He was 28 years old at the time. A gifted visual and performance artist who was of short stature and blessed with dark brown, clear, and brilliant skin, Giza reminded me of my grandfather, whose black skin shined the darkest violet in moonlight.

Giza's elegance was within him. He was soft-spoken, gentle, and wise, and on the few occasions that he would articulate a few words, everyone around him would cease their conversations to listen. It was as if he'd had to search deep inside his soul to reach the answers he'd finally uttered. Most of the time I spent with Giza was in silence. We talked little but shared an enormous amount of history. He loved to wrap my head in beautiful cloths from Africa. From Giza, I learned how to make pancakes from scratch and how to appreciate the slow and sweet taste of dark molasses. Giza was more angel than human; he was otherworldly.

So, when he landed in the hospital with *Pneumocystis carinii* pneumonia, a complication of AIDS, I was shocked. Why had Giza kept the truth of his sexuality from me and from some of his closest friends? He exposed me to harm and knew it. For precious months, I neither contacted nor visited him.

The last few words we exchanged were in the hospital. There were more tears than words, actually.

It was a stunning day in New Orleans when I wore the turquoise and gold dress Giza had sewn for me to his funeral. Wearing white robes and a white crown our friend Litina had created for him,

Giza lay in his coffin. Dead at 28, his young, dark-brown skin was still clear and brilliant. AIDS had taken Giza as well.

AIDS came in silence and swept across my friends, picking and choosing who it wanted, and tearing us apart bit by bit, slowly and torturously. AIDS turned my lovemaking into a sinister proposition and was the covert killer waiting for the wrong moment to expose itself to me. A leprosy befitting the twentieth century, AIDS, like the politics of my time, is a plague with a dubious beginning and an uncertain end. AIDS is like some kind of filtering device that is painstakingly filtering out black women, artists, gays, West Africans, and Puerto Ricans from this world.

And so, I wonder, when future generations look back to us, will they see that all that could have been done was done? Will they look back in admiration at how we cared for one another, at how we put profit and greed aside to help each other survive and prosper on this planet? I don't know. What I do know is that I miss my friends. I miss their creativity, their warm hands, their care of me, but most of all, I miss their humanity.

NANCY MERCADO, PHD

Nancy Mercado has a doctoral degree from Binghamton University—SUNY. She is author of *It Concerns the Madness* (Longshot Productions) and the forthcoming *Rooms for the Living: New York Poems*. She lives in New York City.

Chapter 54

Not in My Church

When I was growing up, Jesus Christ was the center of my family life. My faith became stronger, and I accepted the Lord as my salvation and my rock. When the HIV/AIDS epidemic first touched my life, it was a tough pill to swallow. I watched people I cared about and the children of my friends taken out one by one by a disease that was kept in the closet by so many of its victims. They were members of the church who suffered in silence and clung to their religion, but did not believe in their own salvation. They suffered silently, and they kept their HIV/AIDS a secret.

I am Tinuade, and this is my story.

I had just finished working a very long and difficult day at the office. Getting home to get some sleep was my number one priority. After I dragged myself home, I warmed up some leftovers, quickly ate my dinner, and went to bed. Sleep came easily that night. My tranquil sleep was about to be interrupted.

My phone rang, jarring me out of my deep sleep. It rang about three times before I fumbled around in the dark and picked it up. It was about two in the morning when I heard a soft, but stern, voice beckoning to me for help. It was Jonathan. He was depressed and told me he was standing on a street corner in the middle of Hollywood and needed me to come get him. I wondered why he was calling me. Jonathan was a church-going, God-fearing young man who struggled with his Christianity and his homosexuality. He told me he had no one else to turn to for help. I couldn't believe what I was hearing at two in the morning. As tired as I was, I couldn't turn my back on this young brother.

When I pulled up to the corner where Jonathan had said he was waiting, I didn't see anyone at first. Then he came out of the shadows of one of the storefronts. He got into my car, and I took him home.

Jonathan could talk to me, but he said he couldn't talk to his parents. He had struggled for years with his sexual orientation. Now, he told me he was struggling with the fact he had full-blown AIDS. Now, this put me in a difficult situation. He was depressed, and I wasn't a clinical therapist. He was afraid to tell his parents, who were my friends. He was afraid to talk with his pastor, because he feared the stigma of shame that would be cast down on him. I thought, "Lord, give me the strength to help this young brother through this."

How could this have happened? What do we do now? Where do we go for help? What will people say? These are the common concerns of newly diagnosed HIV/AIDS patients. Like Jonathan, many people with HIV/AIDS first think they may have the flu, as they experience symptoms like fever, muscle and joint pains, swollen lymph nodes, nausea, and diarrhea. Many will seek medical attention when these symptoms don't go away and get worse.

Until recently, the diagnosis of HIV/AIDS was a death sentence. But today there is now hope for a prolonged life with medication that slows the progression of HIV to full-blown AIDS. After they receive their diagnoses, many patients choose a combination of available treatments, as they desperately want to find an effective solution. They will turn to physicians for traditional drug therapy by taking antiretroviral drugs (zidovudine, lamivudine, efavirenz, ritonavir, indinavir)—usually in a combination of three of the drugs. Due to the high cost of medicine in the U.S., many head south or north of the border to get more affordable medication. Others are so paralyzed by the thought of taking so many drugs that they withdraw, hoping it will go away.

Some also seek alternative approaches in order to lessen the symptoms of the disease and the side effects of the medications. The use of herbs, vitamins, yoga, relaxation exercises, spiritual involvement, acupuncture, body massages, support groups, and homeopathic medicine have proven to be effective for HIV/AIDS patients. When they talk about these alternatives with their doctors, patients feel less helpless and more in control of their lives. It is also important to inform doctors of all treatments, because treatments must blend together to achieve the best outcome.

Receiving an HIV/AIDS diagnosis is life-altering, emotionally challenging, and psychosocially charged, and for many it can be overwhelming. Many patients find that once they tell people about their illness, it changes everything, including personal goals, family relationships, employment, and social life. Unlike other fatal diseases such as some forms of cancer, AIDS still has a social stigma attached to it which can cause many patients to have shame and guilt and can cause society turn its back to them.

Medical treatment is the key to treating the physical aspects of this disease. However, HIV/AIDS has significant psychological effects on patients as well. Depression, anxiety, denial, anger, shame, and guilt make up some of the psychological fallout that is not uncommon for patients and their families. HIV/AIDS patients experience many of the same emotional stages other people with terminal illnesses go through. However, unlike patients with other terminal illnesses, many HIV/AIDS patients experience anger toward the person who infected them or anger about the way they contracted the disease (sexual contact, shared needles, and blood transfusions) and about a society that sometimes rejects them. Sometimes the psychological affects of HIV/AIDS can become so overwhelming for patients they need to be placed on anti-depressants, anti-psychotics, or anti-anxiety medication.

You may ask, "Why is HIV/AIDS still an epidemic, considering all the public service announcements and information available to people? Why would anyone have unprotected sex or share needles or syringes?" The reality is that most people don't think something like HIV/AIDS will ever happen to them. When AIDS first began to surface and was identified as a threat, people became more aware and started taking precautions. In the African-American community, however, the spread of HIV/AIDS continues at an alarming rate. According the Centers for Disease Control, in

2004, African Americans accounted for 50 percent of all new AIDS cases. Nationally, AIDS is the fourth leading cause of death among African Americans aged 25 to 44. Many of these people are believed to have contracted HIV when they were adolescents, according to the Illinois Department of Public Health.

This is a harsh reality for the African-American community and for the families affected by this disease. What can family members do to help their loved ones who have HIV/AIDS? What can we do as a community? When it comes to family, many will experience anger, shock, and denial. However, it is important to work through these normal emotions in order to help their loved one. It is normal to ask why this disease has affected a family member. Focus your anger on helping, not hurting. Work to support and embrace your infected loved one. You can help them through their depression by providing support, keeping the lines of communication open and being non-judgmental. Go with them to their medical appointments, encourage them when they are ready to attend individual and/or group therapy (make sure it's HIV/AIDS-oriented) In other words, help them prepare for their new journey in life.

As a community, what can we do? Educate, educate, educate! We need to reach out to help, not shame or hinder those with HIV/AIDS. Although many may not agree with the choices or the lifestyles of those infected with this virus, it is still important not to judge. We need to empower our communities through education, provide safe havens for people and free counseling services and support. In the African American community the church is the foundation, but many with this disease feel stigmatized and ostracized by organized religion. Many church leaders who reach out to help the sick and suffering are hesitant to extend their helping hands to those with HIV/AIDS: "Not in my church," YES, HIV/AIDS is in our churches. It is in our families and in our community. If we don't step up to educate people and embrace those with HIV/AIDS, we will lose many of our brothers and sisters.

In many cases like Jonathan's, those with HIV/AIDS need someone there who can give them unconditional support. Unfortunately, like in far too many AIDS cases, Jonathan lost his battle to AIDS. Thankfully, just as I reached out to Jonathan during his final journey, I continue to give support and encouragement to others. Through my faith I find strength, asking God for guidance as I help those who are in need.

CYNTHIA POWELL-HICKS, MA, PHD,
AND JOANNE POWELL LIGHTFORD

Cynthia Powell-Hicks is a psychologist based in Anaheim, California. Together with her sister, JoAnne Powell Lightford, they continue to help out others in need.

► *Chapter 55*

The Last to Know

Atlanta, 2002: I am speaking to the young women of Spelman College, an all-female African-American college in Atlanta, Georgia, and what am I asked to speak about? AIDS. Twenty years later! Twenty years after the arrival of the plague that has taken 50 of my friends and hundreds of thousands from communities no one cared about, I am brought to this college, a pillar of African-American institutions, to talk about HIV/AIDS.

How can this be that I live through this again? Why are black folk always the last to hear, the last to know, and the last to comprehend? My sisters here in America are contracting HIV/AIDS at an alarming rate, while infections among other demographic groups decline.

The statistics are staggering. Black men are seven times as likely to contract HIV/AIDS as white men, and black women are 19 times as likely as white women. Why? Because more and more black men are being incarcerated, having homosexual intercourse while in jails and prisons, and then passing HIV on to women upon their release.

America's criminal justice system has created an insidious subculture of incarceration that further disenfranchises the black community. But within this culture, we must still survive. HIV/AIDS is only one of the effects of the removal and incarceration of men from the African-American community. Their absence forces women to accommodate the void as they survive within this unnatural imbalance.

The accommodation to abuse has an obvious detrimental affect on black women. We learn from an early age to self-sacrifice, ignore, and deny. We have become masters of giving in, and we pass that down to our daughters. Once we accept our plight as normal, and once we accept hopelessness, it is difficult to dig our way out.

It is difficult to tell our men to use condoms. We are punished for that. It is difficult to deny sex. We are beaten for that. It is difficult to ask for monogamy. We are lied to for that. So, we further accept the imbalance.

The stories I hear from young women trying to protect themselves from HIV are that it is all around them, through intravenous drug use, promiscuity, "down-low" lifestyles, and the back-and-forth incarceration of the male population. It all leaves women vulnerable.

Somehow within this crippling prison culture, we as women must reclaim our responsibilities as the wives, sisters, and mothers of our families. I will continue to talk and share my hope and experiences with girls and women across the country. I support the passionate and tireless organizations that work hands-on within communities, educating, feeding, and supporting women living with HIV, like Women at Risk in Los Angeles, California, and those women who are most vulnerable to the disease, like Wilmington, Delaware's The Beautiful Gate.

Such groups teach me how to spread the word of hope and prevention even to my own daughter. Educate yourself. Protect yourself. Love yourself, and live!

JASMINE GUY

Best known for her role as Whitley Gilbert Wayne on the popular sitcom *A Different World,* Jasmine Guy continues to enjoy a successful career in film, theater, and music.

▶ *Chapter 56*

Family Affair

I remember distinctly the first time I was introduced to HIV. It was 1987. My brother, Max, had made history when he was selected as a co-anchor for ABC's "World News Tonight" several years earlier. He was now living in Chicago and anchoring the local news there. I hadn't seen him for months, but we talked at least once a week.

In successive conversations, he had told me he had not been feeling well. The doctors believed it was a flu-like illness, and we didn't think it was anything serious. When I saw Max, it was late in the spring of 1987. I noticed right away that he looked different. Max was 6'2" and normally about 215 pounds; he was a big man. But I noticed that he had lost quite a bit of weight.

A few weeks later, Max entered St. Francis Hospital, and doctors there conducted a battery of tests. All of them, including an HIV test, came up negative. After a period of time went by (days or weeks), the doctors were finally able to nail it down. Max called me. They had retested him, and this time, he had tested positive for HIV.

Of course, we were all devastated. My brother was so young; now, of course, he seems even younger to me than he did then. Max was diagnosed just before or just after his 48th birthday. He died at the age of 49. It wasn't very long after the death of my brother that Arthur Ashe, a friend of mine since childhood, also died. AIDS had claimed two of the people with whom I was closest. Both of these men believed in the power of ideas. They were very principled men, very dedicated men, very idealistic men, and very decent men. For me, they are still alive. Their stories and their struggles with AIDS are the things that survive the flesh. That doesn't really diminish the loss, but it helps to know why one is here for the time we have left to us.

In time, Max became seriously ill with a pneumocystic infection and was readmitted to St. Francis Hospital. My wife, sisters, mother, and I stayed in Chicago so we could be close to him. Max was very near death, but struggling to stay alive. He was in intensive care, hooked up to a life-support machine. It was an awful experience, because he seemed to be in so much pain, and we didn't know what to do. We had to decide whether to take Max off the life-support machine, but we didn't want to do it if there was a chance he would recover.

I remember that Max's doctor was very responsive and solicitous to us. As a family, we pretty much lived in the waiting room during those days. Max was suffering very much, and fighting, with the help of the machine, for every breath. I was being torn apart inside—I desperately wanted him to stay with us, but at the same time wondered if we should let him go, to give him peace. But none of us ever raised the possibility of taking him off the machine. We simply stayed and hoped, and in time his health turned around.

It was absolutely incredible. My brother had gotten better. He left the hospital, returned to his home, and lived for another year. In fact, he decided to move to Washington, DC, where I was living at the time, and in June of 1988 he attended TransAfrica's annual dinner. We had an absolutely wonderful evening. Everything was just as it used to be.

In the fall of 1988, however, Max fell ill again, and checked himself into Howard University Hospital. This time, he never left. In December, my brother died.

I had always been proud of my brother, but never more so than in the final years of his life. Some months before he was diagnosed with AIDS, Max had traveled to Hazelden, a rehabilitation facility in Minnesota, to conquer his alcoholism. And conquer it he did. This was a major victory, because he struggled with alcoholism for a long time. After Hazelden, he never touched another drop of alcohol.

But even that cannot compare to the way he faced AIDS. He was nothing short of heroic. That last year of his life was without question the finest year of his life. His great public life was behind him, but that meant dramatically less to him than the enormous courage with which he faced death. Gripped by the painful reality that we would soon lose Max, our family pulled closer together than it ever had before.

Family members tend to stretch the tethers between one another once the children get married. There is a new kind of centrifugal force powered by the energy of each sibling's new family, and they sometimes spin away from each other—not so much emotionally, but in the functions of their separate lives. Brothers and sisters move to different cities, and don't see each other as often as they once did.

Although my siblings and I talked frequently, we were not involved in each other's lives on a day-to-day basis anymore. But in the last year of Max's life, my family drew closer than we had been since we four siblings were children together in Richmond, Virginia. And we were closer in large part because of the grace with which Max handled his illness. With the reality of his illness a daily companion, Max never once said, "Why me?" In fact, what he said instead was, "I've had an extraordinary life, with a great deal of fame and fortune. When I was at the height of my career, having experiences and privileges few people could even imagine, I never asked 'Why me?' And so I'm not going to ask 'Why me?' now." If Max ever felt sorry for himself, at any time, we never saw it. He was extraordinarily brave as he continued to travel and in general carry on with his life.

During the same period, we as a family were reading everything about HIV/AIDS that there was to be read, and we would clip articles about new AIDS research and send them to Max's doctor. At the time, the only medication for AIDS sufferers was AZT. Unfortunately, the "cocktail" of drugs that HIV/AIDS patients now take was not available at the time. We constantly conversed with Max's doctor about the information we'd found to make sure that he was providing Max with the most up-to-date care.

Max asked that his illness not be made public until after he died. He made this decision in the social context of the late 1980s; it was a time when HIV and AIDS were seen differently than they are now. Max didn't want whatever time remained to him to become a circus because of his public life.

So we didn't talk about it. I thought about this recently because of Peter Jennings's death. Despite our promise, word of Max's illness had gotten around. Peter, Max's colleague and friend, called me some time during the year after Max's diagnosis. Peter said he heard that Max was ill and might have AIDS. I told Peter that I couldn't talk about it and that at the appropriate time I would call him to let him know first. And when Max had only hours to live, and had slipped into a coma, I called Peter. It was just three or four hours before Max died. I shared Max's story with Peter. It was the only public statement we made to anybody about his illness before Max's death.

When a person dies of AIDS, some families want to form a circle of silence and not reveal it to the rest of the world. We had to make a public announcement about Max and his illness. But we had no concern about scrutiny or stigma at all. If you could contemplate such a thing, then you're not as close to the loved one as you would want to be. The point is that any scrutiny or stigma would pale by comparison to the loss of my brother. It mattered little how we lost him. We had lost him. That was the devastating thing. And we found nothing diminishing about his illness. It's an illness.

Time enabled my family to move forward after my brother's death, but there were certain things that kept it fresh for an extended period of time. We had to go to Chicago and settle Max's affairs. He had possessions and an apartment, and all of that had to be taken care of. My sisters and I did all the things we had to do. People don't deal with a loss like ours collectively; each individual deals with it separately. And people have different ways of confronting death. I never talked to my mother or sisters in any great detail about how they were coming to terms with Max's death. They just seemed to be coming to terms with it. We all went on. We all talked about him often. We all kept Max alive in our hearts.

And there were still things for us to do. The Whitman-Walker

Clinic in Washington, DC, wanted to name an HIV/AIDS services facility after him, and the University of the District of Columbia created a journalism scholarship in his honor. As a family, we participate in the selection of the scholarship recipient each year.

My sisters and I managed our involvement, but in these events, I took a less public role. In fact, this essay is the first public reflection I have made in 18 years about my brother's illness. I wasn't terribly sure I was ready to do this; my hope is that writing about my experience with Max can be helpful to someone else. I'm not a naturally public person. I've done my work because I've believed in my work, but I have never liked the public requirements of it. So I was never inclined to have a very public association with an HIV/AIDS effort simply because my brother died of AIDS. Although I am sympathetic to the work of these organizations, it just seemed to accentuate my loss. I have not completely gotten control of these feelings. Sometimes you need time to work its quiet, gradual magic. It's different for everybody, but that's the way it has been for me.

If my brother were alive today, he would be talking about AIDS because he understood that people often feel as though they *actually know* people who are famous. Even though this isn't entirely accurate, that familiarity, whether real or imagined, makes AIDS more tangible and more real, instead of something that affects anonymous people. If his celebrity could be used constructively to fight this disease, I think Max would see that as a good thing. That is entirely consistent with the type of life he tried to lead.

The National Association of Black Journalists posthumously honored Max at a meeting in the fall of 2005. At the meeting, the speakers reflected on what Max had meant to the generation of black journalists that followed him. Max once gave a speech at Smith College about racism at ABC News that put him in real trouble with his superiors at the time. In the final analysis, however, Max's confrontation affected ABC's policies dramatically in the years that followed. Max believed in that sort of thing. Younger black journalists, men and women now in their forties or fifties, have come up to me and expressed their gratitude for my brother. When they were new in the business and fresh out of school, Max was at the height of his powers. He found time to talk to them and counsel them. It is what I saw with my own eyes all the time, but it always means a great deal to me when people share that with me now. And given how Max supported my work and the kinds of things I was trying to do, I know he would have fought this battle if he were he alive to do it. And if his name and his memory can serve to fight HIV/AIDS more effectively, that's what he would have wanted very passionately.

The first thing we need to do is to start talking about HIV/AIDS; I'm not at all surprised that HIV/AIDS has had such a meteoric rise in our community. The world has not even had an open discussion about the origins of the disease. The British researcher Edward Hooper's book *The River* details research that was done in the Congo that indicates that HIV had man-made origins. According to Hooper, in the 1950s, researchers were working with monkeys to develop a vaccine for polio, but an accident occurred, and HIV's jump from monkeys to humans was the result. Subsequently, there has never been any serious discussion about this revelation. Hooper's work was reviewed in major newspapers, but public discussion of it died with the reviews. It never went further than that. You can generate ink on a lot of things. But apparently, this was a story that had "no legs." It was of no real interest to the people who manage America's news industry. I'm not sure if I would say "the establishment" came in to hasten its silence, but nothing ever came of it. Hooper's book was not dismissed by the scientific community; he is a serious, respected writer and researcher who obviously knew whereof he spoke. But Hooper was the only one speaking.

Even if you can set the origins of the disease aside, you cannot deny what has happened since, particularly among people of African descent. The numbers have grown geometrically in Africa in general, and southern Africa in particular. In some areas of sub-Saharan Africa, the infection rate reaches 40 percent. The disease is passed between men and women through heterosexual contact just as frequently as it is any other way. In the American context, recent infection rates, particularly among black women, are staggering.

There are also high rates of HIV/AIDS transmissions in American prison populations. When these men come home, there are often, therefore, sad and tragic consequences for the women who are waiting for them. Yet there seems to be no major public focus on or outrage at what America's criminal-justice system, with its disparate sentencing and incarceration of almost 1 million black men, is doing to us as a people. The implications—short-, medium-, and long-term—are truly terrifying. Yet there is no resounding outcry nationwide against this, even among the so-called black political and religious leadership. It doesn't make any sense.

I can't say I have all the answers. Sometimes we do talk about these issues, but there is simply no coverage of it in the media. We don't know who else is talking about it. We think nobody else is talking about it. We have less control and influence over the media than we used to have. Various consolidations have occurred in the news industry; it often seems that everything has been turned into a Fox show. The media has fewer independent parts than it did before. It has moved to the right and is less interested in reporting about the black community and its interests.

Having said that, I find it unforgivable that a presidential campaign can go by and not even the *Democratic* candidates are required to present some analysis and policy prescriptions for the multidimensional crisis that is HIV/AIDS. It just doesn't come up. I'm not suggesting there is any conspiracy going on here, but trying to get some in-depth public discussion going on HIV/AIDS is like banging your head against a brick wall.

Other communities have effectively mobilized to combat this disease. It is interesting that the black community has not done likewise. I think there is a "not in my family" element to this. There are some class implications as well. As we embarked upon the civil-rights movement, we were all in the same boat, and class was meaningless. It didn't make a difference what you had or didn't have. We were together in our fight because we had no choice.

When the lid of Jim Crow was lifted, some of us were in a position to go up and out. Some of us did cleave from that part of the black community that remained stuck on the bottom. As a result, major black organizations don't take up the cudgel for prisoners, even though many of them are in jail for no good reason. The statistics are incredible—66 percent of the cocaine users in the U.S. are white, but 80 percent of those tried and convicted for possession of crack cocaine are black. Blacks account for 12 percent of drug users in America, but 70 percent of those incarcerated for drug use are black. Institutional racism has gripped the judicial system in America. The criminal-justice system operates in a way that guarantees black overrepresentation in these prison populations. And America's booming prison industry is creating jobs and economic opportunities for many white communities across America. It's not a stretch to call the prison industry the new slavery. But nobody is talking about this. Perhaps this is because those who do the talking for us are not the ones who are directly affected.

Let's use the war in Iraq as an analogy. We would not *still* be in Iraq if the United States were drafting soldiers. We simply would not be there. We are there now because we have a volunteer army full of poor black, brown, and white people who are a) desperate, and b) have no voice in the corridors of power. If every member of Congress had to send his or her children to Iraq, we wouldn't be there. That's an indisputable fact. And this economic schism is mirrored in what black organizations say and do, versus what they won't say and won't do. If you asked a member of the general black population what the NAACP and the Urban League were focusing on now, I don't think that one of ten could give you an answer. In the old days, everybody could give you an answer.

Perhaps the black community did not cleave into two visible public parts, but two very separate parts are there, nonetheless. It seems that the top does not work as vigorously on behalf of those who are stuck on the bottom as it did when we were all in the same boat together.

Getting black America and its leaders to talk about HIV/AIDS is not enough; we must also be cognizant of how we talk about the disease. Despite perception and ignorant assumptions about the disease, the demographics of HIV/AIDS are shifting to include children and women of all economic strata. There has to be a change in how the community works to combat HIV/AIDS because it threatens the future existence of the entire black community. Everybody is affected by this now. We cannot afford to discuss HIV/AIDS as an isolated issue or distinguish HIV/AIDS from the other complex problems black people are facing. It is now a part of a compound problem. HIV/AIDS is part of America's health care crisis. You can't talk about HIV/AIDS in Africa without discussing poverty. You can't talk about HIV/AIDS apart from infrastructural powerlessness. If funds for public education are not available because of a corporate-controlled Congress, rapacious globalization, and a multitude of other unresponsive macroprocesses, you simply cannot effectively combat HIV/AIDS. All of these things are interrelated and need to be talked about accordingly.

People who believe that they are isolated from HIV/AIDS—that HIV/AIDS is some sort of peculiar infection that has nothing to do with them—can be made to walk over the bridge if HIV/AIDS is discussed along with the issues that they do care about.

The prison industry is one example. It's both heartbreaking and terrifying to think that one in every eight prisoners *in the entire world* is an African American. We comprise half the entire U.S. prison population—almost a million of us are locked away in America's prisons. Everyone knows there is sex in prison. But in so many of these prisons, condoms are not allowed. Some states, including North Carolina, have a prohibition on them, and as a result, infection rates in prisons have skyrocketed.

But a disproportionate number of black men are in cages as a result of social inequality in America. We put them in cages in the physical prime of their lives and deny them condoms. If you know that sex takes place in prison, then you also have to know that there will be a high incidence of HIV/AIDS. If you know that these men are going to be released one day and you know that there are women waiting for them, then if you do nothing, you are part of the awful business of spreading the disease. It's an awful business that sends its profits to white Americans that are employed by prisons or buy stock in companies that own prisons. As long as this thing happens in the shadows, then those of us who know about it, but say nothing, are responsible for spreading the disease too. But this "awful business" ought to be our business, and the black church's business, and the Congressional Black Caucus's business, and the business of the NAACP, the Urban League, and the SCLC. All of these institutions need to talk about what threatens to destroy black people in America, if not the world.

We have to talk to—and speak out for—each other.

When my brother died, I received two long handwritten letters that I did not expect. Men will occasionally surprise you with solicitousness because conventional wisdom dictates that men are not capable of such sensitivity. One letter was from Bishop John Walker, who was then the head of the Washington National Cathedral, and the other was from Congressman Charles Rangel. Both John and Charlie had lost a brother, though in neither case to AIDS. They just wanted to share their experiences of losing a brother with me. Their messages were very helpful to me, because there's really nothing quite like losing a sibling prematurely. The greatest tragedy, of course, is to lose a child. If you follow the normal sequence of life, you expect parents to die before their children. But it's also a great tragedy to lose a sibling while he or she is still relatively young. It is like losing a part of your body. There were always four of us; that was how you saw the world. It was almost like the four of us were an organism with parts that joined together. Then Max was gone, and it was very difficult to come to terms with that loss. I can say with absolute certainty that not a day has gone by in 18 years that I have not thought about him. But the letters I received from Bishop Walker and Charles Rangel gave me comfort, because I knew there were others feeling what I was feeling.

I don't know if we will conquer HIV/AIDS or the other quandaries that affect our community in my lifetime, but the answer to all these problems has to do with information. We have to seek out information. We have to share our information and our stories with one another. You can't expect people to beat the drum on issues that they don't have a chance to know anything about. We must give each other that chance.

RANDALL ROBINSON

Lawyer, author, and activist Randall Robinson is noted for his actions against South African apartheid and the mistreatment of Haitian immigrants via the organization TransAfrica Inc., which he founded in 1977. He currently lives on the island of St. Kitts.

Chapter 57

Innocence, Love, and Loss to AIDS

Dear God, bring to remembrance all that I may have chosen to forget. Allow me to be open and honest about the conversations and circumstances surrounding my story. Help me to not be ashamed as I spiritually undress myself and stand naked before many, bruised, scarred, and sometimes uncertain. Help others not to judge, but instead for each to reflect upon their own persons in hopes of becoming better people. Allow us as humanity to grow into the knowledge and truth of who You are and the gift of life You have given us through Your dear son, Jesus Christ. I pray You get the glory through my story.

Andrea and I were two brown-skinned girls, aged 11, each beautiful but different in her own way. We were having a conversation about boys. The conversation turned to a teenage girl we both knew: "She acts like a slut. It's gross all the guys she has sex with. I would never be like her." ("Judge not, that ye be not judged." Matthew 7:1)

I can hardly recall Andrea's comment, but what I said next changed my life forever. "She's gonna end up with AIDS."

This, I remember. Andrea asked, "What would you do if she had AIDS?"

"Are you crazy? I would disown her."

"Why?"

"Only homos and perverts get AIDS."

"What if I told you I have AIDS?"

"Ha-ha-ha. You're stupid! You don't have AIDS!"

"Shawna, I have AIDS."

"Don't even play like that. It's not funny," I stammered.

The look on her face was so serious. I could feel a huge lump in my throat.

Andrea continued, "I wouldn't play like that. Go ask my dad."

When I did, his eyes got wide and glazed over as he looked past me to Andrea. He said, "You told her?" With that, my whole life changed.

I met Andrea when we moved down the street from her in Long Beach when I was three years old. She was bright, precocious, and a little mischievous, and we were inseparable. When I was seven, our family moved to Pasadena. Our parents drove us back and forth to spend weekends and holidays with each other because we were best friends and could not live without each other.

My life screeched to a halt the day I learned I would have to live without her. I just remember my heart collapsing into my stomach and the tears streaming down my cheeks with a feeling of hopelessness. At that time, we weren't very educated about HIV/AIDS. In my mind, life with her would soon be over. That beautiful, strong, sweet, spirited child wrapped her arms around me and told me to stop crying. The doctors had caught the virus in its early stage, ARC. She said it would be many years before it became full-blown AIDS, and that she was going to live a long time.

"I'm not dead yet, and I'm not dying tomorrow. I ain't goin' nowhere for a long time," she exclaimed with boldness and her cute little giggle that brought a smile to my face.

Two years earlier, in the early '80s, Andrea had fallen out of a tree. The fall resulted in an open fracture of her arm. She had been given a blood transfusion, and the transfusion was the reason for her HIV infection. This was just before all donated blood began to be tested for HIV.

In an instant, my whole perspective on AIDS changed because I knew Andrea. She wasn't gay and certainly was not a nine-year-old pervert. My understanding became that the innocent and pure in heart could contract this deadly virus. People didn't choose it. It could indiscriminately choose them.

The next ten years were life as usual. We grew up. We spent every

New Year's Eve together. She had invited me to my first ballet class when we were four, and our classes continued until I was 19. The first time we smoked cigarettes, we were together. She was the first person I told about my first sexual encounter, and I was the first person she told about her first sexual encounter. I was with her the first time I got high. She took me to my first and only Prince concert. My first trip to New York, we were together. She was my maid of honor when I got married and the godmother to my firstborn child. She was on her deathbed when I was pregnant with my second child, who of course is named Andrea, and my third child carries her middle name, Marie.

On her deathbed ... that wasn't as hard for me as I had anticipated. I think it was because she was so full of life. Even when she was very sick, she was always determined to live her life to the fullest. She went on vacations and exposed herself to different cultures. She was a collector of various styles of art and was artistically creative herself. I still have things that she and her mom, my godmother, made for me. She was always taking pictures, and we constantly were writing each other letters and poems. It was as though our life together was simply preparation for life apart. Andrea used to say to me, "Always together, never apart, maybe in distance, but never in heart."

Her last days on earth were hard for her and her family. Andrea was very uncomfortable and in a lot of pain, and on that last night before she died, her doctors planned to run some more tests the following day that would cause her more pain. I went home and prayed, "Dear God, please just take her. Don't let her go through any more pain. Take her where she can be healthy and happy again. Please, God." It was at 2:00 A.M. that my mom came in my room and told me, "Andrea's gone. She passed this morning." At first, I felt tremendously guilty because I prayed for her to die, but suddenly a peace came over me that at the time I could not explain. I know my best friend was healthy, happy, smiling down on me, and looking out for me like she always had. She was and is my angel.

Toward the end of her life, Andrea talked a lot about Jesus through her poetry. I had been brought up in a church-going family, so I certainly knew who God was. It wasn't until later in my life, however, that I truly began to experience a relationship with my Heavenly Father through my Lord and Savior, Jesus Christ. I have had much opposition that attempted to keep me disconnected from God. After Andrea passed away, I recognized that God had strategically placed this natural experience of friendship and unconditional love before me and then allowed me to make the choice to come to Him in faith, motivated by love and self-sacrifice. It was a selfless prayer to ask God to take her, for her sake. A selfish prayer would have been for him to heal her so she would still remain here on earth with us. My heart desired perfection and glory for her, because she had already given so much to so many. To me, she gave enough love to sustain me for the rest of my life. Andrea will always hold her place in my heart.

She died on March 10, 1996, three days before my 21st birthday. She was 20 years old. The faith that had grown through my relationship with Andrea doesn't allow me to experience life without her. She is still and will always be a part of my daily blessings. To this day, I speak to Momma (her mother) on a regular basis, and my children call her "Nana." I dated Andrea's younger brother for five years. Her family is my family, and the common denominator of love has been, and will always be, Andrea.

Dear God, thank you for allowing me the opportunity to live, laugh, and cry with Andrea once again through my story, her story, and our story. I love you, Drea!

SHAWNA C. ERVIN, AKA VIRTUE

Shawna C. Ervin is a popular hairstylist who resides in Los Angeles, California.

▶ *Chapter 58*

My Shining Light

When I think of my brother, so many feelings come to mind. For one, he has always been a major guidepost in my life. As a young boy, I would follow him around our house, imitating every move he made. Only five years my elder, he has nevertheless always been my hero. Through his life, he opened doors to new realities and possibilities in my life.

Our parents were simple people. Both from the rural South, they provided us with a comfortable life made all the better by the abundance of love that they showered on each of us. Since we were young boys, our psyches were constantly infused with the will and confidence to pursue whatever goals we might want to achieve in life. That said, neither really knew the details of what it takes to reach those goals beyond the time-honored advice to stay in school, off drugs, and close to God.

On the other hand, I've always thought of my brother as a trail-blazer in our family. Coming of age in the late seventies and early eighties, he ventured out far beyond our cloistered surroundings in black Los Angeles in pursuit of tastes and adventures that were unknown to our family.

A "fashionista" way before the word came into vogue, my brother would use his allowance and earnings from a part-time job to bring home the hippest clothes to wear on his escapades. He soon began to use school holidays for trips with his friends to San Francisco and Dallas. It was around this time that he started to pull away from our family circle and make the moves that signaled his independence as his transition to adult life began to take shape.

Even at a young age, I knew that my brother was gay. Although we didn't directly discuss the matter until much later, it was obvious that he was different from the other men in our family. If my parents shared similar suspicions, they never shared them with me, nor did they ever voice comments either way about the gay lifestyle. Their reticent stance on the issue made the subject a non-issue for me.

Secrets Revealed

An atmosphere of candor and understanding has always permeated my relationship with my brother. It was characteristic of the close relationship we have that he revealed that he was HIV positive to me. The memory of that moment is permanently etched in my head; the shock and dread of his news sent shock waves of doom through my soul that still live with me to this day. Up until that point, on an intellectual level at least, I believed that the two of us would outlive our parents, and he would be in my life forever. His confession shattered that belief and left my spirit torn to shreds. I interpreted his words to mean that he was actually telling me that he was going to die.

During the weeks, months, and years following his diagnosis, it seemed as if my family was under a constant deathwatch with my brother. In response to his illness, our family immediately circled the wagons, furiously researching information and resources that would result in a cure or, at the very least, an extension of his life. Through the years, our proactive response to his illness has been subjected to jarring setbacks—notably, the ongoing deaths of his many friends. However, as a family we have persevered, and it's my belief that in no small way our diligence is responsible for the longevity he's been blessed with in the face of this disease.

It has now been more than 20 years since I learned about my brother's HIV status. I am happy to report that for the most part he is well; today he suffers primarily from the normal woes associated with someone his age.

Overall, from what I've witnessed, my brother has lived his life with remarkable grace in the face of the constant threats to his health. In the years since his diagnosis, he's developed a Zen-like disposition about his circumstances; this has kept him and our family from crumbling. That said, he has also had to survive major bouts of depression and anguish, but he has always come through those crises stronger and with a better understanding of his purpose in life.

From the standpoint of advocacy, he has been on the front lines for creating awareness and understanding about HIV/AIDS. From the moment he was first diagnosed, he has been unrelenting in lending his voice to this struggle, and has been unashamed and unapologetic about his life and how he's lived it. Watching him do so has made me exceedingly proud.

Given the life cycle that most associate with this disease, I have sometimes wondered why and how my brother is still here with us today. As the world continues to spin around us, literally millions of people have died from this disease; the lingering question I've often asked is, "When will it be his turn to die, and mine to grieve?"

When to grieve about my brother and his illness is a question I've often asked myself. Over the years, I've watched many others move through the pain and loss of death into a state of renewal. For a long time now, I have lived my life under a constant cloud of grief, always mournful of his condition and what his loss will do to me and to my family. Getting past my grief has been hard; in fact, it has perhaps been the most difficult aspect for me in dealing with his circumstances.

Living with AIDS is a very lonely life, both for the sufferer and those who love him or her. Watching someone you love die is never easy, but when you factor in the stigmatization and fear associated with this disease, you're left with an atmosphere of silence that can be truly stifling. Even when taking into account the show of love and support an extended family and friends can provide, the day-to-day pressures of living with HIV-positive status on a personal level is still is something that must be faced alone.

In my case, getting past my grief really meant learning to accept my brother's illness. As I've reached this realization, I've discovered an appreciation for his longevity and ability to enjoy each moment simply for what it is. I've taken the guessing game out of my repartee and have replaced it with gratitude for each day that I physically have him in my life. My new axioms are: "Deal with today, not tomorrow," and also, "Accept the things over which I have no control." Arriving at this space has not been easy, but it has enabled me to reach my own state of renewal.

Fortunately, our family has not experienced the pain felt by many who have lost a loved one afflicted by this disease, but I would be remiss if I failed to note the consequences of our living with his HIV status for over 20 years.

Our father died six years ago, and although his death was from natural causes, I sometimes wonder if stress related to my brother's illness may have contributed to his health problems. In my mother, I can clearly see the real influence of his disease. Although she is still a somewhat active and vibrant woman, I do believe that the burden of living with the constant threat that AIDS presents has taken an observable physical toll on her body.

As for myself, I'm not really sure. Knowing my brother's HIV status has weighed heavily on me. However, as farfetched as it sounds, his illness has also brought tremendous value to my life. For one, always knowing that his time may be short has made me grow up and take stock of my life's goals and objectives. His illness (in addition to our father's death) has also given me a profound appreciation for life. It's amazing that even through his illness, my brother continues to have a profound influence over my life.

Even though the life that I have crafted for myself has offered me the opportunity to live out many of my greatest dreams and meet great people, my brother Jeffrey is still the most remarkable person that I've ever known. His strength, passion, and commitment to life leave me in awe of the power of the human spirit. Knowing that our lives are just blips on the wave of time makes me feel blessed to be connected to someone so extraordinary.

GIL L. ROBERTSON IV

◆ PART V

Appendices

Glossary of HIV/AIDS–Related Terms

ACQUIRED IMMUNE DEFICIENCY SYNDROME (AIDS): The most severe manifestation of infection with the human immunodeficiency virus (HIV). The Centers for Disease Control and Prevention (CDC) lists numerous opportunistic infections and neoplasms (cancers) that, in the presence of HIV infection, constitute an AIDS diagnosis. There are also instances of presumptive diagnoses when a person's HIV status is unknown or not sought. This was especially true before 1985 when there was no HIV-antibody test. In 1993, the CDC expanded the criteria for an AIDS diagnosis to include CD4+ T-cell count at or below 200 cells per microliter in the presence of HIV infection. In persons (aged 5 and older) with normally functioning immune systems, CD4+ T-cell counts usually range from 500 to 1500 cells per microliter. Persons living with AIDS often have infections of the lungs, brain, eyes and other organs, and frequently suffer debilitating weight loss, diarrhea, and a type of cancer called Kaposi's sarcoma. Since AIDS is a syndrome, it is incorrect to refer to it as the AIDS virus.

ADHERENCE: The extent to which a patient takes his/her medication according to the prescribed schedule (also referred to as "compliance").

AFFECTED COMMUNITY: Persons living with HIV and AIDS, and other related individuals including their families, friends, and advocates whose lives are directly influenced by HIV infection and its physical, psychological, and sociological ramifications.

AFRICA UNION: http://www.africa-union.org

AIDS CARRIER: Any person living with HIV/AIDS. This term is stigmatizing and offensive to many people living with HIV/AIDS. It is also incorrect; the effective agent is HIV.

AIDS-DEFINING ILLNESS: Any of a series of health conditions that are considered, in isolation or in combination with others, to be indicative of the development of AIDS. These conditions occur at a late stage of HIV infection. Quite often, it is only at this particular stage that many individuals discover that they are infected by HIV. Such conditions may be grouped in four categories: opportunistic infections, brain and nerve diseases, certain cancers, and AIDS wasting syndrome.

AIDS DEMENTIA COMPLEX (ADC): Disturbance in brain function that is thought to be due to HIV infection in the brain. ADC may impair a person's ability to function in social or work settings.

AIDSINFO DRUG DATABASE: An online database service of the U.S. National Library of Medicine, with information about drugs undergoing testing against AIDS, AIDS-related complex, and related opportunistic diseases. Internet address: http://sis.nlm.nih.gov/HIV/HIVDrugs.html.

AIDSLINE: The former online database service of the US National Library of Medicine, with citations and abstracts covering the published scientific and medical literature on AIDS and related topics, now incorporated into MEDLINE. Free MEDLINE searches are available through the NLM Gateway. Internet address: http://gateway.nlm.nih.gov/gw/Cmd.

AIDS MEDICINES: AIDS medicines include antiretroviral medicines, anti-infective medicines to treat or prevent opportunistic diseases, anti-cancer medicines to treat frequent malignancies in people living with HIV/AIDS, and palliative medicines to relieve pain and discomfort. The *WHO Model Formulary* (2002) includes comprehensive information on all HIV-related medicines contained in the WHO Model List of Essential Medicines. It presents information on the recommended use, dosage, adverse effects, contra-indications and warnings of these medicines.

AIDS-RELATED CANCERS: Malignancies including certain types of immune-system cancers known as lymphomas, Kaposi's sarcoma, and anogenital cancers that are more common or more aggressive in people living with HIV/AIDS. HIV, or the immune suppression it induces, appears to play a role in the development of these cancers.

AIDS-RELATED COMPLEX (ARC): A variety of symptoms and signs found in some persons living with HIV. These may include recurrent fevers, unexplained weight loss, swollen lymph nodes, diarrhea, herpes, hairy leukoplakia, and/or fungal infection of the mouth and throat. Also more accurately described as symptomatic HIV infection. More specifically, a variety of symptoms that appear to be related to HIV infection. They also include an unexplained, chronic deficiency of white blood cells (leukopenia) or a poorly functioning lymphatic system with swelling of the lymph nodes (lymphadenopathy) lasting for more than three months without the opportunistic infections required for a diagnosis of AIDS. *See also AIDS WASTING SYNDROME.*

AIDS SERVICE ORGANIZATION (ASO): A health association, support agency, or other service involved in the prevention and treatment of AIDS.

APPROVED DRUG: Any registered or licensed drug, or any drug having marketing authorization.

ASYMPTOMATIC: Without symptoms. Usually used in the HIV/AIDS literature to describe a person who has a positive reaction to one of several tests for HIV antibodies but who shows no clinical symptoms of the disease.

BODY FLUIDS: Any fluid in the human body, such as blood, urine, saliva (spit), sputum, tears, semen, mother's milk, or vaginal secretions. Confusion about the body fluids that can transmit HIV is a common cause of misunderstanding and fear about HIV and continues to cause discrimination against people living with HIV/AIDS. Always explain which body fluids contain HIV in sufficient concentration to be implicated in HIV transmission (e.g. blood, semen, pre-ejaculate, vaginal fluids, and breast milk). HIV cannot be transmitted through body fluids such as saliva, sweat, tears or urine.

CENTERS FOR DISEASE CONTROL AND PREVENTION (CDC): The U.S. Department of Health and Human Services agency with the mission to promote health and quality of life by preventing and controlling disease, injury, and disability. The CDC operates 11 centers including the National Center for HIV, STD, and TB Prevention (NCHSTP). The CDC assesses the status and characteristics of the HIV epidemic and conducts epidemiologic, laboratory, and surveillance investigations.

COFACTORS:
1. Substances, microorganisms, or characteristics of individuals that may influence the progression of a disease or the likelihood of becoming ill.
2. A substance, such as a metallic ion or coenzyme, that must be associated with an enzyme in order for the enzyme to function.
3. A situation or activity that may increase a person's susceptibility to AIDS. Examples of cofactors are: other infections, drug and alcohol use, poor nutrition, genetic factors, and stress. In HIV immunology, the concept of cofactors is being expanded and new cofactors have been identified. A recent example is the discovery of the interaction of CXCR4 (fusin) and CD4 to facilitate entry of HIV into cells.

COMBINATION THERAPY: (For HIV infection or AIDS.) Two or more drugs or treatments used together to achieve optimal results against infection or disease. For treatment of HIV, a minimum of three anti-retrovirals is recommended. Combination therapy may offer advantages over single-drug therapies by being more effective in decreasing viral load. An example of combination therapy would be the use of two nucleoside analogue drugs (such as lamivudine and zidovudine; see entries for these drugs) plus either a protease inhibitor or a non-nucleoside reverse transcription inhibitor.

DRUG REGULATORY AUTHORITY: A national body that administers the full spectrum of drug regulatory activities, including at least all of the following functions:

- marketing authorization of new products and variation of existing products
- quality-control laboratory testing
- adverse drug reaction monitoring
- provision of drug information and promotion of rational drug use
- good manufacturing practice (GMP) inspections and licensing of manufacturers, wholesalers, and distribution channels
- enforcement operations
- monitoring of drug utilization

DRUG RESISTANCE: The ability of some disease-causing microorganisms, such as bacteria, viruses, and mycoplasmas, to adapt themselves, to grow, and to multiply even in the presence of drugs that usually kill them.

EPIDEMIC: A disease that spreads rapidly through a demographic segment of the human population, such as everyone in a given geographic area, a military base, or similar population unit; or everyone of a certain age or sex, such as the children or women of a region. Epidemic diseases can be spread from person to person or from a contaminated source such as food or water.

EPIDEMIOLOGY: The branch of medical science that deals with the study of incidence, distribution and control of a disease in a population.

ESSENTIAL DRUGS: Essential medicines (as defined by the WHO Expert Committee on the Selection and Use of Essential Medicines) are those that satisfy the priority health care needs of the population. They are selected with due regard to public-health relevance, evidence on efficacy and safety, and comparative cost-effectiveness. Essential medicines are intended to be available within the context of functioning health systems at all times in adequate amounts, in the appropriate dosage forms, with assured quality and adequate information, and at a price the individual and the community can afford. The implementation of the concept of essential medicines is intended to be flexible and adaptable to many different situations; exactly which medicines are regarded as essential remains a national responsibility.

GENDER AND SEX: The term "sex" refers to biologically determined differences, whereas the term "gender" refers to differences in social roles and relations between men and women. Gender roles are learned through socialization and vary widely within and between cultures. Gender roles are also affected by age, class, race, ethnicity and religion, as well as by geographical, economic, and political environments.

HIGH-RISK GROUPS/GROUPS WITH HIGH-RISK BEHAVIOR: These terms should be used with caution as they can increase stigma and discrimination. They may also lull people who don't identify with such groups into a false sense of security. 'High-risk group' also implies that the risk is contained within the group, when in fact, all social groups are interrelated. It is often more accurate to refer directly to "sex without a condom," "unprotected sex," "needle-sharing," or "sharing injecting equipment," rather than to generalize by saying "high-risk group."

HIGHLY ACTIVE ANTIRETROVIRAL THERAPY (HAART): The name given to treatment regimens recommended by leading HIV experts to aggressively suppress viral replication and progress of HIV-related disease. More recently, a new drug has been developed to prevent the virus from entering the cell. The usual HAART regimen combines three or more different drugs, such as two nucleoside reverse transcriptase inhibitors (NRTIs) and a protease inhibitor, two NRTIs and a non-nucleoside reverse transcriptase inhibitor (NNRTI), or other combinations. These treatment regimens have been shown to reduce the amount of virus so that it becomes undetectable in a patient's blood. (See http://www.aidsinfo.nih.gov, a service of the U.S. Department of Health and Human Services.)

HIV DISEASE: During the initial infection with HIV, when the virus comes in contact with the mucosal surface and finds susceptible T-cells, the first site at which there is truly massive production of the virus is in lymphoid tissue. This leads to a burst of massive viremia with wide dissemination of the virus to lymphoid organs. The resulting immune response to suppress the virus is only partially successful, and some virus escapes. Eventually, this results in high viral turnover that leads to destruction of the immune system. HIV disease is, therefore, characterized by a gradual deterioration of immune functions. During the course of infection, crucial immune cells, called CD4+ T-cells, are disabled and killed, and their numbers progressively decline.
See ACQUIRED IMMUNE DEFICIENCY SYNDROME; HUMAN IMMUNODEFICIENCY VIRUS TYPE 1.

HIV INCIDENCE: HIV incidence (sometimes referred to as cumulative incidence) is the proportion of people who have become infected with HIV during a specified period of time. UNAIDS normally refers to the number of people (of all ages) or children (age 14 and under) who have become infected during the past year.

HIV-INFECTED: As distinct from HIV-positive (which can sometimes be a false positive test result, especially in infants of up to 18 months of age), the term HIV-infected is usually used to indicate that evidence of HIV has been found via a blood or tissue test.

HIV-NEGATIVE: Showing no evidence of infection with HIV (e.g., absence of antibodies against HIV) in a blood or tissue test. Synonymous with seronegative.

HIV-POSITIVE: Showing indications of infection with HIV (e.g., presence of antibodies against HIV) on a test of blood or tissue.

Synonymous with seropositive. Test may occasionally show false positive results.

HIV PREVALENCE: Usually given as a percentage, HIV prevalence quantifies the proportion of individuals in a population who have HIV at a specific point in time. UNAIDS normally reports HIV prevalence among adults, aged 15 to 49.

HIV SET POINT: The rate of virus replication that stabilizes and remains at a particular level in each individual after the period of primary infection.

HIV VIRAL LOAD: *See VIRAL LOAD TEST.*

HUMAN IMMUNODEFICIENCY VIRUS (HIV): The virus that weakens the immune system, ultimately leading to AIDS. Since HIV means 'human immunodeficiency virus,' it is redundant to refer to the HIV virus.

HUMAN IMMUNODEFICIENCY VIRUS TYPE 1 (HIV-1): The retrovirus isolated and recognized as the etiologic (i.e., causing or contributing to the cause of a disease) agent of AIDS. HIV-1 is classified as a lentivirus in a subgroup of retroviruses. Most viruses and all bacteria, plants, and animals have genetic codes made up of DNA, which uses RNA to build specific proteins. The genetic material of a retrovirus such as HIV is the RNA itself. HIV inserts its own RNA into the host cell's DNA, preventing the host cell from carrying out its natural functions and turning it into an HIV factory.

HUMAN IMMUNODEFICIENCY VIRUS TYPE 2 (HIV-2): A virus closely related to HIV-1 that has also been found to cause AIDS. It was first isolated in West Africa. Although HIV-1 and HIV-2 are similar in their viral structure, modes of transmission, and resulting opportunistic infections, they have differed in their geographical patterns of infection.

IMMUNE DEFICIENCY: A breakdown or inability of certain parts of the immune system to function, thus making a person susceptible to certain diseases that they would not ordinarily develop.

IMMUNE RESPONSE: The activity of the immune system against foreign substances.

IMMUNE SYSTEM: The body's complicated natural defense against disruption caused by invading foreign agents (e.g., microbes, viruses). There are two aspects of the immune system's response to disease: innate and acquired. The innate part of the response is mobilized very quickly in response to infection and does not depend on recognizing specific proteins or antigens foreign to an individual's normal tissue. It includes the complement system, macrophages, dendritic cells, and granulocytes. The acquired, or learned, immune response arises when dendritic cells and macrophages present pieces of antigen to lymphocytes, which are genetically programmed to recognize very specific amino acid sequences. The ultimate result is the creation of cloned populations of antibody-producing B-cells and cytotoxic T lymphocytes primed to respond to a unique pathogen.

KAPOSI'S SARCOMA: An AIDS-defining illness consisting of individual cancerous lesions caused by an overgrowth of blood vessels. Kaposi's sarcoma (KS) typically appears as pink or purple painless spots or nodules on the surface of the skin or oral cavity. KS also can occur internally, especially in the intestines, lymph nodes, and lungs, and in this case is life threatening. The cancer may spread and also attack the eyes. There has been considerable speculation that KS is not a spontaneous cancer but is sparked by a virus. A species of herpes virus also referred to as Kaposi's sarcoma herpes virus (KSHV) or HHV, similar to the Epstein-Barr virus, is currently under extensive investigation. Up to now, KS has been treated with alpha interferon, radiation therapy (outside the oral cavity), and various systemic and intralesional cancer chemotherapies.

LYMPHOID INTERSTITIAL PNEUMONITIS (LIP): A type of pneumonia that affects 35 to 40 percent of children with AIDS, which causes hardening of the lung membranes involved in absorbing oxygen. LIP is an AIDS-defining illness in children. The etiology (cause) of LIP is not clear. There is no established therapy for LIP, but the use of corticosteroids for progressive LIP has been advocated.

MACROPHAGE: A large immune cell that devours invading pathogens and other intruders. Stimulates other immune cells by presenting them with small pieces of the invader. Macrophages can harbor large quantities of HIV without being killed, acting as reservoirs of the virus.

MICROBICIDE: An agent (e.g., a chemical or antibiotic) that destroys microbes. New research is being carried out to evaluate the use of rectal and vaginal microbicides to inhibit the transmission of sexually transmitted infections, including HIV.

MSM: Acronym for "men who have sex with men."

MTCT: Acronym for "mother-to-child transmission."

MYCOBACTERIUM AVIUM COMPLEX (MAC):
1. A common opportunistic infection caused by two very similar mycobacterial organisms, *Mycobacterium avium* and *Mycobacterium avium intracellulare* (MAI), found in soil and dust particles.
2. A bacterial infection that can be localized (limited to a specific organ or area of the body) or disseminated throughout the body. It is a life-threatening disease, although new therapies offer promise for both prevention and treatment. MAC disease is extremely rare in persons who are not infected with HIV.

NELFINAVIR (NFV): A protease inhibitor antiretroviral medicine used for the treatment of HIV infection in combination with two other antiretroviral medicines.

NEUTROPENIA: An abnormal decrease in the number of neutrophils (the most common type of white blood cells) in the blood. The decrease may be relative or absolute. Neutropenia may be associated with HIV infection or may be drug-induced.

NEVIRAPINE (NVP): A non-nucleoside reverse transcriptase inhibitor used in HIV infection in combination with at least two other antiretroviral drugs; used in prevention of mother-to-child transmission in HIV-infected patients.

NON-NUCLEOSIDE REVERSE TRANSCRIPTASE INHIBITORS (NNRTIs): A class of drugs that inhibit an enzyme used by HIV called "reverse transcriptase." The non-nucleoside reverse transcriptase inhibitors include efavirenz and nevirapine. They interact with a number of drugs metabolized in the liver; the dose of protease inhibitors may need to be increased when they are given with efavirenz or nevirapine. Nevirapine is associated with a high incidence of rash and occasionally fatal hepatitis. Rash is also associated with efavirenz but is usually milder. Efavirenz treatment has also been associated with an increased plasma cholesterol concentration.

OPPORTUNISTIC INFECTIONS: Illnesses caused by various organisms, some of which usually do not cause disease in persons with healthy immune systems. Persons living with advanced HIV infection suffer opportunistic infections of the lungs, brain, eyes, and other organs. Opportunistic infections common in persons diagnosed with AIDS include *Pneumocystis jiroveci* pneumonia; Kaposi's sarcoma; cryptosporidiosis; histoplasmosis; other parasitic, viral, and fungal infections; and some types of cancers.

PALLIATIVE CARE: Palliative care is an approach to life-threatening chronic illnesses, especially at the end of life. Palliative care combines active and compassionate therapies to comfort and support patients and their families who are living with life-ending illness. Palliative care strives to meet physical needs through pain relief and maintaining quality of life while emphasizing the patient's and family's rights to participate in informed discussion and to make choices. This patient- and family-centered approach uses the skills of interdisciplinary team members to provide a comprehensive continuum of care including spiritual and emotional needs.

PEOPLE LIVING WITH HIV/AIDS (PLWHA): With reference to those living with HIV/AIDS, it is preferable to avoid certain terms:

AIDS patient should only be used in a medical context (most of the time, a person with AIDS is not in the role of patient); the term AIDS victim or AIDS sufferer implies that the individual in question is powerless, with no control over his/her life. It is preferable to use "people living with HIV/AIDS (PLWHA)," since this reflects the fact that an infected person may continue to live well and productively for many years. Referring to PLWHA as innocent victims (which is often used to describe HIV-positive children or people who have acquired HIV medically) wrongly implies that people infected in other ways are somehow deserving of punishment. It is preferable to use PLWHA, or "people with medically-acquired HIV," or "children with HIV."

PERINATAL TRANSMISSION: Transmission of a pathogen, such as HIV, from mother to baby before, during, or after the birth process. Ninety percent of children reported with AIDS acquired HIV infection from their HIV-infected mothers.

PHASE I TRIALS: Involve the initial introduction of an investigational new drug into humans. Phase I trials are closely monitored and may be conducted in patients or in healthy volunteers. The studies are designed to determine the metabolism and pharmacological actions of the drug in humans, safety, side effects associated with increasing doses, and, if possible, early evidence of effectiveness. The trials also can include studies of structure-activity relationships, mechanisms of action in humans, use of the investigational drug as a research tool to explore biological phenomena, or disease processes. The total number of patients included in Phase I studies varies but is generally in the range of 20 to 80. Sufficient information should be obtained in the trial to permit the design of well-controlled, scientifically valid Phase II studies.

PHASE II TRIALS: Include controlled clinical studies of effectiveness of the drug for a particular indication or indications in patients with the disease or condition under study, and determination of common, short-term side effects and risks associated with the drug. Phase II studies are typically well controlled, closely monitored, and usually involve no more than several hundred patients.

PHASE III TRIALS: Expanded controlled and uncontrolled studies. They are performed after preliminary evidence of drug effectiveness has been obtained. They are intended to gather additional information about effectiveness and safety that is needed to evaluate the overall benefit-risk relationship of the drug and to provide adequate basis for physician labeling. These studies usually involve anywhere from several hundred to several thousand subjects.

PHASE IV TRIALS: Post-marketing studies, carried out after licensure of the drug. Generally, a Phase IV trial is a randomized, controlled trial that is designed to evaluate the long-term safety and efficacy of a drug for a given indication. Phase IV trials are important in evaluating AIDS drugs because many drugs for HIV infection have been given accelerated approval with small amounts of clinical data about the drugs' effectiveness.

PNEUMOCYSTIS JIROVECI **PNEUMONIA (PCP):** An infection of the lungs caused by *Pneumocystis jiroveci,* which is thought to belong to protozoa but may be more closely related to a fungus. *P. jiroveci* grows rapidly in the lungs of persons with AIDS and is a frequent AIDS-related cause of death. *P. jiroveci* infection may sometimes occur elsewhere in the body (skin, eye, spleen, liver, or heart). The standard treatment for persons with PCP is a combination of trimethoprim and sulfamethoxazole (TMP/SMX, also known as co-trimoxazole), dapsone, or pentamidine.

PROPHYLAXIS: Preventive therapy; "primary prophylaxis" is given to at-risk individuals to prevent a first infection by, say, PCP; "secondary prophylaxis" is given to prevent recurrent infections.

PROTEASE: An enzyme used by HIV to process new copies of the virus after it has reproduced; drugs specifically aimed at this enzyme are called "protease inhibitors" (see below). Human cells also use protease enzymes, but they are different from the HIV protease.

PROTEASE INHIBITORS: Antiviral drugs that act by inhibiting the virus protease enzyme, thereby preventing viral replication. Specifically, these drugs block the protease enzyme from breaking apart long strands of viral proteins to make the smaller, active HIV proteins that comprise the virion. If the larger HIV proteins are not broken apart, they cannot assemble themselves into new functional HIV particles. The protease inhibitors include amprenavir, indinavir, lopinavir, nelfinavir, ritonavir, and saquinavir. Protease inhibitors are associated with lipodystrophy and metabolic side effects.

PROTOCOL: The detailed plan for conducting a clinical trial. It states the trial's rationale, purpose, drug or vaccine dosages, length of study, routes of administration, who may participate, and other aspects of trial design.

RESISTANCE: The ability of an organism, such as HIV, to overcome the inhibitory effect of a drug, such as AZT or a protease inhibitor.

RETROVIRUS: A type of virus that, when not infecting a cell, stores its genetic information on a single-stranded RNA molecule instead of the more usual double-stranded DNA. HIV is an example of a retrovirus. After a retrovirus penetrates a cell, it constructs a DNA version of its genes using a special enzyme called reverse transcriptase. This DNA then becomes part of the cell's genetic material.

REVERSE TRANSCRIPTASE: This enzyme of HIV (and other retroviruses) converts the single-stranded viral RNA into DNA, the form in which the cell carries its genes. Some antiviral drugs approved by the FDA for the treatment of HIV infection (e.g., AZT, ddI, 3TC, d4T, and ABC) work by interfering with this stage of the viral life cycle. They are also referred to as reverse transcriptase inhibitors (RTIs).

RITONAVIR: A protease inhibitor antiretroviral medicine used in HIV infection as a booster to increase the effect of indinavir, lopinavir, or saquinavir, and in combination with two other antiretroviral medicines.

SAQUINAVIR (SQV): A protease inhibitor antiretroviral medicine used in HIV infection in combination with two other antiretroviral medicines and usually with a low-dose ritonavir booster.

SENTINEL SURVEILLANCE: This form of surveillance relates to a particular group (such as men who have sex with men) or activity (such as sex work) that acts as an indicator of the presence of a disease.

SEROCONVERSION: The development of antibodies to a particular antigen. When people develop antibodies to HIV, they "seroconvert" from antibody-negative to antibody-positive. It may take from as little as one week to several months or more after infection with HIV for antibodies to the virus to develop. After antibodies to HIV appear in the blood, a person should test positive on antibody tests.

SEROLOGIC TEST: Any of a number of tests that are performed on the clear portion of blood. Often refers to a test that determines the presence of antibodies to antigens such as viruses.

SEROPREVALENCE: As related to HIV infection, this term refers to the proportion of persons who have serologic (pertaining to serum) evidence of HIV infection at any given time.

SEROSTATUS: A generic term that refers to the presence/absence of antibodies in the blood. Often, the term refers to HIV antibodies.

SEXUALLY TRANSMITTED INFECTION (STI): Also called venereal disease (VD), an older public-health term, or sexually transmitted disease (STD). Sexually transmitted infections are spread by the transfer of organisms from person to person during sexual contact. In addition to the "traditional" STIs (syphilis and gonorrhea), the spectrum of STIs now includes HIV, which causes AIDS; Chlamydia trachomatis; human papilloma virus (HPV); genital herpes; chancroid; genital mycoplasmas; hepatitis B; trichomoniasis; enteric infections; and ectoparasitic diseases

(diseases caused by organisms that live on the outside of the host's body). The complexity and scope of STIs have increased dramatically since the 1980s; more than 20 organisms and syndromes are now recognized as belonging in this category.

SEX WORKER: This term is preferable to "prostitute," "whore," and "commercial sex worker," which have negative connotations. The term "sex worker" is non-judgmental and recognizes the fact that people sell their bodies as a means of survival or to earn a living.

SUSCEPTIBLE: Vulnerable or predisposed to a disease.

SYMPTOMS: Any perceptible, subjective change in the body or its functions that indicates disease or phases of disease, as reported by the patient.

SYNDROME: A group of symptoms as reported by the patient and signs as detected in an examination that together are characteristic of a specific condition.

SYSTEMIC: Concerning or affecting the body as a whole. A systemic therapy is one that the entire body is exposed to, rather than just the target tissues affected by a disease.

T4 CELL: (Also called T helper cell.) An antibody-triggered immune cell that seeks and attacks invading organisms. Macrophages summon T4 cells to the infection site. There the T4 cell reproduces and secretes its potent lymphokines that stimulate B-cell production of antibodies; signal natural killer or cytotoxic (cell-killing) T-cells; and summon other macrophages to the infection site. In healthy immune systems, T4 cells are twice as common as T8 cells. If a person has AIDS, the proportion is often reversed. The virus enters T4 cells through its receptor protein and encodes its genetic information into the host cell's DNA, making T-cells virtual viral factories. HIV-infected T4 cells may not die, but rather may cease to function. They also begin to secrete a substance known as Soluble Suppressor Factor that inhibits the functioning of even unaffected T-cells.

T8 CELL: Also called killer cells. Immune cells that shut down the immune response after it has effectively wiped out invading organisms. Sensitive to high concentrations of circulating lymphokines, T8 cells release their own lymphokines when an immune response has achieved its goal, signaling all other participants to cease their coordinated attack. A number of B lymphocytes remain in circulation in order to fend off a possible repeat attack by the invading organism. With HIV, however, the immune system's response system does not work. T4 cells are dysfunctional, lymphokines proliferate in the bloodstream, and T8 cells compound the problem by misreading the oversupply of lymphokines as meaning that the immune system has effectively eliminated the invader. So while HIV is multiplying, T8 cells are simultaneously attempting to further shut down the immune system. The stage is set for normally repressed infectious agents, such as PCP or CMV, to proliferate unhindered and to cause disease.

TESTOSTERONE: A male hormone (also present in females, in lower concentrations) that affects muscle mass; it can be used therapeutically in people with HIV infection to promote weight gain and improve sex drive.

THERAPEUTIC HIV VACCINE: Also called treatment vaccine. A vaccine designed to boost the immune response to HIV in persons already infected with the virus. A therapeutic vaccine is different from a preventive vaccine, which is designed to prevent a disease from becoming established in a person.

THRUSH: Sore patches in the mouth caused by the fungus *Candida albicans*. Thrush is one of the most frequent early symptoms or signs of an immune disorder. The fungus commonly lives in the mouth, but only causes problems when the body's resistance is reduced either by antibiotics that have reduced the number of competitive organisms in the mouth, or by an immune deficiency such as HIV disease.

TOXOPLASMOSIS: A parasitic infection of the brain, caused by an organism called a protozoan. Many people are infected by this bug without knowing it. Symptoms include fever, headache, confusion, seizures, and, if untreated, coma. Toxoplasmosis is a risk for those with very low T-cell counts. If one becomes infected, one must take medication indefinitely, to prevent the infection from recurring.

VACCINE: A substance that contains antigenic components from an infectious organism. By stimulating an immune response but not the disease, it protects against subsequent infection by that organism. There can be preventive vaccines (e.g., measles or mumps) as well as therapeutic (treatment) vaccines.

VIRAL BURDEN: The amount of HIV in the circulating blood. Monitoring a person's viral burden is important because of the apparent correlation between the amount of virus in the blood and the severity of the disease: Sicker patients generally have more virus than those with less advanced disease. A new sensitive, rapid test called the viral-load assay for HIV-1 infection can be used to monitor the HIV viral burden. This procedure may help clinicians to decide when to give anti-HIV therapy. It may also help investigators determine more quickly if experimental HIV therapies are effective.

VIRAL-LOAD TEST: In relation to HIV, a test that measures the quantity of HIV RNA in the blood. Results are expressed as the number of copies per milliliter of blood plasma. Research indicates that viral load is a better predictor of the risk of HIV disease progression than the CD4 count. The lower the viral load, the longer the time to AIDS diagnosis and the longer the survival time. Viral-load testing for HIV infection is being used to determine when to initiate and/or change therapy.

VIRUS: Organism composed mainly of nucleic acid within a protein coat, ranging in size from 100 to 2000 angstroms (unit of length; one angstrom is equal to one hundred-millionth of a centimeter). When viruses enter a living plant, animal, or bacterial cell, they make use of the host cell's chemical energy and proteins' and nucleic acid's synthesizing ability to replicate themselves. Nucleic acids in viruses are single-stranded or double-stranded, and may be DNA (deoxyribonucleic acid) or RNA (ribonucleic acid). After the infected host cell makes viral components and virus particles are released, the host cell is often dissolved. Some viruses do not kill cells but transform them into a cancerous state; some cause illness and then seem to disappear, while remaining latent and later causing another, sometimes much more severe, form of disease. In humans, viruses cause, among other illnesses, measles, mumps, yellow fever, poliomyelitis, influenza, and the common cold. Some viral infections can be treated with drugs.

ZIDOVUDINE (ZDV or AZT): A nucleoside reverse transcriptase inhibitor antiretroviral medicine, zidovudine was the first antiretroviral drug to be introduced. Used in HIV infection in combination with at least two other antiretroviral drugs, and in monotherapy of maternal-fetal HIV transmission.

National HIV/AIDS Hotlines

Alabama
Local Access Number: 334-206-5364
Toll Free Access Number: 800-228-0469

Alaska
Local Access Number: 907-276-4880
Toll Free Access Number: 800-478-2437

Arizona
Local Access Number: 602-230-5822
Toll Free Access Number: 800-342-2347

Arkansas
Local Access Number: 501-661-2408
Toll Free Access Number: 800-342-2437

California
Local Access Number: 415-863-2437/916-445-0553
Toll Free Access Number: 800-367-2437/800-922-2437

Colorado
Local Access Number: 303-782-5186
Toll Free Access Number: 800-252-2437

Connecticut
Local Access Number: 860-509-7800
Toll Free Access Number: 800-203-1234

Delaware
Local Access Number: 302-652-6776
Toll Free Access Number: 800-422-0429

District of Columbia
Local Access Number: 202-938-7822
Toll Free Access Number: 202-332-2437

Florida
Local Access Number: not available
Toll Free Access Number: 800-352-2437

Florida—Spanish
Local Access Number: not available
Toll Free Access Number: 800-545-7432

Florida—Haitian Creole
Local Access Number: not available
Toll Free Access Number: 800-243-7101

Georgia
Local Access Number: 404-876-9944
Toll Free Access Number: 800-551-2728

Hawaii
Local Access Number: 808-733-9010
Toll Free Access Number: 800-321-1555

Idaho
Local Access Number: 208-321-2777
Toll Free Access Number: 800-677-2437

Illinois
Local Access Number: 217-785-7165
Toll Free Access Number: 800-243-2437

Indiana
Local Access Number: 800-342-2437
Toll Free Access Number: 800-342-2437

Iowa
Local Access Number: 515-244-6700
Toll Free Access Number: 800-445-2437

Kansas
Local Access Number: 785-296-6036
Toll Free Access Number: 800-342-2437

Kentucky
Local Access Number: 502-564-6539
Toll Free Access Number: 800-221-0446

Louisiana
Local Access Number: 504-821-6050
Toll Free Access Number: 800-992-4379

Maine
Local Access Number: 207-774-6877
Toll Free Access Number: 800-851-2437

Maryland
Local Access Number: 410-837-2437
Toll Free Access Number: 800-638-6252

Massachusetts
Local Access Number: 617-536-7733
Toll Free Access Number: 800-235-2331

Michigan
Local Access Number: 313-547-3655
Toll Free Access Number: 800-872-2437

Minnesota
Local Access Number: 651-373-2437
Toll Free Access Number: 800-248-2437

Mississippi
Local Access Number: 601-576-7723
Toll Free Access Number: 800-826-2961

Missouri
Local Access Number: 753-751-6439
Toll Free Access Number: 800-533-2437

Montana
Local Access Number: 406-444-3565
Toll Free Access Number: 800-233-6668

Nebraska
Local Access Number: 402-552-9255
Toll Free Access Number: 800-782-2437

Nevada
Local Access Number: 775-684-5900
Toll Free Access Number: 800-842-2437

New Hampshire
Local Access Number: 603-271-4576
Toll Free Access Number: 800-752-2437

New Jersey
Local Access Number: 609-984-5874
Toll Free Access Number: 800-624-2377

New Mexico
Local Access Number: 505-266-0911
Toll Free Access Number: 800-545-2437

New York
Local Access Number: 716-845-3170
Toll Free Access Number: 800-872-2777

North Carolina
Local Access Number: 919-733-3039
Toll Free Access Number: 800-342-2437

North Dakota
Local Access Number: 701-328-2378
Toll Free Access Number: 800-472-2180

Ohio
Local Access Number: 614-466-6374
Toll Free Access Number: 800-332-2437

Oklahoma
Local Access Number: 918-834-4194
Toll Free Access Number: 800-535-2437

Oregon
Local Access Number: 503-223-2437
Toll Free Access Number: 800-777-2437

Pennsylvania
Local Access Number: 717-783-0573
Toll Free Access Number: 800-662-6080

Rhode Island
Local Access Number: 401-222-2320
Toll Free Access Number: 800-726-3010

South Carolina
Local Access Number: 803-898-0625
Toll Free Access Number: 800-322-2437

South Dakota
Local Access Number: 605-773-3737
Toll Free Access Number: 800-592-1861

Tennessee
Local Access Number: 615-741-8530
Toll Free Access Number: 800-525-2437

Texas
Local Access Number: 512-490-2535
Toll Free Access Number: 800-299-2437

Utah
Local Access Number: 801-487-2100
Toll Free Access Number: 800-366-2437

Vermont
Local Access Number: 802-863-7245
Toll Free Access Number: 800-882-2437

Virginia
Local Access Number: 804-371-7455
Toll Free Access Number: 800-533-4148

Washington
Local Access Number: 360-236-3425
Toll Free Access Number: 800-272-2437

West Virginia
Local Access Number: 304-558-2950
Toll Free Access Number: 800-642-8244

Wisconsin
Local Access Number: 414-273-2437
Toll Free Access Number: 800-334-2437

Wyoming
Local Access Number: 307-777-5800
Toll Free Access Number: 800-327-3577

HIV Testing Facilities

Alabama
AIDS Alabama
P.O. Box 55703
Birmingham, AL 35255
Phone: 205-324-9822
Confidential Help Line: 800-592-2437

Alaska
Office Alaskan AIDS Assistance Association
1057 W. Fireweed, Suite 102
Anchorage, AK 99503
Phone: 907-263-2050
Fax: 907-263-2051

Arizona
AIDS Project Arizona
1427 N Third St, Ste 125
Phoenix, AZ 85004-1636
Phone: 602-253-2437

Arkansas
Arkansas AIDS Foundation
518 East 9th Street
Little Rock, AR 72202
Phone: 501-376-6299

California

San Francisco AIDS Foundation
995 Market St #200,
San Francisco. CA 94103
Phone: 800-367-AIDS

Minority AIDS Project
5149 W Jefferson Blvd
Los Angeles, CA 90016
Phone: 323-936-4949 (main) and 800-922-2437 (toll free)

Colorado

Colorado AIDS Project
2490 W. 26th Ave., Building A
Suite 300
Denver, CO 80211
Phone: 303-837-0166
Fax: 303-861-8281
info@coloradoaidsproject.org
www.coloradoaidsproject.org

Connecticut

Community Care Center
Living with HIV/AIDS Program
Conklin Bldg Ste 205
Hartford, CT 06106-3300
Phone: 860-545-5398 (main)
info@harthosp.org
www.aidsprojecthartford.org

Delaware

AIDS Delaware
New Castle County Office
100 West 10th Street, Suite 315
Wilmington, DE 19801
Phone: 302-652-6776
www.aidsdelaware.org

Washington, District of Columbia
The AIDS Institute
1705 Desales Street NW, Suite 700
Washington, DC 20036
Phone: 202-835-8373
www.theaidsinstitute.org

Florida
Shisa Incorporated
Community Education Center
323 1/2 Macomb St
Tallahassee, FL 32301-1017
Phone: 850-224-8718 (main)
info@shisa.org
www.shisa.org

North Central Florida AIDS Network, Inc.
3615 S.W. 13th Street, Suites 3&4
Gainesville, FL 32608
Phone: 352-372-4370 and 800-824-6745
ncfan@afn.org

University of South Florida College of Medicine
17 Davis Boulevard, Suite 403
Tampa, FL 33606
Phone: 813-258-5929

South Beach AIDS Project
306 Lincoln Rd
Miami, FL 33139-3103
Phone: 305-532-1033

Georgia
AID Atlanta
1605 Peachtree Street NW
Atlanta, GA 30309-2955
Phone: 404-870-7700
www.aidatlanta.org

Hawaii
Kalihi-Palama Health Center
915 N King St
Honolulu, HI 96817-4544
Phone: 808-848-1438 (main)
kphcadmin@loihi.com
www.healthhawaii.org

Idaho
Allies Linked for the Prevention of HIV and AIDS
500 West Idaho Street, #220 (5th and Idaho, above Flying M)
Boise, ID 83702
Phone: 208-424-7799
www.alphaidaho.org

Illinois
AIDS Foundation of Chicago
411 S. Wells, Suite 300
Chicago, IL 60607
Phone: 312-922-2322
www.aidschicago.org

Indiana
The Damien Center
1350 N. Pennsylvania
Indianapolis, IN 46202
Phone: 317-632-0123
info@damien.org
www.damien.org

Iowa
Rapids AIDS Project
6300 Rockwell Dr NE
Cedar Rapids, IA 52402-7220
Phone: 319-393-9579

Kansas
Wyandotte Co. Health Dept.
619 Ann Avenue
Kansas City, KS 66101-3099
Phone: 913-321-4803

Kentucky
Louisville Metro Health Department
400 East Gray Street
Louisville, KY 40202
Phone: 502-574-5600
Fax: 502-574-6699
www.health.loukymetro.org
www.louisvilleky.gov/health

Louisiana
Baton Rouge AIDS Society
4550 North Blvd Ste 101
Baton Rouge, LA 70806-4050
Phone: 225-923-2437

Maine
The Maine AIDS Alliance
1 Weston Ct.
Augusta, ME 04330
Phone: 207-621-2924
maa@gwi.net
www.maineaidsalliance.org

Maryland
Baltimore City Health Department Administrative Office
210 Guilford Ave
Baltimore, MD 21202
Phone: 410-396-1403
BCHD@baltimorecity.gov
www.ci.baltimore.md.us/government/health

Massachusetts
AIDS Action Committee of Massachusetts, Inc.
294 Washington Street, 5th Floor
Boston, MA 02108
Phone: 617-437-6200
info@aac.org
www.aac.org

Michigan
APM Downtown Detroit,
2751 E Jefferson Ave, Ste 301
Detroit, MI 48207-4100
Phone: 313-446-9800
info@aidspartnership.org
www.aidspartnership.org

Minnesota
Minnesota AIDS Project
1400 Park Avenue S.
Minneapolis, MN 55404
Phone: 612-341-2060
info@mnaidsproject.org
www.mnaidsproject.org

Missouri
Specialized Testing
8131 Manchester Rd
St Louis, MI 63144-2819
Phone: 800-450-3980 (main)
Phone: 877-837-8669 (toll-free)
www.areuatrisk.com

Montana
Yellowstone AIDS Project
2906 First Ave. North Suite 200
Billings, MT 59101
Phone: 406-245-2029
becca@yapmt.org / www.yapmt.org

Mississippi
Hinds County Health Department
Jackson Medical Mall
350 W. Woodrow Wilson, Ste. 411
Jackson, MS 39213
Phone: 601-364-2666

Nebraska
NAP Omaha & Watanabe Wellness Center
139 South 40th Street
Omaha, NE 68131
Phone: 402-552-9260
info@nap.org
www.nap.org

Nevada
Aid for AIDS of Nevada
2300 S. Rancho Drive, Suite 211
Las Vegas, NV 89102
Phone: 702-382-2326
Fax: 702-366-1609
afan@afanlv.org
www.afanlv.org

New Hampshire
Greater Manchester AIDS Project
77 Pearl St
Manchester, NH 03101
Phone: 603-623-0710

New Jersey
Buddies of New Jersey
Franklin A. Smith Resource Center
149 Hudson Street
Hackensack, NJ 07601
Phone: 201-429-2900
njbuddies@aol.com

New Mexico
New Mexico AIDS Services
625 Truman St. NE
Albuquerque, NM 87110
Phone: 505-938-7100 and 888-882-2437
www.nmas.net

New York
AIDS Center/Jack Martin Fund Clinic
The Mount Sinai Hospital
Annenberg Building, B1-Level
Madison Avenue @ 10th Street
One Gustave L. Levy Place, Box 1009
New York, NY 10029
Phone: 212-241-6159
www.mountsinai.org

Strong Memorial Hospital
601 Elmwood Ave.
Rochester, NY 14642
Phone: 585-275-2100
Strong_WebContact@urmc.rochester.edu
www.stronghealth.com

North Carolina
UNC Center for AIDS Research,
Lineberger Cancer Center
Chapel Hill, NC 27599
Phone: 919-966-8645
cfar@med.unc.edu

North Dakota
North Dakota Department of Health
HIV/AIDS Program
600 E. Boulevard Ave., Dept. 301
Bismarck, ND 58505-0200
Phone: 701-328-2378
Toll Free: 1-800-472-2180 (in-state callers only)

www.ndhiv.com/contact/

Ohio
The AIDS Taskforce of Greater Cleveland
3210 Euclid Avenue
Cleveland, OH 44115
Phone: 216-621-0766
www.aidstaskforce.org

Ohio AIDS Coalition
48 W. Whittier Street
Columbus, OH 43206-2503
Phone: 800-226-5554
Phone: 614-444-1683
www.ohioaidscoalition.org

Youngstown City Health District STD Clinic
Oak Hill Renaissance Place, Second Floor
345 Oak Hill Ave.
Youngstown, OH 44502
Phone: 330-743-3333 (Ext. 262)

Oregon
Cascade AIDS Project
620 SW Fifth Avenue, Suite 300
Portland, OR 97204
Phone: 503-223-5907
www.cascadeaids.org

Oklahoma
Tulsa C.A.R.E.S.
3507 E Admiral Pl
Tulsa, OK 74115-8211
Phone: 405-232-2437 or 800-285-CARE
www.tulsacares.org

Pennsylvania
ActionAIDS
1216 Arch Street, 6th Floor
Philadelphia, PA 19107

Phone: 215-981-0088
info@actionaids.org / www.actionaids.org

Pittsburgh AIDS Task Force (PATF)
905 West Street, Fourth Floor
Pittsburgh, PA 15221
Phone: 412-242-2500
Toll Free: 1-888-204-8821
info@patf.org
www.patf.org

Rhode Island
AIDS Project Rhode Island
Adams Clinic
293 Oxford Street
Providence, RI 02905
Phone: 401-781-0665
www.aidsprojectri.org

South Carolina
Lowcountry AIDS Services
3547 Meeting Street Road
North Charleston, SC 29405
Phone: 843-747-2273
fblunt@aids-services.com
www.aids-services.com

South Dakota
Project Takoja
625 Sitting Bull
Rapid City, SD 57701
Phone: 605-343-8762

Tennessee
Friends for Life
43 N. Cleveland
Memphis, TN 38104
Phone: 901-272-0855
www.friendsforlifecorp.org

Nashville Cares
501 Brick Church Park Drive
Nashville, TN 37207
Phone: 615-259-4866
HEARTLine: 800-845-4266
www.nashvillecares.org

Chattanooga CARES
P.O. BOX 4497
Chattanooga, TN 37405
Phone: 423-265-2273
Hotline: 800-960-AIDS
contactus@chattanoogacares.org
www.chattanoogacares.org

Texas
AIDS Foundation Houston, Inc.
3202 Weslayan Annex
Houston, TX 77027
Phone: 713-623-6796
info@AFHouston.org
www.aidshelp.org

University of Texas
Southwestern Medical Center at Dallas
Department of Internal Medicine
Community Prevention and Intervention Unit
400 S Zang Blvd, Ste 520
Dallas, TX 75208-9150
Phone: 214-645-7300
www.utsouthwestern.edu/utsw/cda/dept103192/files/159065.html

Utah
Utah AIDS Foundation
1408 South 1100 East
Salt Lake City, UT 84105
Phone: 801-487-2323
mail@utahaids.org

www.utahaids.org

Vermont
Vermont Cares
361 Pearl Street
Burlington, VT 05401
Phone: 802-863-2437
800-649-2437 toll free
www.vtcares.org

Virginia
VCU HIV/AIDS Center
Box 980147
1001 East Broad St.
Richmond, VA 23219-1928
Phone: 804-828-2210
www.hivcenter.vcu.edu

Washington
People of Color Against AIDS
2200 Rainier Avenue South
Seattle, WA 98144
Phone: 206.322.7061
Fax: 206.322.7204
pocaan@pocaan.org
www.pocaan.org

West Virginia
West Virginia Department of Health and Human Resources
Bureau of Public Health
Berkeley County Health Department
800 Emmett Rousch Dr
Martinsburg, WV 25401-6313
Phone: 304-263-5131
berkeleylhd@wvdhhr.org
www.wvdhhr.org

Wisconsin
AIDS Resource Center of Wisconsin
820 North Plankinton Avenue
Milwaukee, WI 53203
Phone: 414-273-1991
Phone: 800-359-9272
www.arcw.org

Wyoming
Wyoming AIDS Project
PO Box 50662
Casper, WY 82605.0662
Phone: 307-237-7833
Phone: 800-675-2698
wyaidsproj@wyoming.com

ABOUT THE AUTHOR

Gil L. Robertson IV is a journalist whose work has appeared in *Essence, Billboard, Black Enterprise, The Source,* the *Los Angeles Times,* and the *Atlanta Journal-Constitution*; he has also appeared on the *Tavis Smiley Show,* CNN, and BET. His syndicated column, "The Robertson Treatment," appears in more than 30 newspapers and reaches more than 2 million readers across the country.